MW01105235

The First and Seventh Joys of Our Lady

Bilingual Texts of Two Dutch Biblical Plays

MEDIEVAL AND RENAISSANCE
TEXTS AND STUDIES

VOLUME 475

EARLY EUROPEAN DRAMA TRANSLATION SERIES

VOLUME 3

The First and Seventh Joys of Our Lady

Bilingual Texts of Two Dutch Biblical Plays

Edited and Translated by

Elsa Strietman

and

Peter Happé

ARIZONA CENTER FOR MEDIEVAL

ACMRS

AND RENAISSANCE STUDIES

Tempe, Arizona
2017

THE ARIZONA CENTER FOR

MEDIEVAL &
RENAISSANCE

STUDIES

Published by ACMRS (Arizona Center for Medieval and Renaissance Studies),
Tempe, Arizona.
© 2017 Arizona Board of Regents for Arizona State University.
All Rights Reserved.

Library of Congress Cataloging-in-Publication Data

Names: Strietman, Elsa, editor, translator. | Happé, Peter, editor, translator.
Title: The first and seventh joys of Our Lady : bilingual texts of two Dutch
     Biblical plays / Edited and Translated by Elsa Strietman and Peter Happé.
Other titles: Eerste van Bliscap van Maria. | Sevenste Blyscap van Onser
     Vrouwen. | Eerste van Bliscap van Maria. English. | Sevenste Blyscap van
     Onser Vrouwen. English.
Description: Tempe, Arizona : ACMRS, 2016. | Series: Medieval and
     Renaissance Texts and Studies ; volume 475 | Series: Early European drama
     translation series ; volume 3 | Includes bibliographical references.
Identifiers: LCCN 2016015236 | ISBN 9780866985284 (pbk.)
Subjects: LCSH: Mary, Blessed Virgin, Saint--Drama.
Classification: LCC PT5440 .F5 2016 | DDC 839.312/05160801--dc23
LC record available at https://lccn.loc.gov/2016015236

Cover Illustration:
Hans Memling, *Annunciation* (c. 1480).
Metropolitan Museum of Art, New York.
Image is in the Public Domain.

∞

This book is made to last. It is set in Adobe Caslon Pro,
smyth-sewn and printed on acid-free paper to library specifications.
Printed in the United States of America

TABLE OF CONTENTS

INTRODUCTION

To commemorate the transfer of the statue of the Virgin Mary from Antwerp to Brussels in 1348, the Brussels authorities began to support an annual procession (*ommeganc*) on the Sunday before Pentecost in her honour, and by about a century later a dramatic element had been added in the form of a play concentrating each year upon one of the Joys of Mary. There was an extensive development of cycle plays in the mid-fifteenth century in several European countries, especially France, England, and some German states, but the Dutch example, which may owe something to the growing popularity of such performances, has many independent features, of which the focus on the Virgin is the most remarkable.[1] Instead of a narrative structure stretching from Creation to Judgement Day, as in the cycle plays written and performed at York and Chester, or one focused upon the Passion, as was more commonly the case in France, especially that by Jean Michel performed in Angers in 1486, the *Bliscapen* (*Joys*) were arranged into seven episodes, one of which was celebrated each year in connection with the procession on the Sunday before Pentecost in Brussels. This combination of a procession followed by a dramatic play was probably established in 1448, when a codifying regulation by the city authorities set out the requirements for the occasion, and it continued to be followed in a seven-year cycle until 1566. W. H. Beuken, to whose edition of the two surviving episodes, the *First* and *Seventh Joys*, the present work is much indebted, has assembled a great deal of useful background information, but it must be admitted that knowledge of many aspects of the original versions and their performance remains rather patchy.[2]

---

[1] In the surviving fragments of the *Passion d'Auvergne* there is a pattern in which Christ communicates with his mother at the end of each day, but these contacts are not related to the Joys: see Graham A. Runnalls, ed., *La Passion d'Auvergne* (Geneva: Droz, 1982), 19–20. Part of the *N Town Cycle* is adapted from a smaller sequence of plays centring on the Virgin; see Peter Meredith, *The Mary Play from the N Town Manuscript* (London: Longman, 1987).

[2] W. H. Beuken, ed., *Die Eerste Bliscap van Maria en Die Sevenste Bliscap van Onser Vrouwen* (Culemborg: Tjeenk Willink/Noorduijn, 1973). Page references are to this edition. The regulation is quoted from the Brussels archive on p. 12. See also Bart Ramakers, "5 mei 1448. Begin van de traditie van de jaarlijkse opvoering van een van de zeven *Bliscapen* in Brussel: toneel en processies in de late middeleeuwen," in *Een theatergeschiedenis*

However, the extant texts do provide some indications about the overall scheme in the prologues and epilogues. These give emphasis to the devotion to the Virgin as a special protector of the city of Brussels (1/1–7) and note the importance of the public ceremony and the political allegiance of the community. They outline the cyclic structure and the annual performance, and at the end of the last play, the seven Joys are briefly recapitulated in the order of their presentation over the seven-year cycle: the Annunciation, the Nativity, the Three Kings, Christ in the Temple, the Resurrection, Pentecost, and the Assumption of the Virgin (7/1701–22). In itself this arrangement does present a chronological sequence for the Joys and covers the life of Mary from her conception to her Assumption. The rather self-conscious interest in the structure of the plays is discernible elsewhere, as when the prologue to the *First Joy* explains that the fall of Lucifer through Pride will not be shown (1/49–51), and when the prologue to the *Seventh Joy* refers to the (lost) *Sixth* performed in the previous year, but explains that it will not now be recalled in detail (7/16–18). Such references would, nevertheless, serve to bring to mind for many the narrative content of the previous year. These plays are conceived as urban drama and they are seen as a contribution to the spiritual welfare of the city (1/15–25). The Prologue to the *Seventh* is careful to emphasize the orthodoxy of what is to be presented by referring to 'scripture and some learned clerks' (7/41).[3] The procession, with carts showing episodes in the Christian story in chronological order, took place through the city in the morning, and in the afternoon the appropriate play for the year was performed in the Grote Markt. It appears from the 1448 municipal regulation that the same stage set was used for all seven texts.[4]

The author or the original planners of the cycle may well have drawn upon the growing European interest in such large-scale plays in a number of ways, especially the extensive scope of the narrative as well as decisions about performance and the mise-en-scène, but there are many features which suggest that they were constructing their own independent variation. One of their most remarkable achievements was the inventiveness of the narrative structure. Many details of the sequences adapted in the plays come from traditional sources like the *Gospel of Nicodemus* and the *Legenda Aurea*.[5] The use of such traditional elements may well have arisen in other fifteenth-century cycles with orthodox objectives, especially as the early evolution of large-scale cycles was, in all likelihood, part of a process of asserting traditional values against heresy in that

der Nederlanden. Tien eeuwen drama en theater in Nederland en Vlaanderen, ed. by R. L. Erenstein (Amsterdam: Amsterdam University Press, 1996), 42–49.

[3] Catholic orthodoxy is indicated in Envy's reference to the exercise of free will by Lucifer 1/486–92.

[4] Beuken, 24.

[5] Beuken, 27.

period.[6] But the two Dutch plays we have show inventiveness in the ways in which such elements are integrated. Thus the episodes dealing with the tree of Paradise and Seth's journey back to it, the rod of Joachim in the temple, Mary's exemplary behaviour in the temple, and the summoning of the disciples to be present at her death — all of which are apocryphal and yet requiring to be regarded as cherished and valuable stories for their own sake — are integrated into continuous narratives which are special to the cycle, as far as we can tell. In the *First* the author has chosen a structured sequence whereby Adam's appeal for release from hell is taken up by the others suffering there and this in turn is paralleled by the allegorical appeal of Bitter Misery and the plea for mercy from Passionate Prayer which stimulate the debate in heaven and the ultimate solution in the Incarnation. The managing of these episodes, which are intermixed with strictly biblical elements such as the Annunciation and the Nativity, gives rise to potent interrelationships. Since the overall design is to weave such narratives around one particular joy of Mary for each play, the combination of minor narratives with the Joy itself would have to be worked out separately for each play. Even though only two plays survive, they are sufficient to show that a process of association and recapitulation is going on in each of them. In doing so these plays make use of the exploitation of memory which is inherent in cycle plays.[7] For example, in Limbo, Eve recalls her disastrous advice to Adam in Paradise (1/788–91) and, as she grows older and weaker, Mary reminds John (and the audience) on two occasions of Christ's words on the cross in which he committed her to John's care (7/95–100 and 689–710). By such devices, the chronological sequence characteristic of the English mystery cycles and the French and German *Passions* geographically surrounding the Netherlands, which must have been well-known in the fifteenth century, is eschewed and new significances are generated, centring upon the role of Mary and the contemplation of her virtues, together with recurring pleas for intercession. It need hardly be said that the worship of Mary was central to Catholic orthodoxy, and as such, it was something which later was to come under pressure from the reformers. The author did not confine himself simply to the episode of the individual Joy: his practice was to expand and contextualize it by interweaving other narratives around it.

This inventiveness in the narratives, which was directed towards the contemplation and celebration of the Joys, shows itself differently in the incorporation of abstract characters in the *First*, though it is not discernible in the *Seventh*. Envy is particularly emphatic as an allegorical elaboration of the scriptural

---

[6] See Peter Happé, "Genre and Fifteenth-Century English Drama: The Case of Thomas Chaundler's *Liber Apologeticus*," *Medium Aevum* 82 (2013): 66–80.

[7] For the relationship between memory and locations in performance see Glenn Ehrstine, "Framing the Passion: Mansion staging and visual Mnemonic," in *Visualizing Medieval Performance: Perspectives, Histories Contexts*, edited by Elina Gertsman (Aldershot: Ashgate, 2008), 268–77 (267–69).

desire of Lucifer to emulate the divinity.[8] Some physical attributes of his characterisation are mentioned, including the traditional one of his gnawing at himself (1/109–110 and 396). He is given dramatic initiative over the temptation of
Adam and Eve. Later in the play, there is an allegorical episode in which Bitter
Misery is made to represent the suffering of the faithful in limbo and has to be
helped by Passionate Prayer to make her supplications effective in heaven. The
outcome of this sequence is the debate of Mercy, Truth, Peace, and Justice that
leads ultimately to the Incarnation. Such a debate is indeed to be found in other
cycles, including those by Eustache Marcadé and Arnoul Gréban and the English *N Town Plays*. These share with the *First* an elaborate development of argument, but the sequencing of this particular Dutch version is unique. Elsewhere,
the virtuous Mary, as a child, is given four young companions named Wisdom,
Humility, Purity, and Obedience (1/1674–77). The use of abstract characters
here may well have anticipated the popularity and frequency of allegories in the
contemporary plays of the rhetoricians (the *Spelen van Sinne*), which rely extensively upon such inventive sequences and the ingenious creation of interrelated
abstract characterisation.

Like many other cyclic plays, the *Bliscapen* have passages featuring devils.
The association between Envy and Lucifer in the *First* carries a significant part of
the narrative and at times the devils have an opportunity for celebration. However, how serious these should be is a matter for speculation as, presumably, the
ultimate defeat of the devils was known and expected by the faithful, and yet
theatrically their participation commonly borders on the comic. Notwithstand-
ing the widespread fear of Hell and torment, there is no doubt that here, as in
other cycle plays, the devils are rather ridiculous and their participation in a
dramatic performance is so theatrically effective that one can hardly see them as
entirely threatening in this context. Their entertainment value was no doubt too
high to be overlooked. In our translation we have left open the possibility that
they would have had a comic aspect and that would be part of their theatrical
success. A great deal more might have been apparent from the way in which they
might have been costumed. Probably there would have been a grotesque element
which would increase the push towards comedy.

The drama of the two plays contains exhortation, reflection, debate, and
preaching, but it also shows several passages of closely constructed dialogue
which have the effect of making the actions seem very human. An example is
the conversation between the Neighbours of Ephesus who have been witnesses
to St. John's preaching and now provide a commentary on his miraculous departure (7/572–639). The tone of the exchanges here is not comic: these are not
yokels. Yet they strike the listener as human and normal in the face of the mar-
vellous spectacle which is going on at the same time: 'It's not exactly simple / To

---

[8] Envy, one of the Seven Deadly Sins, has been attributed to Lucifer on the basis
of Isaiah 14:14.

understand what this will mean' (7/585). There is a similar conversation between the Young Men in the Temple in the *First* (1/1850–1912).[9]

Besides the extensive use of music discussed below, the dramatic mode is enhanced by metrical virtuosity and poetic language. The latter is especially potent in emotional passages and also in rhetorical address. The dramatist took over one special linguistic feature from other cyclic drama, particularly in France, in his use of rondeaux, formally patterned groups of lines, beginning with eight lines rhyming *abaaabab*. These are especially effective in creating the emotional effect of a passage or in providing a moment of poise before a contrasting episode begins.[10] Such are the lines which confirm the bond between St. John and Mary (7/157–64), Mary's relief at not having to meet the Devil at her death (7/494–501), the praise of Mary by the disciples (7/982–88), and their thanks to God for his care for her (7/1342–49).[11]

The manuscripts of the two surviving plays are closely related to performance and were written by the same scribe using the same script, c. 1455. They are not thought to be authorial autographs. These copies were used for many years and were modified by as many as nine different hands including that of Franchoys van Ballaer, the director in 1559 (Beuken, 18 and 21). Many of the alterations were dictated by the necessities and changes which arose in performance. By that time, the predominantly Catholic nature of the enterprise with its special emphasis upon the Virgin was coming under some pressure from the new learning inspired by the Reformation, and Ballaer may have intervened to restrict some of the praise for her.[12] The details about performance that can be derived from these texts are supplemented by other documents, including a cast list for the *First* showing the names of some actors with the parts they played, some having more than one role, and a list of props for the *Seventh* in 1559 (Beuken, 23 and 25).

Some further details in the account written by Calvete de Estrella of what actually happened on 2 June 1549 give evidence about the procession and the dramatic performance of the *Fourth*, which is otherwise unknown and for which

---

[9] The similarity of these passages increases the probability that the two plays had a common authorship. Beuken further supports this view by his reference to similarities in the rhyming, word formation, and poetic language, 48–49.

[10] For the dramatic versatility of rondeaux in France, see Véronique Dominguez, *La scène et la croix : le jeu de l'acteur dans les passions dramatiques françaises (XIVe–XVIe siècles)* (Turnhout: Brepols, 2007), 237–48.

[11] Beuken cites the interlocked pattern of *abaaabab* for twenty-five lines at 1/1376–1400, and suggests that the complexity of the verse forms in the *Bliscapen* was influenced by the versification in the *Mystères*, 42.

[12] Cf. Ramakers, 46–47.

no text is extant.[13] On that occasion there were thirteen wagons, which showed the following episodes in dumbshow with some mimetic activity but no speech: the Birth of Mary, Mary and the Infant Jesus, the Presentation in the Temple, the Annunciation, the Birth in the Stable, the Shepherds, the Circumcision, the Kings, the Purification, the Resurrection, the Ascension, Pentecost, and the Assumption.[14] These include most of the seven Joys but they also widen the scope of the stories presented beyond them. There does not appear to be any special emphasis in the procession upon the fourth Joy of Mary concerning Christ in the Temple which was to be performed later on that day. As there is no wagon specifically dedicated to that particular Joy, it is possible that it was the custom to leave out the topic which was to appear in fully dramatic form. The absence of information about the contents of the procession in the six other years makes it difficult to tell whether this variation was customary, but it remains a possibility.[15] Nor is it apparent whether the components of the procession would have been different from Estrella's account in the six years focussed upon the other Joys. The information he does give clearly indicates that the mimes on some of the wagons included movement and gestures.[16]

As far as the dramatic performance is concerned, his observation that it took place in an area like a Coliseum suggests that the method was to have a large open space with specific locations so that the action could be shown at individual specialised sites and in the spaces in between. The word suggests a large arena with many people looking on. It is also possible that some of the audience might have moved about the square. In all probability the Dutch performance matches the custom of using a public square in many examples found in France, Switzerland, and the German states. One of the chief effects of such a method is to superimpose the events of the past upon the circumstances of the present in as much as the town square was the site of many everyday experiences, but it also functioned as the place of municipal display, intense commercial activities and often the location for the administration of justice, including executions.[17]

---

[13] For a Dutch version, see P. Leendertz, *Middelnederlandsche dramatische poëzie* (Leiden: Sijthoff, 1907), 493–94.

[14] Unlike the order of the plays in the cycle, Estrella's list does not follow the chronological order of events in Mary's life.

[15] B. A. M. Ramakers, *Spelen en figuren: Toneelkunst en processiecultur in Oudenaarde tussen Middeleeuwen en Moderne Tijd* (Amsterdam: Amsterdam University Press, 1996), 415.

[16] A mixture of dramatic performance and mimed activity is a feature of the Lille Plays: see Alan E. Knight, ed., *Les Mystères de la Procession de Lille*, 6 vols (Geneva: Droz 2001-) 1.42.

[17] On the active tension between the fictive localities of the past envisaged in performance compared with the later reality of the contemporary circumstances, see Sarah Beckwith, *Signifying God: Social Relation and Symbolic Action the York Corpus Christi Plays* (Chicago: University of Chicago Press 2001), 36–38.

From the play texts themselves, it is possible to deduce a number of the fixed locations and to appreciate how they might have been used. The presence of fixed locations in a large acting area became a standard feature and there were conventions which lay behind their use. The presence of Heaven and Hell was common. Here, Heaven is a particularly complex station and it is used extensively in both plays. Beuken has suggested that there were at least three parts to it: one for God, one for the angels, and one for the other inhabitants of Heaven.[18] The place for God functions as a place in which the actor could remain, being opened to reveal the deity in splendour when he is needed to participate in the action: *Meanwhile they will open the heaven where God sits and says to the Angel Gabriel* (7/326sd). It was apparently high up because Gabriel is sent *down* from heaven to carry out the divine will, as when he descends for the Annunciation (1/1965–2012), and for its complement later when, carrying a palm branch, he again descends to inform Mary of her coming death and to conduct her up into heaven (7/364–67).

One of the most remarkable episodes occurs in the allegorical passage in which Bitter Misery is helped by Passionate Prayer. In order to carry a message, she makes a hole with a drill or auger in the floor of heaven and ascends herself to make her plea to Mercy (1/916sd). At this point, Bitter Misery, who is on crutches because her legs are broken, must have been unable to ascend herself. It is not clear whether a particular mechanism was used for these movements upwards or downwards.[19] Some latitude is apparent in the actual relationship in terms of location between God and other characters for when he addresses his host he is to speak 'from above or below' (7/1137sd). This rather anomalous instruction may have arisen because at this point he is actually to speak to a large number of performers and there may have been some special requirements in arranging a suitable grouping of a large number of characters.

The fixed and conventional locations are supported by other designated places to which characters have to move. Such movements are an integral part of the dramatic experience in that they act as dividing lines between episodes and often positively introduce a change of mood or atmosphere.[20] In the *Seventh* the approaching death of Mary is played at a fixed location and the disciples are drawn from other places in the acting area to be present. This movement is dra-

---

[18] This is derived from the list of properties reproduced by Beuken, 25.

[19] In the York Cycle, the Mercers guild apparently had a lifting mechanism on their pageant wagon, see Alexandra F. Johnston and Margaret Rogerson, *York*, Records of Early English Drama, 2 vols, (Toronto: University of Toronto Press), 1979) 1.55.32–40, and Pamela M. King, *The York Mystery Cycle and the Worship of the City* (Cambridge: Brewer, 2006), 12.

[20] For movements between fixed locations, see Vicki L. Hamblin, "Performing the Text: A Comparative Analysis of Three French Mystery Plays," in *Mainte belle oeuvre faicte. Etudes sur le théâtre médiéval offertes à Graham A. Runnalls*, edited by Denis Hüe, Mario Longtin and Lynette Muir (Paradigme: Orléans, 2005), 191–205 (196–200).

matically important as it leads to the emotional climax of the reunion with her. Most notable is Saint John's transition from Ephesus where he is preaching to the people. The stage direction indicates that the journey was meant to be visible and spectacular:

> Here two angels will come with a cloth and wrap it around
> Saint John and the cloth will shine like a cloud. And so
> covered, they will transport him to Maria's door, or in another
> way, as it seems best. (7/571sd)

This movement is an all the more impressive illustration of the divine intention because of the comments of the Neighbours in Ephesus who watch the miraculous journey taking place (7/572–81) and of Saint John's own observations as he is moved by power he does not understand (7/641–43). However, it remains open to speculation exactly how this and the movements of the other disciples were actually managed. The stage direction suggests that there was some uncertainty.

The changes of location for the action are sometimes underlined by musical emphasis as when attention is shifted from Joachim's humiliation in the temple to God's initiative over the birth of Mary (1/1461sd).[21] Indeed, the ends of episodes where attention has to be switched to another location are often marked by music, as when Seth finally brings a remedy, which offers hope to the descendants of Adam (1/738), or when the souls in limbo are made aware of the possibility of release (1/838). The switch to hellish episodes, however, can be accompanied by grimmer noises (1/766sd, 770sd).[22]

Among the other important locations are the house of Mary at the foot of Mount Sion[23] and her grave in the *Seventh*, and the elaborate concept of Paradise from which Adam and Eve are ultimately excluded by the angel and which contains the tree with the forbidden fruit. This is the tree to which Seth returns later in order to bring hope to his dying father, Adam (1/699–702). Mary has a speech at the beginning of the *Seventh* in which she expresses her desire to visit the places associated with her son's sufferings and triumphs. It is not clear whether or when she does this, but the Jews, in conspiring against her, mention such movements later (7/132–43 and 170–71).

As noted above the plays had a political role in part, evident in the address to the ruling authorities, but they also reflect political and religious change. In

---

[21] See W. H. M. Hummelen, "*Pausa* and *Selete* in the *Bliscapen*," in *Urban Theatre in the Low Countries, 1400–1625*, edited by Elsa Strietman and Peter Happé (Turnhout: Brepols, 2006), 53–76. He proposes that the term *selete* is used for singing and *pausa* for instrumental music, and he notices that music is also used for the passage of time, 58.

[22] The noises from Hell and some of the dialogue set there, as at 1/404–61, are a feature which the *Bliscapen* share with other cycle plays, especially the French and German versions.

[23] Hummelen suggests that this house had two stories, 61–62.

part they are an assertion of religious orthodoxy, and at the same time, echoing widespread contemporary practice in other countries, they give an insight into the way resourceful and innovative dramatization of traditional material could stimulate as well as express religious experience. But within this extensive and well established objective, the texts can also reveal in places the pressure on the old religion which was brought to bear in the sixteenth century.

DIE EERSTE BLISCAP VAN MARIA

DIERSTE PROLOGHE

Maria, voncke ende rayende licht
Des hemels, die den toren swicht
Vander heileger Drievuldicheyen,
Ic bidde u, minlijc aengesicht,
Dat ghi u gracie soe in ons sticht,   5
Dat uwen lof daer by moet breyen
Sonder verbeyen. Reyn suver kersouwe,
Wilt onsen prince ende oec sijn vrouwe,
Ende Charloot, onsen jongen heere,
Met sijnder vrouwe, behueden vor rouwe.   10
Ende alle haer vruende, jonge en ouwe,
Moet God bescermen van allen seere;
Ende oec voort meere sijn lant, sijn steden,
Dorpe, slote, wil God in vreden
Altoes behueden vor mesval;   15
Ende alle de ghene, om cort gebeden,
Diere geerne tslants profijt in deden.
Vor Bruessel biddic boven al!
Voert gruetic u minlic groet en smal:
Sijt willecome, edele en gemeyne,   20
Die hier dus minlic sijt versaemt
In desen melodyosen pleyne.
Sijt willecome, edele en gemeyne!
Tprieel uut Troyen, den edelen greyne,
Gegroyt, gebloeyt, es Bruesel genaemt.   25
Wy grueten u minlic, groet en cleyne,
Die tonser feesten hier sijt versaemt.
Sijt hier welcomen, soet betaemt.
Want dat lieflijc beelde lofsam,
Dwelc hier noch opten Savel steet,   30
Van Antwerpen te Bruesel quam
By miraculen, soet menich weet,
Soe souden wi u geerne, ende sijns bereet,

The First Joy of Maria

THE FIRST PROLOGUE
Maria, spark and radiant light
Of heaven, who calms the wrath
Of the Holy Trinity,
Beloved face, I pray to you
That you pour your mercy into us in such a way   5
That your praise may thereby be spread
Without ceasing. Pure, unblemished marguerite,
May you guard our prince, and also his lady,
And our young lord, Charles,
And his lady, from grief.   10
May God protect all their friends,
Young and old, from all suffering;
And may he also keep his land, his towns,
His villages and his castles in peace,
And guard them always from misfortune;   15
And protect all those—to keep my prayer short—
Who diligently work for the realm's advantage.
I pray above all for Brussels!
And now I kindly greet you, great and small;
Be welcome, nobles and commoners,   20
Who are here thus amicably gathered
In this delightful place.
Be welcome, nobles and commoners!
The bower grown from the noble seed of Troy
Has blossomed, and is named Brussels.   25
We greet you kindly, great and small,
Who are gathered here for our feast.
Be welcome here, as it befits.
Because that lovely statue, worthy of praise,
Which still stands here, on the Zavel,   30
And came from Antwerp to Brussels
By a miracle, as many know,
We would gladly, and readily

In love der hemelscher tresorie,
Figuerlic speelwijs doen besceet   35
Die eerste bliscap die haer gescye:
Hoe dat die suete maecht Marie
Ontfinc den Gods sone onbesmet,
Ende loste ons vanden ewigen strie
By singels salute te Nazaret.   40
Ende altemet jaerlix, soet hoert,
Sonder verlet ende sonder discoert,
Soe meinen wier vort, ter stat beveelne,
Verstaet mijn woert, noch .vj. te speelne.
Al es de boetscap tprincipale   45
Ons speels, tes noot datmen verhale
Waer omme dat God, tot onsen behouwe,
Menscelicheit aen nemen wouwe.
Niet min, wi laten overlien
Lucifers val met sijnre partien,   50
Die hen bi hoverdien gesciet.
Dies bliven si ewelic int verdriet,
Int ewige demster, sonder verlaet;
Om een gepeys waest sonder daet.
Maer want de viant met scalkere liste   55
Den mensce benijdde, om datti wiste
Dat hi ter gracien was vercoren,
Soe de hi hem Gods gebod verhoren,
Dwelc Adam ende alle sijn geslachte
Moeste besueren, tot dat dit brachte   60
Dontfermicheit Gods tot enen vree.
Dit was de sake daert God om dee,
Dat hi in donbesmette zeborie
Wou rusten ende bringen ons tsijnder glorie.
Dus, eerbaer notabele, lieve geminde,   65
Ic woude dat yegelic wel versinde:
Ons meyn es reyn, slecht es ons conste.
Verstaedt ende vaedt ons goede jonste.
Wy doent uut minnen, wilt dat bekinnen,
Om vruecht vermeeren;   70
Gode ende der stat, ic segt u plat,
U allen ter eeren.
Dus yegelic wilt dan duegdelic keren,
Ende nement danckelic nu ter tijt.
Wi gaen beginnen, hoert en swijt.   75

Show you figuratively in our play
Through love for her, the heavenly treasure,　　　　35
The first joy which she received:
How the sweet virgin, Maria,
Conceived immaculate the Son of God,
And so freed us from eternal strife
Through the angel's salutation at Nazareth.　　　　40
And every year following, as it should,
Without omission and without discord
So we mean to perform, by order of the town,
Believe me, six further plays.
Even though the annunciation is the main message　　　45
Of our play, it's necessary to explain
Why God for our salvation
Wished to become incarnate.
Nevertheless we do not show
The fall of Lucifer and his pack,　　　　50
Caused by evil pride.
Thus they remained in eternal grief
In eternal darkness, without relief;
Doomed by unfounded envy.
But the devil, with low cunning　　　　55
Envied mankind because he knew
That man was chosen for grace,
And he made Adam ignore God's command,
For which mankind and all his kin
Were made to suffer, until God's Mercy　　　　60
Brought the torment to an end.
This was the reason why God decided
That he wished to rest in the immaculate vessel
And thus bring us all into his glory.
Thus, noble audience and dear friends,　　　　65
I would like all to be fully aware
That our intention is pure, and our art simple.
Share with us our cherished art.
Please understand we'll do it for love
That pleasure in our art may grow;　　　　70
I tell you plain, it's in honour
Of God and the town, and all of you.
May everybody receive it as worthy,
And accept it with grace.
We shall now begin: listen and be silent.　　　　75

NIJT   Och Lucifer, meester, hoe ghevaren?
                Wy, die daer aen gescreven waren
                Int boeck des levens metten here,
                Sijn nu gecondampneert met sere
                Die ewige doot te liden, wachermen,   80
                Sonder verganc ocht sonder ontfermen
                Van hem, die ons hier neder velde
                Om dat wy boven sijn ghewelde
                Ons wilden verheffen. Dies moeten wi bliven
                In dit verdriet!
LUCIFER   Ja, als keytiven,   85
                Diene by minen rade vererreden.
                By uwen consente, Nijt, wi ontferreden
                Der bliscap ende der ewiger erven.
                Dies wi hier ewelic moeten sterven
                In swaerder ellinden, in groter smae.   90
                Ons mochts wel rouwen!
NIJT   Neen, dats te spae,
                Meester, van onsen berou te sprekene.
                Maer dbest es: pinen wijs ons te wrekene
                Ende met ons int strec te bringene,
                Die nu bi hem sijn, ic weetse te ringene!   95
                Ja meester, op dat ghijs radich sijt,
                Ic crijchse by ons.
LUCIFER   Jaic seker, Nijt,
                Ic hulpse u bringen oec int sneven.
                By ons was den raet bedreven,
                Dat wi ons stelden tegen de weerden   100
                Des heren, bi nide ende bi hoverden.
                Dus es ons dit mesluc gesciet,
                Dat wi sijn comen int verdriet.
                Dus dan, Nidicheit, soe ghi gesproken
                Hebt, hulpt dat wi worden gewroken,   105
                Ende brinctse bi ons int jammer dal,
                Die de here vercoes.
NIJT   Vrilic, ic sal!
                Soe uterlic sere eest mi spitende,
                Dat ic mi selven ga al verbitende:
                Uut rechter hatyen etic mijn hande   110
                Van ongenuechten.

ENVY	Oh Lucifer, master, what's happening?	
	We, who have been entered	
	Into the book of life with the host of angels	
	Are now grievously condemned	
	To suffer eternal death, alas,	80
	Without ending and without pity	
	From him, who imprisoned us down here	
	Because we wanted to raise ourselves	
	Above his sovereignty, and so we must remain	
	In this misery!	

LUCIFER   Yes, like wretches   85
          Who angered him on my advice.
          Through your council, Envy, we robbed ourselves
          Of joy and our eternal heritage.
          We must endure in perpetuity
          Extreme misery, great shame.   90
          We have reason to regret it!

ENVY   No, it's too late,
          Master, to speak of our remorse.
          But the best thing is if we exert ourselves in revenge
          And bring into the noose with us
          Those who are now with him,   95
          Then I know how to catch them!
          Yes master, if you are of the same mind
          I'll win them over.

LUCIFER   Yes, for sure, Envy,
          I'll help you to bring them down.
          We had conceived the plan
          That we rebelled against the power   100
          Of the lord out of envy and arrogance.
          Thus this misfortune has befallen us
          So that we have come to grief.
          Now then, Envy, as you've said,
          Help us so we'll be avenged   105
          And bring with us into the vale of tears
          Those whom the lord elected.

ENVY   Surely I will!
          It gnaws at me so terribly
          That I'm eating myself up with spite:
          From true hate I gnaw my hands   110
          Out of anger.

LUCIFER   Dat scijnt uwen tande,
            Die ghi dor cnauwelt hebt en versleten
            Van groten spite.
NIJT   Ic heb, seg, gheeten
            Mi selven, alsoet oec wel es scinende
            Aen mijn fautsoen: ic ga al dwinende   115
            Tot eender scaduwen, soe nipet my,
            Dat iemen bat varen soude dan wi.
            Ende na mijn macht salict bevellen
            Tot ewigen tiden.
LUCIFER   Ghi sijt der hellen
            Seer profitelic, claerlic, Nijt!   120
            Maer segt, wies dat ghi tornich sijt,
            Ende wien ghi sout, quaemt tuwen wensche,
            Bi ons hier stieren.
NIJT   Wat? trouwen den mensche;
            Dien hopic, canic, te verdullene,
            Dien God gestelt heeft te vervullene   125
            Bi sijnre hoger caritaten
            De stoele, daer wi als ingele saten.
            Daer benic op uut, om dien te geckene
            En hier int demster bi ons te treckene.
            Lucifer, meester, dit hebbic voren   130
            Te trapeneerne!
LUCIFER   Constu dat gelaboren,
            Nijt, ons saken die souden versconen
            Ende sere versoeten!
NIJT   Ic salne wel honen.
            Laet mi gewerden, ic saelt wel coken!
            Hoverdie, Giericheit selent oec stoken   135
            Bedectelijc, ic weed dbedrijf
            Wel bi te bringene.
LUCIFER   Tempteret dwijf:
            Si en es so vast niet als de man
            Van wederstane.
NIJT   Ic brinct haer best an
            Biden serpente, dat onbevlect   140
            Nu bi haer es; het gaet ende sprect
            In dat eerdsche paradijs.
            Oec eest seer listich, subtijl en wijs.
            By dien soe hopic stille ocht lude
            Den mensce te bedriegene.

LUCIFER   It shows in your teeth,
                    Which you've chewed up and worn down
                    Out of intense rancour.
ENVY   I tell you I have consumed
                    Myself, as is very obvious
                    From my appearance: I'm wasting away   115
                    To a shadow—it bugs me so—
                    That anyone should fare better than we do.
                    And with all my might I'll fight against this
                    Into eternity.
LUCIFER   You are clearly
                    Of great benefit to hell, Envy!   120
                    But tell me, about whom are you angry,
                    And whom you would, if you had your desire,
                    Steer in our direction?
ENVY   What? Well mankind, of course;
                    That's the one I hope to lead astray if I can,
                    The one whom God has placed to fill,   125
                    Through his great charity,
                    The chair on which we sat as angels.
                    That's what I'm after, to fool mankind
                    And lure him with us into the dark.
                    Lucifer, master, that's a plot I plan   130
                    To hatch cunningly.
LUCIFER   If you could manage that,
                    Envy, our cause would improve no end
                    And be rather the sweeter!
ENVY   I'll make fools of them.
                    Let me get busy, I'll cook 'em.
                    Pride and avarice will stoke it up   135
                    Secretly; and I'll know
                    How to pull it off.
LUCIFER   Tempt the woman:
                    She's not as steadfast as the man
                    In resisting.
ENVY   I'd better do this
                    By involving the serpent, which is now   140
                    Innocently at her side: it moves and speaks
                    In that earthly paradise.
                    It's very cunning, subtle and wise.
                    In that way I hope, by and by,
                    To lead mankind astray.

LUCIFER	Dat worden de crude	145
	Dier toe dienen, seker soe doent.	
	Scoey duvel, scoey! Ten doech gesermoent	
	Niet langere; hets den besten sin	
	Tot onzen profite.	
NIJT	Tword groet ghewin	
	Der ganser hellen, maecht soe gescien.	150
	Dits wech.	
	Ic heb de stat versien	
	Daer de here na sijn gelieven	
	In heeft gestelt Adam en Yeven,	
	Om daer te verdienen, sonder lac,	
	De vroude daer hi ons selve uut stac,	155
	Dwelc ons te lidene es onsoete.	
	Tsus, laet geworden: yuust te gemoete	
	Comt mi tserpent; dat lopic smeeken	
	Mit bliden geveerte. Dits wel .j.teeken	
	Van voortgange mijns bedrijfs geveyst.	160
	Zerpent, hoord mi: ic heb ghepeyst	
	Nutte saken, reyn int becliven,	
	Tot uwen orbore.	
TSERPENT	Consti die bedriven,	
	Daer wildic toe hulpen en pinen eenpaerlic,	
	Haddics de macht.	
NIJT	Jaghi soe, claerlic.	165
	Ja, wildi werken bi minen avise?	
	In midden van desen paradise	
	Daer steet een boem, si u gewaecht,	
	Die orborlike vruchten draecht.	
	Wiste Adam hoe datse smaken,	170
	Hi soudse plucken.	
TSERPENT	Wat connen si maken,	
	Die vruchten alsoe hoge gepresen,	
	Ochtse Adaem nutte?	
NIJT	Soe wordhi genesen	
	Vander natuerliker doot.	
	Oec wordhi verheven en also groot,	175
	Volmaect en van so hoger weerden,	
	Al es diene hier sciep van eerden.	
	Ende voord soe soudi onverspleten	
	Alle die grote sciencien weten,	
	Die liggen verborgen inden here,	180
	Diene hier stelde.	

LUCIFER	Those are the ingredients	145
	Which will bring this about, I'm sure of it.	
	Be off, devil, be off! It's no use sermonising	
	Any longer; it's the best plan	
	For our good.	
ENVY	It's going to be a great scoop	
	For the whole of hell, if it would turn out like this.	150
	I'm off.	
	I've marked the place	
	Where the lord has seen fit	
	To put Adam and Eve,	
	In order to deserve innocently	
	The joy from which he has banned us,	155
	Which we greatly resent.	
	Now then, wait a sec: in fact, here comes	
	The serpent towards me. I'll go and butter him up	
	In a friendly way. This is a sign	
	That my plan will work.	160
	Serpent, listen to me: I've thought	
	Of some really useful things, bound to work	
	To your advantage.	
THE SERPENT	If you could bring them off	
	I'd be glad to help and make a real effort,	
	If it lies in my power.	
ENVY	Yes, you do clearly.	165
	Now, do you want to follow my advice?	
	In the middle of this paradise	
	There stands a tree, you ought to know,	
	Which produces very useful fruits.	
	If Adam knew how they tasted	170
	He would pick them.	
THE SERPENT	So what can they do,	
	These fruits you praise so highly,	
	Were Adam to eat them?	
ENVY	He will then be cured	
	Of natural death.	
	Also he will be raised and become very powerful,	175
	Perfect and of such high worth,	
	As is he who created him out of clay.	
	Furthermore he would have complete knowledge	
	Of all the great learning	
	Hidden in the lord	180
	Who put him here.	

TSERPENT   Nu dan, ic keere
                    Tot Yeven. Canicser toe beringen,
                    Si salre Adame wel toe bringen,
                    Niet jegenstaende dat God verbood.
                    Der vrouwen list es alsoe grood,   185
                    Dat si volcomen selen haer saken,
                    Al souden sire qua note om smaken.
                    Dus werdet best soe aen geleit
                    Om voordganc te hebbene.
NIJT   Hets claer besceit.
                    Gaet vrou Yeven aen subtylic,   190
                    Het sal volcomen.
TSERPENT   Gheerne, vrilic;
                    Ic saelt besorgen op een cort.
                    Vertrec! ic meent ons orboer wort.

                    Yeve, vrouwe van desen vergiere,
                    Die hier de here reyn van bestiere   195
                    By sijnre groter gracien wrachte,
                    Om dat ghi ende al u geslachte
                    Verdienen sout, om cort verclaren,
                    De glorie, daer dingele in waren,
                    Ja, vrouwe, bi sijnre groter genade —   200
                    Maer wildi werken bi minen rade,
                    Ic weet u selc avijs te gevene,
                    Dat u ewelic steet te levene,
                    Ende selt oec weten hoe ende watte
                    Van allen wijsheden.
YEVE   Serpent, wats datte?   205
                    Waert soe, daer wildic mi toe pinen!
                    Wats de sake?
TSERPENT   Van goeder minen
                    Staet hier een boem in desen pleyne,
                    Wies appele soe soet sijn ende soe reyne,
                    Diere nutte, hi leefde emmermeere.   210
                    Oec soude hi sijn gelijc den here
                    In vruechden, in vreden, sonder verdriet,
                    Teewigen dagen.

THE SERPENT	Now then I will go
	To Eve. If I can persuade her,
	She will convert Adam,
	Although God has forbidden it.
	Women's cunning is so great 185
	That they will persist with their plans
	Even though they suffer for it.
	So this is the way to do it
	To get what we want.
ENVY	That's quite clear.
	If you tackle lady Eve with cunning, 190
	It'll all work.
THE SERPENT	Gladly and truly;
	I'll get to it at once.
	Let's go! I think this will help us.

[The Serpent approaches Eve.]

Eve, you are lady of this garden,
Which the lord, perfect creator,   195
Has made through his plentiful grace,
So that you and all your descendants
Would deserve, to put it briefly,
The glory in which the angels dwelt—
Yes, lady, through his great mercy.   200
But if you would follow my counsel,
I would then give you such advice,
That you would live for ever,
And would also know the ins and outs
Of all wisdom.

EVE	Serpent, what do you mean? 205
	If that were true, I would try hard for it!
	What exactly are you saying?
THE SERPENT	There's a fine tree here
	In this pleasant garden
	Whose apples are so sweet and so pure,
	That whoever eats from them will live forever. 210
	And also he would equal the lord
	In joy, in peace, without sorrow
	Everlastingly.

YEVE   Na dijn bediet
                              Serpent, waert groet om ons, vorwaer!

                              Adam, verstaet mijn redene claer: 215
                              Ic bringe u meere, die emmer geproeft
                              Moet sijn ende die ons sere behoeft
                              Te doene, want wijs selen genesen
                              Vander doot.
ADAM   Wat soude dat wesen,
                              Vrou Yeve, dat ghi met nernste begeert   220
                              Aen mi? Eest dat ghijt mi vercleert,
                              Ic salre in doen sonder verdrach
                              Tuwer liefden, dies ic vermach.
                              Want noode so soudic u vererren,
                              Soet redelic si.
YEVE   Dan sonder merren,   225
                              Adam, so wilt na mijn begeren
                              Deser vrucht nutten, sonder ontberen,
                              Van die in midden staet gegroyt
                              Den paradise; want claerlic doyt:
                              Ghi werter bi, dats wel mijn weten,   230
                              Ontsterfelic en groot.
ADAM   Ja? hebdi vergheten
                              Dat ons de here sonder genoet
                              Van diere vrucht te eten verboet?
                              Ende dat wi elder na ons gevoech
                              Van allen vruchten nutten genoech,   235
                              Maer dat wi emmer niet en daden
                              Teghen tgebod?
YEVE   Laet u geraden,
                              Lieve Adam! Op alle trouwe,
                              Et vander vrucht.
ADAM   Ach weerde vrouwe,
                              Wi en hebben emmer geen noot van dien,   240
                              Te doene tegen des heren verbien.
                              Hier staet soe menegen boem seer liefflic
                              Gegroyt, wiens vruchten sijn gerieflic
                              Van scine, van roke, ende oec van smaken.
                              Wat node waers, dat wy dan braken   245
                              Tgebod Gods ende tegen sijn woerden
                              In contrarien dan overhoerden,

EVE	As I understand you,
	Serpent, for us that would be something indeed.

[Eve turns to Adam.]

	Adam, listen, I've heard something special:	215
	I bring you a message, surely which must surely be	
	Tested, and on which, without fail,	
	We must act, for through it we will be freed	
	From death.	
ADAM	What could it be then,	
	Lady Eve, that you so earnestly desire	220
	From me? If you can explain it to me	
	Then I will do without delay	
	Whatever I can, for love of you.	
	I couldn't bear to anger you,	
	Unless you ask something unreasonable.	
EVE	Without further ado,	225
	Adam, do as I ask you	
	And immediately eat this fruit,	
	From the tree which stands in the middle	
	Of paradise. For it is clear	
	That through this fruit, I'm certain of it,	230
	You will be mighty and immortal.	
ADAM	What! Have you forgotten	
	That our peerless lord	
	Forbad us to eat that fruit?	
	And that anywhere else, as we like	
	We can eat plenty of all other fruit,	235
	As long as we do not act	
	Against his command?	
EVE	Please listen to me,	
	Dear Adam! Trust me,	
	And eat of this fruit.	
ADAM	O dearest lady,	
	We really don't need to do this,	240
	And go against the lord's command.	
	There are so many lovely trees	
	Growing here, whose fruits are pleasing	
	To look at, to smell and also to taste.	
	What need have we then to break	245
	God's command and in defiance of his words	
	Be rebellious in disobedience	

	Die ons tsier liesten heeft besneden	
	Te deser hoecheyt?	

YEVE   Keeren, sijt te vreden
         Adam! Wi selen den here wel payen.   250
         Getroest u dies, laet u gerayen.
         Wi selender vrame bi ontfaen,
         Dat hopic. Hout, siet!
ADAM   Ic saelt bestaen,
         Al eest mi tegen; maar tuwen begeerne
         En willic mi niet pinen te weerne. —   255
         Ie hebt gedaen. God laet ons vromen
         Ende tenen salegen ynde comen!

                                              Selete cort.

GOD   Ic, die ben ende hebbe ghemaect
         Alle dinc ende van nieute omstaect
         Ende op rechtverdicheit gescepen,   260
         Ben nu bi redenen in dien begrepen,
         Dat ic justicie sal doen baren
         Op hen, die overhorich waren
         Mijns geboots, reyn int behagen.
         Dies selen sire penitencie om verdragen   265
         Soe lange, als recht met redenen brieft,
         Dats hem van desen boete gelieft.
         Dan sal mijn gramscap sijn geswicht
         Ende peys dan weder tot hen ghesticht
         Vanden sonden, die si in my   270
         Hebben bedreven.
                          Adam, waer sy?

                              Adam sal comen met eenen
                              blade gedect, ende Yeve oec.

ADAM   Here, ic hoorde u stemme ende wert in vare,
         Mids dat ic naect dus ben int clare.
GOD   Adam, wie hevet u doen weten,
         Dat ghi naect waert? Dan, du hebs gheten   275
         Der vrucht des houts, dwelc ic verboet?
ADAM   Dwijf, die ghi als mijn genoet
         Teenre ghesellinnen hebt gegeven,
         Gaf mi den raet.
GOD   Twi hebstuut bedreven?

To him who out of love has created us
In such a favoured position.

EVE   Jesus! Be content,
Adam! We'll square it with the lord.   250
Come on then, don't worry.
We will benefit from this,
As I hope. Look, take this!

ADAM   I'll do it, then,
Though it goes against the grain; but I don't want to strive
Against what you eagerly desire—   255
There, it's done. May God protect us
And bring us to a blessed end.

A brief Selete.

GOD   I, who am and have created
All things, and made them out of nothing
And founded them on my righteousness,   260
Have now come to the befitting decision
That I shall implement justice
Against those who have proved disobedient
To my wholly beneficial command.
Therefore they shall have to endure penance   265
For as long as is reasonable and fair,
And suitable for this offence.
Then my anger will be assuaged:
Once they have paid for their offences
Peace will be restored to them   270
Once more.
            Adam, where are you?

Adam will appear covered by a leaf, and Eve also.

ADAM   Lord, I heard your voice and I was afraid,
Because I was naked, as you can see.

GOD   Adam, who told you
That you were naked? You must have eaten   275
Of the fruit of the forbidden tree.

ADAM   It was the woman, whom you gave me
As a companion;
She told me to do it.

GOD [*To Eve.*]   Why have you done this?

YEVE   Tserpent heeft mi bedrogen int waen   280
              Mids sinen rade.
GOD   Wantstuut hebt gedaen,
              Serpent, soe seldi vermalendijt
              Sijn ende bliven tewiger tijt
              Onder alle dieren ende beesten ter erden.
              Ende tusscen di ende dwijf sal werden   285
              Viantscap, ende haren ende uwen sade,
              Ende u hoet sal vroech ende spade
              Bedruct wesen onder haer voete.
              Ende Yeve, ic sal di onsoete
              Vermenichfuldegen u ermoe.   290
              In arbeide seldi spa ende vroe
              Dijn kinder baren, ende sonder fijn
              Seltstu onder tsmants macht sijn.
              Adam, om dat ghi sonder noot
              Uut uws wijfs rade, dwelc ic verboot,   295
              Aet vanden bome, sal deerde, wilt merken,
              Vermalendijt sijn in uwen werken:
              In arbeide seldi van haer gevoet sijn.
              Dornen, distelen, aldus moet sijn,
              Sal si u bringen; crude seldi eten   300
              Der eerden; oec seldi int zweten
              Dijns aenscijns dijn broet eten vornoemt,
              Tot dat ghi weder ter erden coemt.
              Want van slike ende van eerden
              Sidi gemaect, ende weder selt werden,   305
              Mids dien dats tu dus hebt gebroken
              Mijn hoge gebod; tmoet sijn gewroken,
              Des en can nyemen doen beweerte.
              Bi mi moet risen rechts begeerte;
              So wel hem diet volcht ende na mi hayt.   310
              Waer sidi, mijn ingele? Hebdi genayt
              Van desen besondegen haer lieder cleere,
              Soe ict beval?
EEN INGEL   Siet, ja wi, here.
              Si sijn bereet tot uwen vermane,
              Soet redelic sy.
GOD   Nu, doetse hen ane.   315
              Ic sal hem hulpen decken haer lee
              Ende slutense hier uut deser stee,
              Daer van nu voert na desen tijt
              Ne geen natuerlic mensce en blijt,

EVE	The serpent has deceived me, I realise,	280
	With his advice.	
GOD	Because you have done this,	
	Serpent, you will be cursed	
	And remain so forever,	
	Alone among all animals and beasts on earth.	
	And between you and the woman shall arise	285
	Enmity, and between her and your seed.	
	And your head shall be at all times	
	Crushed under her feet.	
	And Eve, I shall mercilessly	
	Multiply your misery.	290
	In labour you will always	
	Bear your children, and forever	
	You will be in the power of the man.	
	Adam, because you needlessly	
	Followed your wife's advice, and ate from the tree	295
	Which I forbade, the earth, take note,	
	Will be cursed, as will your work:	
	Through labour you will earn your living.	
	Thorns and thistles, thus shall it be,	
	Will she bring you; you shall eat the herbs	300
	Of the earth; and you shall eat your bread	
	By the sweat of your brow,	
	Until you return to dust.	
	For out of clay and dust	
	You were created, and you will return to it;	305
	And because you have so broken	
	My high command, it must be avenged:	
	No one can avert that.	
	Through me must arise the desire for justice;	
	Blessed be he who follows this and longs for me.	310
	Where are you, my angel? Have you sown	
	The clothes for these sinners	
	As I commanded?	
AN ANGEL	Yes, we have, lord, look.	
	They are ready as you decreed	
	And as is just.	
GOD	Clothe them both.	315
	I shall help them to cover their members	
	And exclude them from here, from this place,	
	Where from now on and forever	
	No normal human being will live:	

Ja, sonder enege die int versterken   320
Mijn prophecie selen vol werken,
Ter vramen van hem die na dbehoren
In minen name werden herboren
Int salege doepsel, sonder verlaet,
Tot haren behouwe. Nu, Adam, gaet!   325
Hier uut moetti gesloten werden
Ewelic, om u overterden.
Ghi hadt te wensche al uwen cuere.
Serubin, blijfter staende vuere.`
Met uwen zwerde, sonder sparen,   330
Seldi dese suver stat bewaren.
Hets mijn bevelen dat ghijt doet.

DINGEL CHERUBIN *blijft staende tot Adams doot.*

O here vol gracien, in uwer oetmoet
Ghevic mi over, sonder verdrach.
Ghi hebbet al in uwer behoet,   335
Want ghi in uwer genaden soet
Hebt doen verscheeden nacht ende dach.
Van uwer groetheit niemen en mach
Te vollen begripen, benic wel vroet.
Ghi blijft ende waert, eer oude plach.   340
Grondeloes vloyende soe es u vloet.
Dies men u lof toe scriven moet.

Selete; sanc of spel.

ADAM   O laes, wat salic nu bestaen,
              Erm, onsalich knecht, vol rouwen!
              Wat salic maken, waer salic gaen?   345
              Hoe hebdijt, erm keytijf, gebrouwen?
              In weelden haddi u mogen houwen,
              Daer ghi nu ellindich blijft.
              Die duecht wilt lonen met ontrouwen,
              Hets redelic dat hijs druc bedrijft.   350
              Ic heb gesteken ende ghekijft
              Tegen den meester der meesteren gemeene.
              My selven hebbicker mede ontlijft
              Ende ewelic brocht in bitteren weene.

	Yes, except some who will work towards	320
	The fulfilment of my prophecy,	
	To the benefit of those who, as is proper,	
	Are reborn in my name	
	Through everlasting holy baptism,	
	To safeguard their salvation. Now, Adam, go!	325
	You shall be kept away from here	
	For ever, because of your offence.	
	You had all that you could desire.	
	Cherubim, stay and guard the gates.	
	With your swords, without fear or favour;	330
	You shall protect this holy place.	
	It is my command that you do so.	

AN ANGEL OF THE CHERUBIM remains standing until Adam's death.

	O Lord, full of grace, I yield myself	
	To your benevolence, without restraint.	
	You hold everything in your power,	335
	For you in your sweet mercy	
	Have made separate night and day.	
	No one can wholly comprehend	
	Your greatness, of that I'm certain:	
	You are and were before time began.	340
	Unfathomable flows your stream.	
	Therefore we must offer you praise.	

Selete, singing or playing.

ADAM	Alas, what shall I do now,	
	Poor wretch that I am, full of grief!	
	What shall I do, where shall I go?	345
	How did you come to this, poor slave?	
	You could have remained in prosperity	
	While now you are in misery.	
	If betrayal is the recompense for goodness	
	Then it's right I should suffer grief.	350
	I have fought and striven	
	Against the lord of lords.	
	Myself I have undone by this,	
	And brought forever into bitter tears.	

YEVE	Ay laes, nu vinden wi ons alleene,	355
	Die tierst van Gode waren bevrijt!	
	Tserpent, die scalke beeste onreene,	
	Heeft ons by rade aldus ontwijt.	
	Wy moesten emmer sijn benijt,	
	Om dat wi dus in eren saten.	360
	Wi hebben ons qualic daer in gequijt.	
	Dies sijn wi nu aldus verwaten!	
ADAM	Vrou Yeve, ten can ons niet gebaten,	
	Dat wi veel meer rouwen dreven.	
	Maer hopen wi inder caritaten,	365
	Die ons de here van desen wil geven.	
	Wi hebben ons selven brocht int sneven	
	Onversien, bi dommen rade.	
	Dies laet ons bidden den here verheven,	
	Dat hi ons toene sijn genade.	370
YEVE	Gheminde man, hout, nemt dees spade,	
	Daer mede soe moetti wercs beginnen.	
	Met bitteren arbeide ende met smade	
	Soe moeten wi onsen nootdorst winnen.	
ADAM	Laes, int paradijs daer bynnen	375
	En hadden wi des ne genen noet,	
	Want alle vruchten, na tsheren verzinnen,	
	Die wiesen alsoe hise geboet,	
	Eer hi ons dus daer buten sloet.	

Selete: pause.

NIJT	O Lucifer, meester, verhuecht u, lieve!	380
LUCIFER	Hoe gevaren, Nijt?	
NIJT	Juust tonsen gerieve	
	Eest comen, wi en souden cume anders wenscen.	
LUCIFER	Eest waer, duvel, eest waer?	
NIJT	Jaet, alle menscen	
	Die moeten nu sterven, dats verloren!	
	Ende dan selense ons toebehoren	385
	Ende bliven bi ons hier inder qualen,	
	Ocht thoechste recht sal moeten falen	
	Ende dat voertstel des groets heren.	
	Maer hemel ende erde soude eer verkeren,	
	Eer hi veranderde luttel of yet	390
	Die regle van rechte.	

EVE	Alas, now we find ourselves deserted,	355
	We who before were protected by God!	
	The serpent, that deceitful, unclean beast,	
	Has by his counsel desecrated us.	
	We were bound to be envied	
	Because we dwelt in honour.	360
	We have conducted ourselves badly	
	And that's why we are now accursed!	
ADAM	Lady Eve, it will not help us a jot	
	To go on lamenting.	
	But let us hope for charity,	365
	That the lord may want to give us.	
	We have brought this fall upon ourselves	
	Recklessly, and through stupid counsel.	
	So let us pray the lord almighty	
	That he will show us his mercy.	370
EVE	Beloved husband, here, take this spade:	
	With it you must begin your work.	
	With harsh labour and with shame	
	We will have to make our living.	
ADAM	Alas, in paradise itself	375
	We did not want for anything,	
	For all fruits, as God ordained,	
	Grew as he commanded them,	
	Before he drove us out.	

Selete: Pause,

ENVY	O Lucifer, dearest master, rejoice!	380
LUCIFER	How did it go, Envy?	
ENVY	Just as we wanted,	
	It has happened; we couldn't wish for anything better.	
LUCIFER	Is that true, devil, is that true?	
ENVY	Yes, all people	
	Must now die, that's their fate!	
	And then they will belong to us	385
	And remain with us here in misery,	
	Or the supreme justice would have to fail	
	And the divine plan of the Almighty.	
	But heaven and earth would sooner change,	
	Before he would alter one jot or tittle	390
	The rule of justice.	

LUCIFER   Dats wel bespiet!
                    Hulpe longeren, nu horic vry!
                    Comt dus die mensce met ons hier bi,
                    Soe sal hi betalen ons gequel,
                    Dat wi hier lyen!
NIJT   Mijn mager vel,   395
                    Dat ic dus na heb liggen verbiten,
                    Es nu soe vrolic, het waent spliten,
                    Om dies dat ic den mensce, verheven
                    Met Gode, dus heb gebracht int sneven!
                    Hadde hi de vroude beseten so soete,   400
                    Ic hadde af gheeten hande en voete,
                    En haen wijs hem niet connen beweren
                    Haer welvaert.
LUCIFER   En weet mi hoe gebeeren.
                    Mi selven en canic niet bedwingen!
                    Ic sal uut minen velle springen   405
                    Van bliscepen, dat ghise dus uut duechden
                    Hebt getrocken. Soe groten vruechden
                    En hadde noyt duvel vor desen int lijf!
                    Nijt, ic geef u vor dit bedrijf,
                    Dat ghi aen Adame hebt bedreven,   410
                    Dat ghi voert ewelic selt leven
                    Op deser werelt ende daer na erfelic
                    Seldi wesen altoes onsterfelic;
                    Oec blijfdi hier met mi gecroent
                    Inder hellen.
NIJT   Soe worden gehoent   415
                    Veel sielen, die ic noch sal betrapen.
                    Ende clerke, moencke, canoenke, papen,
                    Die pittereren selen te strie
                    Op anderen, bi giericheien en bi nie,
                    Die salic hier noch met hopen bringen   420
                    En doense in onsen ketel springen
                    Van boven neder, bi menegen cudde
                    Ongetelt!
LUCIFER   Ic lache dat ic scudde,
                    Om dat de mensce, die was verheven,
                    Aldus der gracien es ontdreven,   425
                    Die hem die here dor sijn gena
                    Verleende, ende sal nu moeten met sma
                    Bi ons sijn. Twas een abel practike,
                    Dat ment soe coecte!

LUCIFER   You've done that well!
                          Dammit, I'm pleased to hear that!
                          So, if mankind will join us here,
                          That will make up for the torment
                          That we suffer here!
ENVY   My scraggy hide,   395
                          Which I have been chewing up
                          Is now so cheerful, I'm going to burst,
                          Because I have got man, so favoured
                          By God, brought into perdition.
                          If he had possessed that joy so sweet   400
                          I would have eaten my hands and feet,
                          Should we not have not been able to prevent
                          His well-being.
LUCIFER   I'm beside myself with joy.
                          I can't control myself at all!
                          I'll jump out of my skin   405
                          With pleasure, that thus you have dragged them
                          Out of bliss. Such great joys
                          No devil ever felt before!
                          Envy, I grant you for the misfortune
                          That you have imposed on Adam   410
                          That from now you will live forever
                          In this world and after that your inheritance
                          Will be eternal life;
                          And also you'll remain here by my side, crowned
                          In hell.
ENVY   So are deceived   415
                          Many souls, whom I will still trap.
                          And clerks, monks, canons, priests,
                          Who exert themselves to prey
                          On others, out of avarice and envy,
                          I will pile up here,   420
                          And make them jump down into our kettle
                          From above, in numbers
                          Uncountable!
LUCIFER   I'm shaking with laughter
                          Because mankind, who was exalted,
                          Has thus been robbed of grace,   425
                          Which the lord had granted him
                          Through his mercy, and must now be with us
                          In shame. That was a wonderful trick,
                          Which cooked his goose!

j DUVEL   Noyt des gelike
                        En hoorde geen duvel singen noch lesen   430
                        Van liste! Nijt, ghi sult claer wesen
                        Lucifers raet in allen dingen;
                        Ghi selt allene meer wercs toe bringen
                        Dan al de duvels of neckers broet
                        Der ganser hellen. De sake eyscht spoet   435
                        Om te vervolgene tot meer profijts,
                        Hoe dat verkeerde.
LUCIFER   Nu toe, in tijts
                        Vor den rechtere, soet behoert,
                        Eer dat vercoele; wi selen hem dwoert
                        Verhalen, dat hi hen lieden spelde,   440
                        Als hise int paradijs ierst stelde.
                        Dan als wijt hem aldus vor bringen,
                        Hi en saels niet loechenen.
NIJT   Hi en canse niet verdingen
                        Bi rechte; ende anders in genen kere
                        Dan redene ende recht en gheert de here.   445
                        Tegen recht en ginchi niet een hoy
                        Om hemel en eerde.
LUCIFER   Scoy duvel, scoy
                        Tot vor den rechtere; het geeft wel vrame
                        Ter stont te besoekene. Brinct met Adame,
                        Dat hi sijn vonnesse hoer. Laet sien,   450
                        Na sijn mesdragen sal recht gescien,
                        Dat hopic aen die gerechtiche
                        Des groets heren.
NIJT   Nu ghi moet me,
                        Adam, aenhoren tvonnesse van Gode.
                        Ghi hebt contrarie sinen gebode   455
                        Bi uwen consente willen sondegen.
                        Dies seldi van ons horen becondegen
                        Wat boeten datter toe behoert
                        Tselker mesdaet; ende ghi, tert voert,
                        Yeve. Ghi hebt bedreven tfeit,   460
                        Dus moettier oec an.
ADAM   Het es de waerheit,
                        Dat wi bi onversienen rae
                        Tgebod braken; des hoert genae
                        Des heren ter saken, om cort verclaren.
                        Want wiere doch verleit in waren   465
                        Van u, viant, die ons uut spite

FIRST DEVIL   No scheme like it
                        Was ever heard, sung or read,   430
                        By any devil! Envy, you'll clearly be
                        Lucifer's advisor in all things.
                        You alone will bring more work
                        Than all the devils in Old Nick's brood
                        In the whole of hell. This success   435
                        Needs to be pressed home
                        Even though we've made such a good start.
LUCIFER   Come on, it's time
                        To go before the judge, as is proper,
                        Before things cool off. We shall rely on
                        The word that he spelled out for them   440
                        When he first placed them in Paradise.
                        If we then confront him with that
                        He won't be able to deny it.
ENVY   He cannot defend this well
                        In truth; for nothing else in any respect
                        Desires the lord but reason and justice.   445
                        He would not go against justice by one jot
                        For all heaven and hell.
LUCIFER   Quick, devil, quick,
                        Bring it before the judge; it's a great advantage
                        To make a case without delay; and bring Adam
                        To hear the verdict. Let it be seen   450
                        That his wickedness receives due punishment;
                        I expect that from the justice
                        Of God almighty.
ENVY   Now you have to come,
                        Adam, and hear God's judgement.
                        You have, in defiance of his command,   455
                        Deliberately, giving consent.
                        And so you will hear us claim
                        The punishment which is fitting
                        For such a crime; you too, come forward,
                        Eve. You have done this deed,   460
                        And must take the consequences.
ADAM   It is the truth,
                        That we, through an error of judgement,
                        Broke God's command; in short
                        Such a case should attract his mercy.
                        For we were tempted to it   465
                        By you, fiend, who from spite

                 Brocht hebt aldus te Gods verwite.
                 Ende uut u es, lude en stille,
                 Geresen den swaren overwille,
                 Die wi in mensceliker natie   470
                 Broesscelic wrachten; dies hort wel gracie
                 Vanden rechtere. Dit aengesien,
                 Hopix genade.

LUCIFER   Neen, wacht u van dien!
                 Van gracien en wasser niet gesproken.
                 In rechte begeric, dat si gewroken   475
                 Die sonde des overwils, bedreven
                 Van u beiden, en dat int sneven
                 Ghi ende u afcomst gemeene
                 Ewelic bliven selt in weene,
                 Want ghi verhoert hebt den volleestere   480
                 Des hemels enter erden.

NIJT   Alsoe waest, meestere!
                 Dat sijn de crude, vor waer soe sijnt!
                 Al waerdi van ons in dien gepijnt,
                 Dat ghi dit deet en hebt gedaen,
                 Ghi haddet mogen wederstaen,   485
                 Want ghi van Gode hadt uwen wille
                 Te doene; aldus te desen gescille
                 En hoert geen gracie, ic zegt u plat.
                 Ende oft ghi uwen wille hadt
                 Te doene, en consti dan ons bezwaringe   490
                 Niet wederstaen, tes al plaringe
                 Dat ghier tegen te seggen moegt weten.
                 Bi rechte salment u af meten.
                 Tes verloren veel gemaut
                 Ocht gepluert.

LUCIFER   Mi hoert, alst naut,   495
                 Oec daer in te sprekene een woert.
                 O alder rechtverdichste rechter, hoert!
                 Ic bid u, dat ghi hier op let:
                 Ghi hebt den mensce gegeven .j.wet
                 Ende in menichfuldegher wyse   500
                 Gestelt in uwen paradyse
                 Ende hem geseit en weten laten:
                 Te wat uren si vanden houte aten,
                 Dat daer in midden der pleyne stoet,
                 So sou hi sterven. Dus, rechter goet,   505
                 De mensce heeft ongehorsamheit

	Have delivered us into God's wrath.	
	From you has arisen, without a doubt,	
	That grave disobedience	
	Which we, as fragile human beings,	470
	Did commit; mercy is appropriate for this	
	On the part of the judge. Taking this into account	
	I hope for mercy.	
LUCIFER	No, watch what you're saying!	
	Mercy is out of the question.	
	In justice I desire that the sin of disobedience	475
	Committed by you both	
	Be avenged, and that by your fall	
	You and all your descendants	
	Will always remain in grief	
	Because you have defied the creator	480
	Of heaven and earth.	
ENVY	That's how it was, master!	
	That is the crux, for sure it is!	
	Even if we tempted you to it,	
	An offence that you did commit,	
	You ought to have resisted.	485
	For you received from God the power	
	To exercise free will; and in this conflict	
	Mercy has no place, I tell you straight.	
	And if you had your free will	
	To exercise, and you could not withstand	490
	Our temptation, then it's all nonsense	
	Whatever you have to say against it.	
	Justice shall be meted out to you.	
	It's no use complaining	
	Or getting into a rage.	
LUCIFER	It's fitting, when it comes to it	495
	For me to add my pennyworth.	
	O most just judge, hear this!	
	I implore you to pay heed to it:	
	You have given mankind a law,	
	You have established him in your Paradise	500
	With many blessings,	
	And have told him and let him know	
	That whenever he should eat from the tree	
	Standing in the middle of Paradise	
	He would then die. In effect, wise judge,	505
	Mankind has really shown	

          Bewijst ende u gebod weerleit.
          Dies eyschic, datti sterve al voren
          Ende dat mi dan sal toe behoren
          Sijn siele, ende daer na emmermeere   510
          Sijnder nacomers.

NIJT   Tes redelic, heere,
          Want de mensce, also men weet,
          Heeft afgeworpen u zuver cleet
          Ende es uwer gracien contrarie vonden
          Ende ons cleder aen gedaen van sonden.   515
          Ten es geen wonder, dat ghi u bolcht:
          Hijs u ontgaen ende ons gevolcht.
          Ende oft hi, here, aldus int fijn
          Met u niet en wilde, so moesti met ons sijn.
          Want u contrarie in recht bediet   520
          Ons gebod dede ende duwe liet.
          Aldus en can hi hem niet beweren
          Bi genen rechte, na ons vercleren,
          Hi en moet ons ewelic horen toe
          Ende al de sine.

GOD   Lieve Adam, hoe   525
          So hebdi u selven hier toe gegeven?
          Waerdi van mire gracien moe,
          Daer ic u toe hadde verheven?
          Ghi hadt hier binnen mogen leven
          Termijn van redeliken jaren;   530
          Dan haddi ewelic, sonder sneven,
          Daer boven in dewige vruecht gevaren.
          Nu es verloren dijn mesbaren;
          De regle van rechte sal moeten gescien.
          De duvels eysschen om u mesvaren,   535
          Dat ic u wise te hem lien.
          Wetti iet te seggene te dien
          In u behulp op tsviants treeken,
          Sprect op! Elcx sake wel oversien,
          Soe en sal hier niemen geen recht gebreken.   540

ADAM   Lacen, here God, en weet wat spreken!
          Ic kynne, dat ic de sonde dede.
          Maer genadechlic soe wiltse wreken
          Op my ende minen nacomers mede.
          Selen die moeten den ewigen vrede   545
          Derven om onser beider sonden,
          Dan dunct mi geen gerechtichede.

Disobedience and defied your command.
Therefore I demand that he should die
And that his soul should belong
To me, and after that, forever,　　　　　　　　　510
The souls of his descendants.

ENVY　　　　　　　　　　　　　　　Yes, reason demands that, lord,

For mankind, as we know,
Has thrown away your cloak of purity
And has acted in defiance of your mercy
And has put on our garb of sins.　　　　　　　515
You have every right to be angry:
He has forsaken you and followed us.
And if he, lord, does in the end
Not want to be with you, he must be with us.
Because, to be precise, against you　　　　　　520
He did our bidding and ignored yours.
So he cannot defend himself
With any plea, as far as we can see:
He must now be ours forever
And so must all his kin.

GOD　　　　　　　　　　　　　　　　Dear Adam, how is it　　525

That you have given yourself to this?
Had you wearied of my grace
Into which you were lifted?
You could have lived in this place
For as many years as you wanted.　　　　　　530
And then you would, without dying and forever,
Have entered into heaven and its eternal joy.
But now all your grief is in vain;
The rule of law must prevail.
Because of your sin the devils demand　　　535
That I hand you over to them.
If you can think of anything to say
That will help your defence against the devil's tricks,
Speak up! Each side must be heard thoroughly
Then no one shall want for justice.　　　　　540

ADAM　　Alas, lord God, I do not know what to say!

I confess that I committed this sin.
But please avenge it mildly
On me and on my descendants even more.
It is they who will be denied eternal peace　　545
Because we two have sinned:
That does not seem justice to me.

En si mesdadich niet en sijn vonden
Anders dan wise hebben gebonden
In sonden, bi onversienen rade, 550
Mi dunct, hier hoert wel toe genade.

NIJT Antworde van desen, here, wilt verstaen.
Die sondare die moet loen ontfaen,
Na dat es sijn weerdichede
Van hem, daer hi de sonde aen dede. 555
Oec sidi geduerech rechter, here;
Dus moet de beteringe emmermere
Vanden sondare sijn bedreven,
Die tsegen u in sonden sneven.
Oec dor u groetheit, hort wes ic meene, 560
Waer die emende veel te cleene
Van hem gedaen, die tfeit selve wrachte.
Dus moet dan arnen al tgeslachte.
Ende noch, en dade uws selfs gevoech,
En waer u dit niet groet genoech 565
— U grote mogentheit aen ghesien —,
Wistmen meer wraken te doen gescien
Dan aenden mensceliken knecht.
Bi redenen, ende dies versuekic recht,
Here, op een cort, sonder verdrach. 570

GOD O mensce, wat horic van di, o wach!
Rechts soe salic mi moeten bewinden.
Want na dat redene en recht vermach,
En condier geen onscout tegen vinden.
Ic dede u lieden als mijn verminden 575
Ende coes u te mire glorien bequame,
Maer ghi hebt u laten verblinden;
Dies salder u af risen blame.
Want al dat mensceliken name
Voert aen sal dragen, na desen tijt 580
Geboren werdende van Adame,
Die worden van mi vermalendijt
Ende geefse u over in u berijt,
Viant. Wanneer si selen sterven,
Soe seldise om deser sonden spijt 585
Met u inder hellen erven.
Dit vonnesse gevic te deser werven.

LUCIFER Lof, rechter, van uwen rechte vercoren.
Wi dancken ons uwer weerdicheien!

So if they have not been proved guilty
Except that we have bound them
In sin, because of evil advice,   550
I think mercy should here prevail.

ENVY   Answer this, lord, and mark it well.
The sinners, they must receive their due,
According to the dignity
Of him, against whom he sinned.   555
Besides you are the everlasting judge, lord;
And so the atonement must forever,
Be paid by the sinners,
Who will perish by sinning against you.
Because of your greatness — listen to what I mean —   560
The penitence would be much too small
If it were paid only by him, who committed the actual deed.
Therefore all his descendants will have to pay.
And yet, even if that really wasn't your own wish,
And if this were not sufficient penance for you —   565
Taking into account your great power —
Then one should think of a greater revenge
To impose on this man, who is merely a servant.
For these reasons I demand justice in this respect,
Lord, immediately and without delay.   570

GOD   O man, what do I hear about you, alas!
I shall have to mete out justice:
In spite of all that reason and right can do,
You cannot find any justification for this.
I treated you both with great love   575
And chose you to enhance my glory,
But you have let yourselves be blinded;
Therefore shame will beset you.
For all that henceforward
Will bear the name of mankind   580
And who after this will be born from Adam,
Those will be cursed by me,
And I yield them to your power,
Fiend. When they shall die,
They will, because of this dire sin,   585
Share your inheritance in hell.
This is the judgement that I pronounce at this time.

LUCIFER Praise, judge, for your judgement dire.
We thank you for your favours shared!

NIJT	Ghi hebt gemindert onsen toren.	590
	Lof, rechter, van uwen rechte vercoren.	
LUCIFER	Wy selen gaen stampen en smoren	
	Ende tegen hem lieden ons coken bereyen.	
NIJT	Lof, rechter, van uwen rechte vercoren.	
	Wi bedancken ons uwer werdicheyen!	595
LUCIFER	Scoyen wi, duvel, sonder beyen	
	Tot inden groten kakebo!	
	Gawi de plaetse lingen en breyen:	
	Het comter nu al, des ben ic vro!	
NIJT	Het worter bestiert, seg, so, heer, so!	600
	Laet werden, laet wassen Adams tronc.	
	Si moeten alle in desen no	
	Bi ons springen enen spronc,	
	Ja, sijnse out of sijnse jonc!	
LUCIFER	Ghi helle, hoert wes ic doe bekint:	605
	Doet maken alrande instrumint	
	Van ruesters, van craulen en van tangen,	
	Daer ghi den mensce met selt ontfangen,	
	Van cupen, van pannen ende van ketelen,	
	Van pecke en van gloyende zeetelen,	610
	Om yegeliken nae sinen state	
	Tontfane, coninge en prelate.	
	Al saelter comen, rijf en raf!	
	Maect u bereescap en comes af,	
	Sijt blide en vro! Helle, maect feeste,	615
	Het wert al onse, beide minste en meeste!	

Groet gerommel ende geruusch salmen inde helle maken met alrehande geruchte.
                                                       Ende dan selete.

ADAM *seit tot sinen kinderen:*		
	Och lieve geminde kinder vercoren,	
	Wi hebben de gracie Gods verloren.	
	Des moeten wi alle als erme slaven	
	Labueren, luken, dersschen en graven	620
	Ende winnen in regen, in couden, met sere,	
	Daer wy bi leven.	
j KINT	Lof hebbe die Here,	
	Die mach ons troesten van allen hindere!	
ADAM	O laes, mijn uutvercoren kindere,	
	Ic werde versleten, out en cranc.	625
	Dus dese ellinde valt mi te lanc,	

ENVY	You have smoothed away our ire.	590
	Praise, judge, for your judgement dire.	
LUCIFER	We begin to rage and fan the fire,	
	For them our ovens will be prepared.	
ENVY	Praise, judge, for your judgement dire.	
	We thank you for your favours shared!	595
LUCIFER	Let's scamper, devil, without ado	
	Into the vast caldrons of hell!!	
	Go we, to lengthen and widen the place:	
	They're all coming my way—and it's great!	
ENVY	It's all going our way, don't you think, lord?	600
	May Adam's line increase and grow!	
	They'll have to jump	
	In this misery into our trap,	
	Whether they're old or young!	
LUCIFER	Hey, hell, listen to what I make known:	605
	Go and prepare all sorts of instruments	
	Of gridirons, tridents and pincers	
	With which to welcome mankind	
	And vats and pots and kettles	
	Of pitch and red hot seats	610
	To receive everybody	
	According to his state, king and prelate.	
	They're all going to come, all the riffraff!	
	Make your preparations and finish them,	
	Whoopee! Hell, let's have a ball!	615
	They're all going to be ours, great and small!	

Here they make a great racket and clatter in hell, with all sorts of noises.
And then Selete.

ADAM *says to his children:*	O dearly beloved, cherished children,	
	We have lost the grace of God.	
	So all of us, like poor slaves,	
	Must labour and fence, and thresh and dig,	620
	And in rain, in cold, in pain,	
	Eke out a living.	
FIRST CHILD	Praise be to the Lord	
	Who can console us in all misery!	
ADAM	Alas, my cherished children	
	I have become worn out, old and ill.	625
	So this misery lasts too long for me,	

Want ic heb hier in pinen sware
Geleeft over .ix^c. jare.
Dies mijn siecte es ongemeten.
Lacen, nu soudic geerne weten,   630
Wanneer dat ic de medicine
Gecrigen sal van mire pine.
Woude mi yemen den zin ontbinden,
Soe waric vroe.

DANDER KINT   Wildi yet sinden
Ten paradise, datmen daer vrage   635
Om medicine tot onsen behage,
Hoe dat u boete sal gescien
Van uwer qualen?

ADAM   Set, gaet besien
Ten paradise in corten stonde,
Want mi lanct na mijn gesonde.   640
Dies vraecht den ingel, wanneert sal wesen
Dat ic mire qualen worde genesen
Ende hoemen blusschen mochte dmesval.
Gaet, spoet u, lieve.

SET   Wel vader, ic sal
Daerwert lopen met groter haesten   645
Ende besoeken ten alder naesten
Die medicine, die u mach falen.
Adieu, dits wech, om cort verhalen:
God wil u hoeden altijt vor lee.

ADAM   Lieve kinder, mi es soe wee!   650
Mijn herte wert zwaerder dan .j. loot.
Lacen, mi naect de bitter doot!
Mijn aderen crempen, mi cout mijn bloet.
Ic moet van hier.

j KINT   Hebt goeden moet,
Vercorne vader, ic hoep ghi saen   655
Vertroest selt werden.

ADAM   En mach niet ontgaen
Der doot, mi wert soe wee ter herten.
En can niet meer van groter smerten.
Mijn zenuwen crympen, mi faelgeren de sinnen.
Dus leyt mi te mijnder cameren bynnen.   660
Mijn herte bezwijct my, ic werde soe cranc
De doot die noept my.

j KINT   O vaderlijc sceiden, wreet ende stranc,
Die nu den ganc der doot moet terden!

For I have with great hardship
Lived here for more than nine hundred years.
My plight is never ending.
Alas, I would now gladly know, 630
When I shall receive the medicine
Which will soothe my pain.
If anyone could reveal that to me,
Then I should be happy.

SECOND CHILD Would you like to send someone
To Paradise, to seek there 635
For a medicine to comfort us,
And ask what penance would cure you
Of your ills?

ADAM Seth, go and search
In Paradise, as fast as you can,
For I long to be cured. 640
Then ask the angel when it will be
That I will be healed of my ills
And how our griefs may be assuaged.
Go, make haste, dear son!

SETH Yes, father, I shall
Go thither in great haste 645
And search as best I can
For the medicine, which might help you.
Adieu, I'm off without delay:
May God always keep you from grief.

ADAM Dear children, I am so ill! 650
My heart is growing heavier than lead.
Alas, now bitter death approaches me!
My veins contract, my blood runs cold.
I must depart.

FIRST CHILD Be brave,
Beloved father, I hope that soon 655
You will be consoled.

ADAM I cannot escape
My death; my heart becomes so sore.
I cannot go on in this great pain.
My nerves contract; my senses fail.
Now lead me to my chamber. 660
My heart gives way, I become so weak:
Death is now near me.

FIRST CHILD O father, your departure is cruel and harsh,
For you must now tread the path of death!

Haddy mogen verbeyden dontfanc
Van Sed eerlanc, oft ghi verlost mocht werden,   665
Die ten paradise wert es met groten scerden,
Het soude volherden u, hopic, algadere
Al dinen druck.

DANDER KINT   O lieve vadere
Adam, nu sidi, soet God begeerde,
Ghestorven. — Nu laetten ons inder eerde   670
Begraven ende bidden Gode den here,
Dat hi sijn gracie op hem kere.

j KINT   Wel broeder, ic ben bereet tot desen.
O laes, tmoet al gestorven wesen.

DANDER KINT   Orlof Adam, geminde vadere,   675
Tenen sceidene so eest nu comen.
.IX^c.ende.XXX.jaere hebdi geleeft te gadere,
Nochtan hebdi nu inde genomen.
Wat mach den langen tijt dan vromen?

SET   God danc, ic heb so lange geronnen,   680
Dat ic sie blicken gelijc der zonnen
Dat paradijs, groet van gewichte,
Dwelc God met siere hant selve stichte
Tot tsmenscen vrame, reyn int gescien.
Oec hebbic den sconen ingel gesien,   685
Die God dor sijn hoge weerde
Daer voer stelde met enen zweerde.
Des willic hem te desen stonden
Gaen vragen na mijns vader gesonden,
Met groten nernste, sonder versagen.   690
Eerwerdich ingel, ic come u vragen
Na die over sware mesquame
Van minen geminden vader Adame,
Ocht enege medicine tot dien
Bi gracien tsheren sal gescien.   695
Sier quetsen naem hi geerne bet,
Dies bidt hi om raet.

DINGEL *vor tparadijs*   Verstaet mi, Set!
Ic sal u seggen, hoe en waer mede,
Dat hi sire qualen, die hem let,
Gecrigen sal gesondichede.   700
Dit es den boem, daer hi aen dede
De sonde hier inden paradise.
Bi hem soe sal hem oec den vrede

	If you had been able to wait and learn from Seth,	
	Who went to Paradise in great haste,	665
	Whether you could be redeemed:	
	That would have relieved you completely, I hoped,	
	Of all your misery.	
SECOND CHILD	O beloved father,	
	Adam, now you have died	
	According to God's will. — Now let's bury him	670
	In the earth and pray to God, our lord,	
	That he will grant him his mercy.	
FIRST CHILD	Well, brother, I am prepared for this.	
	Alas we all must die.	
SECOND CHILD	Farewell, Adam, beloved father,	675
	Our parting has now come.	
	Nine hundred and thirty years you lived altogether,	
	But now you have reached your end.	
	What signifies such a long life?	
SETH	God be thanked, I have run so long,	680
	That I can now see, shining like the sun,	
	That Paradise, great in extent,	
	And wonderful to behold, which God created	
	With his own hand for mankind's benefit.	
	I have also seen that beautiful angel	685
	With a sword whom God in his high majesty	
	Placed at the threshold.	
	Therefore I would now like to go	
	And ask him about my father's health,	
	With great urgency and without fear.	690
	Noble angel, I come to ask you	
	About the very serious illness	
	Of my beloved father, Adam,	
	And whether there is any medicine,	
	Which, by the grace of god would cure him.	695
	He longs to be cured from his ills,	
	And so he begs for your counsel.	
THE ANGEL *at the gates of Paradise.*	Listen carefully to me, Seth!	
	I shall tell you how and by what means	
	He will regain his health,	
	From the ills which beset him.	700
	This is the tree he offended	
	In Paradise by his sin.	
	This tree will also be the means through which	

Comen in menichfuldeger wise.
Ghi selt verstaen: met desen rise,   705
Die ic van desen bome u trac,
Daer sal Adam, die oude grise,
Bi werden verlost sijn ongemac.
Gaet henen, plant mi desen tac
Uwen vader onder sijn hoet.   710
Hi sal op groyen, sonder lac,
Ende werden een boem scoen en groet.
Adame soe seldi vinden doot.
Dus doet als ic u heb geseit.
Bi desen wert hi verloest sier noot   715
En brocht tot sire gesondicheit
Van selker qualen als hi in leit.

SET
Lof en danc, God, Here bequame,
Soe moet u ewelic toe vloyen,
Dat uten rise tot smenscen vrame   720
Medicine van sonden sal bloyen.
Maer lacen, den ghenen sal seer vernoyen,
Die selen liggen in bitteren clagen,
Na tgene dat God sijn gracie sal spoyen
Op trijs, dat medicine sal dragen.   725
Orlof, her ingel! Na Gods behagen
Soe sal u hoge begeerte gescien.
Doch hopic, sal yemen gebyen den dagen,
Datmen vruchtbarich dit rijs sal sien.
Om te volcomene als van dien,   730
Dat mi die ingel maecte cont,
Soe willic sier hoger begeerten plien
Ende planten trijs in corter stont,
Ten teekene dat noch sal maken gesont,
Bi gracien tsheren, al ons geslachte   735
Ende dier nu bitterlic liggen gewont
Inder demster hellen grachte.
Ic bevele u, rijs, des heren crachte.

Hier salmen singen of spelen,
Ende dan comt Lucifer.

LUCIFER
O duvels alle, versterct u neringe!
Hier wert so over grote geeringe   740
Vanden sielen die hier zweymen,
Wi en selense waer weten heymen.

He will in various ways achieve peace.
You will come to understand: with this twig   705
Which I picked from the tree for you,
Will Adam, old and grey,
Be freed from his illness.
Go forth, plant this branch for me
Under your father's head.   710
It will grow to perfection
And it will be a large and beautiful tree.
Adam, you will find, has died;
So do as I have commanded you.
Through this he will be freed from his misery   715
And restored to health
From such evils as he suffers.

SETH   Praise and thanks God, beloved Lord,
Must eternally come to you
Because from this twig will flower   720
Medicine for sins to man's benefit.
But alas, this will greatly pain those
Who will lie in bitter lament
Waiting for the moment when God will bestow his grace
On to the branch which will carry medicine.   725
Farewell, lord angel! May God grant
That your mighty prophecy will come to pass.
Also I hope that if anyone comes to see that day
He will perceive this branch bearing fruit.
In order to achieve all that,   730
Which the angel revealed to me,
I will comply with his noble wish
And plant this branch immediately,
As a token that, by the grace of God,
All our descendants will be cured   735
Who are now lying bitterly wounded
In the dark pool of hell.
I commend you, branch, to the power of the lord.

Here they will sing or play, and then Lucifer arrives.

LUCIFER   All you devils, let's get on with it!
There's going to be such a mob   740
Of souls who will arrive here,
That we won't know where to put them.

	Mijn buuc sal bersten int verblien	
	Van deser conscilien.	
NIJT	Tmoet hier al lien,	
	Dat vanden geslachte van Adame	745
	Es comen. Dat blijct aen Abrahame	
	Ende Melchisedech, den iersten pape,	
	Die hier oec sit.	
LUCIFER	Hets tonsen betrape,	
	Dat bi naturen geboren es:	
	Jacob, Joseph ende Moyses,	750
	Josue, Sampsoen ende meer andere,	
	Yesse, Salemoen ende Alexandere,	
	David, Job ende Ezechias,	
	Daneel ende oec Ysayas;	
	En soudse half niet connen bedien	755
	Wat hier getont es.	
NIJT	Den duvel van lien!	
	Het comt hier al, eest leec of clerc!	
	Hoe wijs, hoe constich, of hoe sterc	
	Dat si sijn mogen, tcomter al na.	
	En elc sit hier na sinen sta.	760
	Den last valt groet, al doe wijt geerne.	
	Wie saelt ons beletten?	
LUCIFER	Twaer quaet te beweerne.	
	Niemen en mocht ons so verdullen,	
	Wi[ne] selen den groten kakebo vullen!	
	Noit scuere en was so vol gestommelt	765
	Met scoven!	

Groet geruchte inde helle.

	Hoort hoemen rommelt!	
NIJT	Het duncken mi horselen die daer swermen,	
	Soe crijsschen de zielen.	
LUCIFER	Laet criten, laet kermen!	
	Wy selen ons selven aen hem wreken.	
	Scoy wech, laet ons de brander vort steken.	770

Gheruchte.
Dits tclagen ende tkermen
inde Helle vanden vaders.

	My belly is bursting with glee	
	Because of this synod.	
ENVY	They'll all arrive here,	
	All that have sprung from Adam's	745
	Seed. You can tell that because Abraham	
	And Melchisedech, the first priest,	
	Are also here.	
LUCIFER	This is our prey,	
	All who have been born in nature:	
	Jacob, Joseph and Moses,	750
	Joshua, Samson and a host of others,	
	Jesse, Solomon, Alexander,	
	David, Job and Ezekiel,	
	Daniel and also Isaiah;	
	I can't name half of those	755
	Who are stacked away here.	
ENVY	By the devil, what a crowd!	
	They all come here, be they layman or clerk;	
	However wise or clever, or strong	
	They may be, they all end up here.	
	And everybody sits according to his status.	760
	It's a helluva job, even though we do it gladly.	
	And who's going to prevent us?	
LUCIFER	It will be hard to stop us.	
	No one could so deceive us	
	That we could not fill this pit of shit!	
	There was never barn crammed so full	765
	Of sheaves!	

Great tumult in hell.

ENVY	Hear how they rumble!	
	It sounds like a nest of hornets,	
	The way the souls are screaming.	
LUCIFER	Let them shriek, let them groan!	
	We will avenge ourselves on them.	
	Get going; let's get the stakes for burning.	770

Noise.
This is the lamenting and groaning in the hell of the Fathers.

ADAM   O alder rechtverdichste rechter verheven,
                Hort mi, Adam, het dunct mi tijt,
                Want inden boeken so staet gescreven:
                Nader grootheit der sonden bedreven
                Soe moetment beteren sonder respijt.   775
                Ende wie dat in dootsonden blijt
                (Vintmen inder scrifturen claer),
                Die moet der penitencien lijt
                Daer voer gedogen ende int gestrijt
                Der pinen bliven menich jaer.   780
                O here, nu eest wel oppenbaer,
                Dat wi .v^M. jaer tuwer weerden
                Hier hebben geseten, ende op der erden
                .IX^C. jaer oec hebben gedaen
                Penitencie; dies wilt opslaen   785
                U ogen van gracien tonser vrame,
                Here, dor uwen weerdegen name!
YEVE   Eest u bequame, o here, ic, Yeve, bid u om gena
                Der mesdaet, die bi minen ra
                Gesciet es, dwelc alle creaturen   790
                Genieten, dat mi nu rout te spa.
                Ontfermt u onser sonden qua,
                Die donsculdege met ons besueren
                In desen kerkere.
i ANDER   Hoe lange saelt dueren?
                O God, of ghi den hemel scordet,   795
                Soe waer ons allen wel ghesciet,
                Met uwer claerheit tdoncker dorbordet,
                Ende brocht ons daermen ewelic siet!
DAVID   O waer sijn, here, die ontfermicheden,
                Die ghi besworen hebt vorleden   800
                Davitte, dinen knecht getrouwe,
                Die hier nu met bitteren rouwe
                In zwaerder ellinden sit geplaecht?
                Ontfermt sijns, die u dliden claecht,
                Want seker, wi sijn in bitteren sere!   805
JOB   O God, antwordt mi, lieve here,
                Hoe vele gerechticheiden van mesdaden
                Ic, Job, sal moeten liden noch meere,
                Ende wilter mi cortelinge af ontladen!
                Oec toent mi, here, dor u genaden,   810
                Twi ghi u aenscijn bercht dus lange
                Vor my? Hoe moechdi ons dus gestaden

ADAM   O most excellent just judge,
                Listen to me, Adam, the time has come,
                For it is written in the books:
                That according to the gravity of the sins committed
                One has to do penance without ceasing.   775
                And whoever remains in mortal sin
                (This can be found clearly in scripture)
                Must tolerate going
                Through the place of penitence and into the torment
                Of pains for many years.   780
                O lord, it is now quite clear,
                That for five thousand years in compliance with your will
                We have been here, and also on earth
                Have done nine hundred years
                Of penance; therefore please turn   785
                Your merciful eyes to our benefit
                For the sake, lord, of your worthy name!

EVE   If it pleases you, lord, I, Eve, pray your mercy
                For the crime, which came about
                By my counsel and which all creatures   790
                Suffer for, and which belatedly I regret.
                Have pity on our evil deeds,
                For which the innocent suffer with us
                In this dungeon.

FIRST OTHER   How long will it last?
                O God, if you break open heaven   795
                Then it would be well for all of us,
                If your light pierced the dark
                And brought us where one can see eternally.

DAVID   O where are, lord, the mercies
                Which you had granted in the past   800
                To David, your faithful servant,
                Who now in bitter grief, in great misery
                Is here tormented?
                Have mercy on him, who tells you of this suffering,
                For surely we are in bitter pain!   805

JOB   O God, answer me, dear lord!
                How many punishments for my sins
                Must I, Job, still suffer,
                Until you will release me!
                Will you show me, lord, in your mercy,   810
                Why you hide your countenance so long
                From me? How can you allow us

	Te laten inder duvele bedwange?	
	Tverdinken van desen valt mi seer strange!	
	O here, ontbint den zwaren bant!	815
	Ic loefdu met woerden ende met sange;	
	Nu houdi mi, scint, vor uwen viant.	
YSAYAS	Alsoe ic inder scrifturen vant,	
	Doen ic op de werelt was,	
	Doe dedic van doen u allen becant,	820
	Als die prophete Ysayas.	
	Soe seidic u, hoe dat ic las,	
	Dat .j. kint soude sijn geboren	
	Van eenre maecht, sijt seker das,	
	Dat lossen soude dat was verloren.	825
	Dat kint soude na sijn behoren	
	Heten God, na mijn verclaren.	
	Dus vriende, soe ic u seide te voren,	
	Saelt al volscien. Drijft geen mesbaren:	
	Den tijt die naect ons sonder sparen!	830
ADAM	Verhuecht u, vriende, ende blijft in hopen:	
	Die prophecie en mach niet liegen.	
i ANDER	De gracie Gods steet al noch open.	
	Verhuecht u, vriende, ende blijft in hopen.	
DAVID	Hoe ons dees demsterheit mach nopen,	835
	Gods woert en sal ons niet bedriegen.	
ADAM	Verhuecht u, vriende, ende blijft in hopen,	
	Die prophecie en mach niet liegen.	

Sanc of spel.
Bitter Ellinde op crucken, ermelic gecleet.

BITTER ELLENDE	Lof heb de gracie des heren volmaect!	
	Doch benic met groter pinen geraect	840
	Tot op dees werelt, soemen siet,	
	Daer ic eens mijn vriendinne liet,	
	Die mi beloefde hier in mijn stede	
	Te blivene, ende heet Innege Bede,	
	Ende es getrouwe, altoes bereit	845
	Vor de hoghe drievuldicheit	
	Daer willic aen gaen sonder versagen	
	Ende haer dat bitter liden clagen,	
	Die Moyses ende haer vriende gemeene	
	Gedogen in den kerker steene	850
	Der hellen, te haren ongevoege,	

To be left in the power of the devil?
The thought of that I find hard to bear!
O lord, break these heavy shackles!   815
I praised you with words and with song;
Now it seems, you consider me your enemy.

ISAIAH   According to the scriptures,
When I was on the earth
At that time I foretold,   820
As the prophet Isaiah,
And I told you that I had read
That a child would be born
Of a virgin, be sure of that,
Who would save that which was lost.   825
That child would rightfully
Be called God, as I made clear.
Thus, friends, as I told you before,
It will all be fulfilled. Do not lament:
That time now approaches apace.   830

ADAM   Rejoice, my friends, and live in hope:
This prophecy can not be false.

FIRST OTHER   The grace of God is always there.
Rejoice, my friends, and live in hope.

DAVID   However the darkness may oppress us,   835
God's word will not betray us.

ADAM   Rejoice, my friends, and live in hope
This prophecy can not be false.

Singing or playing.
Bitter Misery on crutches, dressed in rags.

BITTER MISERY   Praise be the grace of the Lord unequalled!
But I have come in great torment   840
Into this world, as you can see,
To find my friend once left behind,
Who promised in my place,
To stay. Her name is Passionate Prayer,
And she is faithful, always a link   845
With the might of the Trinity.
I will go to her without delay
And tell her of the bitter grief
Which Moses and also all his friends
Are suffering in the cruel dungeon   850
Of hell, to their great distress,

Op dat sijt vor den hoechsten droege;
Hen souts, dat hopic, gracie gescien.
God danc, doch hebbicse versien!
Dies hopic een sake goet van gewinne.   855
God gruetu, vrouwe!

INNICH GEBET   God loens u, vriendinne.
De gracie des heren wil u bescermen.
Ghi scijnt sere mesmaect.

ELLINDICHEIT   Dat ben ic, wachermen!
Soet blijct en was noit niemen soe wee
Als my.

INNICH GEBET   Hebdi de beene ontwee,   860
Dat ghi soe deerlic, en weet hoe,
U leede sleept?

ELLINDICHEIT   Jaic, en trugbeen toe.
En can gestupen, gecnielen, gebucken.
Dies moetic jammerlic op mijn crucken
Dus henen sweyven in zwaerder allinde,   865
Alsoe ghi siet.

INNICH GEBET   Wie sidi, geminde?
Ghi scijnt so druckich dat ghi mi deert.
Hoe es u name?

ELLINDICHEIT   Dat wert u vercleert,
Wie dat ic ben, van ende tende,
Ende wanen ic come. Och, Bitter Ellende   870
Soe es mijn name. Hort mi vertellen:
Die oude vaders, die inder hellen
Noch liggen moeten [ende] houden stede,
Die namen geerne, Innich Gebede,
Sercoers van haren bitteren lidene.   875
Dus, vrouwe, wistise te verblidene,
Ghi daetter wel aen boven maten.
Want si hebben u hier gelaten
In haer stat om Gods behagen,
Dat ghi haer boetscap sout gewagen   880
Aenden here, die u vermint
Om u snelheit.

INNICH GEBET   Dats waer, ic kint,
Dat si mi te meneger stede
Gelast hebben als Innich Gebede,
Dat ic hen soude sijn bereet,   885
Soet inden soutere ende elder steet,
Die Moyses, Saelmon ende Davit

So that she may bring it to the throne on high;
And that, I hope, will bring them grace.
Thank God that I have found her!
I hope my plea will find favour. 855
God greets you, lady!

PASSIONATE PRAYER God bless you, my friend.
May the grace of the lord protect you.
You seem greatly burdened.

MISERY Alas, I am!
Truly no one ever was so afflicted
As I.

PRAYER Have you broken your legs 860
That you so pitifully—I don't know how —
Drag your limbs along?

MISERY I have, and my spine as well.
I cannot stoop or kneel or bend.
That's why I stumble on my crutches
So wretchedly in heavy pain, 865
As you can see.

PRAYER Who are you, my dear?
You seem so oppressed that it pains me.
What is your name?

MISERY I will explain
Who I am, from beginning to end,
And whence I come. Bitter Misery, 870
That is my name. Here is my story:
The ancient fathers, who are still
Kept chained in hell,
Would greatly desire, Passionate Prayer,
Succour in their bitter torment. 875
So, lady, if you could help
You would bring great consolation.
For they have left you here on earth
To plead with God for their sake,
So that you would carry their message 880
To the lord who loves you
In great haste.

PRAYER It's true, I know,
That they have charged me,
As Passionate Prayer, to be prepared
To serve them in all things, 885
As is described in the psalms and the prophets
Which Moses, Solomon and David

Ordineerden. Maer dat ghijt wit:
Mijn jagen, mijn vliegen ende mijn volgen
En baet niet; de heer es [so] verbolgen,   890
Dat ic hem, vrouwe, in desen saken
En der aenrueren noch genaken.
Hi es verherdicht al in een
Ende ruect mijns lutter.

ELLINDICHEIT   Ach lacen, neen!
Soe bliven si verloren plets,   895
Mijn vriende vercoren.

INNICH GEBET   Sijt niet te wets,
Allindicheit, gheminde vrouwe;
Ic hebber een vriendinne getrouwe
Biden here, die mi te gerieve
Ons tale sal vueren.

ELLINDICHEIT   Wie esse, lieve,   900
Die tuwer talen sal sijn bereit
Vor den meesten?

INNICH GEBET   Ontfermicheit
So es van deser vrouwen den name,
Die vor den here es soe bequame,
Dat onmogelic waer te tellene,   905
Hoe hise vermint.

ELLINDICHEIT   Pijnt u derweert tstellene,
Innich Gebet, ic bids als vuere.
Want saelt gescien, dat wert bi huere,
Dat hopic, ende bi niemen el.
Dus spoetter u mee.

INNICH GEBET   Ellindicheit, wel   910
Ic hope si en sal mi niet verhoren.
Mit minen eggere salic gaen boren
Nernstelic inden hemel een gat
Ende vliegen tot hare.

ELLINDICHEIT   Ghi en moecht niet bat.
Doet de bederve sonder vermien,   915
Datter de ouders af verblien.

> *Sanc of spel, ende Innich*
> *Gebet sal die wile metten*
> *eggere een gat willen*
> *boren inden hemel etc.,*
> *ende seggen boven:*

Composed. But you should know
My efforts, my urgency and my diligence
Are all in vain. God's wrath is so great,   890
Lady, that in this case
I can neither move nor approach him.
He has hardened his heart
And does not heed me.

MISERY   Alas, not so!
Then they will all be lost,   895
My beloved friends.

PRAYER   Do not despair,
Misery, dear lady;
I have a faithful friend
With the lord, who for my sake
Will convey our story.

MISERY   Who is she, my dear,   900
Who for your sake is ready
To go to the highest?

PRAYER   It's Mercy;
That is the name of this lady,
Who is so dear to the lord
That it's impossible to say   905
How much he loves her.

MISERY   Please hasten to her,
Passionate Prayer, I implore you again,
Because if it could happen, it would be through her,
That I hope, and through no one else.
So please make haste.

PRAYER   I hope, Misery,   910
She will not refuse to hear me.
Speedily I will start drilling a hole
In heaven with my drill,
And fly up to her.

MISERY   You could not do better.
Please do all that you can,   915
So that the elders may be gladdened.

Singing or playing. Meanwhile Passionate Prayer will start drilling a hole
into heaven with her drill etc., and from above she says:

INNICH GEBET   O alderhoechste here almechtich,
                Lof heb u gracie, die mi so crechtich
                Maect, dat ic ten hemele dus saen
                Des menscen bederve hier heb gedaen.   920
                Want alsoe sciere als mi vercleert
                De mensce, soe weet die hi begeert,
                Eest God selve, sentinne oft sant.
                Noit snelder bode men en vant
                Dan ic, Innich Gebede, si.   925
                Ontfermicheiden so benic bi.
                Dies willic haer minlic gaen vertogen
                Mijn hoge bederve.
ONTFERMICHEIT   Hoe comdi gevlogen
                Dus snellic, geminde vrou eersame?
                Wanen es ditte?   930
INNICH GEBET   Vrouwe, van Adame
                So comic, die tot mi dede sinden
                Op der erden seer Bitter Allinden
                Die nemmermeer, also si dede gewach,
                Hier boven selve niet comen en mach.
                Dus heefse mi haren sin ontbonden   935
                Ende mi met nernste aen u gesonden
                Om, vrouwe, te nemen met u raet
                Ende dat ghi dan wort haer avecaet,
                Als ghi selve wet, dat es van noe
                Ende haer behoeft.
ONTFERMICHEIT   Sijt willecome, boe,   940
                Maer segt mi Bitter Ellinden bedrijf:
                Esse niet ermelic?
INNICH GEBET   Soe maten wijf
                En sach noit mensce met ogen ane.
                Haer waer seer ongereet te stane,
                Hadsi niet crucken, daer si op leende.   945
                Si hulsde, si bulsde, si crochte, si steende;
                Haer cleeder dorscuert ende al berost,
                Haer scoen dorgaet, haer cousen vermost,
                Haer hoet dorsmeten, haer wangen dorpletst,
                Haer nese dorblutst, haer ogen dorcretst,   950
                Te halven so crupse [met swaren ontluste].
                In .lijᶜ. jaeren en hadse ruste.
                Eest wonder, vrouwe, al es si verbeent
                Van selken tormente?

PRAYER   Most high and powerful lord,
                Praised be your mercy, which gives me such strength
                That I brought to heaven
                As quickly as I have done, mankind's need.   920
                For as soon as mankind makes use of me
                His prayer is conveyed to whomever he intends,
                Whether to God, himself, or any of the saints.
                No faster messenger can be found
                Than me, Passionate Prayer.   925
                Now as I draw near to Mercy.
                I will go and explain to her lovingly
                My strong need.
MERCY   How is it you come, flying
                So fast, beloved honoured lady?
                Why is this?
PRAYER   Lady, I have come   930
                From Adam, who sent to me
                On earth Bitterest Misery,
                Who would never, as she explained,
                Be able to come up here herself.
                So she has revealed to me her aim   935
                And with great urgency sent me to you,
                In order, lady, to consult with you,
                So that you may become her advocate;
                As you yourself know, this is vital
                And most needful.
MERCY   Be welcome, messenger,   940
                But tell me how is Bitter Misery:
                Is she not poorly?
PRAYER   Such an unhappy woman
                Has no man ever seen.
                She could not possibly stand
                If she did not have crutches to lean on.   945
                She wheezes, she coughs, she groans, she moans;
                Her clothes are torn and terribly stained,
                Her shoes all holes, her stockings soiled,
                Her head full of sores; her cheeks are hollowed,
                Her nose is crushed, her eyes are sore.   950
                She can barely crawl from heavy pain.
                For more 5200 years she's had no rest.
                Is it wonder, lady, she's beyond herself
                With such torment?

ONTFERMICHEIT   Och lacen, neent!
                    Mijn sinne verscricken, mijn hert weent bloet,   955
                    Dat si dit liden dus doegen moet.
                    Dies willic van haren overterdene
                    Haer advocaet bestaen te werdene
                    Vor den here gebenedijt.
                    Ic ga tot hem, hets meer dan tijt.   960

                                Selete opt cortste. Die wile
                                salmen Gode bloet sien sitten.

ONTFERMICHEIT *tot Gode*
                    O alderhoechste, mogenste en mechtichste,
                    Rechtverdichste rechter en warechtichste,
                    Ic, Ontfermicheit, die in minnen
                    Wonachtich es tuwer herten binnen,
                    — Noit niemen en coster mi uut gedriven;   965
                    Mijn woninge moet daer ewelic bliven,
                    Ocht de werelt opt corte verginge! —
                    Hoert dan wies ic u sunderlinge
                    Met groten nernste ben vercleerende:
                    Dats dat ic intelic ben begerende,   970
                    Dat ghi de gevangene, die sijn gevaen,
                    Telivereert, here, en wiltse ontslaen.
                    Dies ben ic tu als Ontfermicheit
                    Met nernste biddende.
GHERECHTICHEIT   Ja? al ghereit!
                    Men doe haer gereetscap, si biddes, boye.   975
                    Op dats u, here, niet en vernoye,
                    Mi geliefter oec toe te sprekene
                    Als Gerechticheit, die te verstekene
                    Niet en mach sijn, ic seggu twi:
                    Want also wel benic als si   980
                    In uws selfs herte, here, verlicht
                    Ende op mi hebdijt al gesticht,
                    Dat bevaen heeft hemel en eerde.
                    Aldus dan dor u hoge weerde
                    So sidi mi sculdich dan int clare   985
                    Te hoore, alsoe wel als hare.
                    Haer soetelic spreken mach niet gehoert sijn
                    Sonder mijn antwoorde.
GOD   Wilt niet gestoert sijn
                    Op anderen, weerde lieve vriendinnen.

MERCY   Alas, it is not.
                    My senses are stricken, my heart weeps blood,   955
                    That she must endure such suffering.
                    Because of the terrible state she's in
                    I will become her advocate
                    Before the blessed lord.
                    I'll go to him; the time has come.   960

                    A brief Selete. God is seen clearly on his throne.

MERCY *speaks to GOD.*
                    Most high, most mighty, and most powerful,
                    Most just judge, and most truthful,
                    I, Mercy, who in your love
                    Dwells within your heart –
                    No one could ever drive me from there;   965
                    My dwelling must remain there forever,
                    Or the world would shortly perish! —
                    Hear what I shall now explain to you
                    In great detail and all seriousness.
                    That is, that I passionately desire   970
                    That you deliver, lord, the captives
                    Who are imprisoned, and set them free.
                    This is what I, as Mercy,
                    Implore you most earnestly.
JUSTICE   Yes? Go on then!
                    All of you, do her bidding as she asks.   975
                    If it doesn't annoy you, lord,
                    I'd quite like to say something too
                    As Justice, which cannot
                    Be set aside, and I'll tell you why:
                    Because I am just as important as she is   980
                    And I too am enthroned in your heart, lord,
                    And on me you have founded everything,
                    That is contained in heaven and earth.
                    And because of your own great worth
                    You owe it to me clearly   985
                    To listen to me, as you did to her.
                    Her sweet speech cannot be heard
                    Without my answer.
GOD   Do not be angry
                    With each other, beloved and worthy daughters.

Ghi wet, mijn sinnen vierich dorboert sijn   990
Noyaellic met uwer beider minnen.
Dies seldi mi duegdelic laten bekinnen
Uwer beider gebreke in wedersie;
Ende alsic uws vortstels ben te bynnen,
Soe salic sonder enich envie   995
U beiden payen van desen gestrie.

ONTFERMICHEIT   Te goeder tijt, here, te vreden blivic
In u sentencie; mer noode so kivic
Tegen mire suster Gerechticheit.
Maer scade sceet vrienscap, soemen seit.   1000
Dies sijt mi gunstich van dat mi noest,
Dats dat ghi derme menscen vertroest,
Ocht si moeten gemeynlic alle
Verloren sijn inden mesvalle.
Want David seit ten cleeren bescouwe: 1005
Den tijt comt datmender ontfermen souwe;
Dies benic begerende, dat dan gescie
Vlues op een cort.

GHERECHTICHEIT   Van cleinen bedie
Es u vortstel, soe ghijt bediet.
Ghi hebbet scrifture noch qualic dorwiet,   1010
Want dat God sprac, dats uutgenomen:
Boven alle dander moet dat volcomen.
Hi seide, dat sterven moet groet en cleene,
Adam mit sinen navolgers gemeene.
Van dier tijt, dits ander besceet,   1015
Dat Adam inden appel beet
Toten jonxten dage, seide hi toe.
Cnuwt dat woert wel!

ONTFERMICHEIT   Suster, ic doe.
Al en dadijs so scerpelic niet vermaen,
Ic soudu ten nausten emmer verstaen.   1020
Maer, Gerechticheit, suster, u woerdeken sniden
Als sceerse; mer benic om overliden
Ghestelt, here vader, in uwen moet,
Waertoe soe benic dan te goet?
En magic niet in u gedochte   1025
Volcomen daermen mi toe wrochte,
So blijft de werelt met allen tenden,
Want u Gerechticheit sout al scenden,

	You know that my heart is passionately aflame	990
	With loyal love for both of you.	
	That's why you must let me know clearly	
	Your grievances from both sides;	
	And when I understand both your proposals	
	I will without any prejudice	995
	Try and respond to you both.	
MERCY	In good time, lord, I'll be content	
	With your judgement; but I dislike conflict	
	With my sister Justice.	
	But strife damages friendship, as they say.	1000
	Be generous to me in my need,	
	Which is that you console those poor people	
	Or else they will all together	
	Be lost in their misfortune.	
	For David says, it's very clear:	1005
	The time will come when mercy will be granted;	
	And so I desire that to happen	
	With all speed.	
JUSTICE	Your proposition	
	As you outline it, is of little value.	
	You've badly misread the scripture	1010
	For that which God said is most important	
	Above all else that must come to pass:	
	He said that young and old must die,	
	Adam and all his kind.	
	And something else, this goes back to the time	1015
	That Adam bit into the apple	
	Until the latest day, that's what he said.	
	Mark well these words!	
MERCY	Sister, I do.	
	Even if you did not put it so sharply	
	I would still understand you well.	1020
	But, sister Justice, your words cut	
	Like razors; but if I am to be disregarded	
	Lord father, in your heart,	
	What then is my function?	
	If I cannot in your opinion	1025
	Accomplish that for which I was made,	
	Then the world will come to an end,	
	For your justice would damage all	

Dat wezen sal ende menscelic leeft.
Dies seg ic: neen.

GHERECHTICHEIT   Dwoert dat God heeft   1030
Gesproken, suster, dan mach niet falen.
Al waerdi noch so suet van talen,
U en steet dat Gode niet tontsmekene.
En sal u seggen bi desen tekene:
Worde Adam niet dewige doot besurende,   1035
Gerechticheit en waer niet ewelic durende,
Ende na dat ic gescreven vinde,
So es Gods waerheit sonder ynde.
Ende aldus dan na u verstaen,
Soe soude de waerheit Gods vergaen.   1040
Ontfermicheit, suster, dan mach niet sijn,
Dat wetti selve wel.

ONTFERMICHEIT   Verstaet den fijn.
Tscrifture seit, daer ics mi aen houwe:
God sciep den mensce, om datti souwe
De glorie besitten, alsoe ic las,   1045
Daer Lucifer uutgeworpen was.
Daer was hi toe geordineert,
Vander Gods gracien geviseert,
Ende te bescouwene die ewige claerheit
Van Gods aenscine; nu na de waerheit,   1050
Daer ghi, Gerechticheit, op dinct,
Eest dat ghi dit den mensce niet en gehinct,
So en zal de wille noch de macht fijn
Van sinen makere niet volbracht sijn,
Want hijs niet, soe ic seide te voren,   1055
En maecte om te bliven verloren.
Maer wilde hine ter glorien maken,
Hi moet sijns makers wille dan smaken.
Dan can hem niemen wederstaen,
Of Gods wille moet falen.

GHERECHTICHEIT   Hoert mijn vermaen,   1060
Suster Ontfermicheit: dat ghi segt
Luyt vremde, want na dat ghi sprect,
Soe soude de mensce van sinen mesdaden
Ongecorrigeert bliven en bi genaden
Quijt gaen van dat hi mesdoet.   1065
So dadense hem so lief quaet als goet.
Ghi en ergeweert niet, suster, versinde ghijt,
Na u voertstel.

That is alive and ever will be.
Thus I say no.

JUSTICE   The word that God has   1030
Spoken, sister, that cannot fail.
However sweet spoken you might be,
It isn't fitting to ask this of God.
And I shall give you proof of this:
If Adam did not suffer eternal death,   1035
Then Justice would not prevail forever,
But, as I find written in scripture,
God's truth knows no end.
However, according to your interpretation
God's truth would perish.   1040
Mercy, my sister, that cannot be,
And you know it too.

MERCY   Let's get this straight.
Scripture says, and I stick to it:
God created man so that he would
Possess the glory, as I read,   1045
From which Lucifer has been excluded.
For that was man's destiny,
Intended by God's grace,
And he was to behold the eternal clarity
Of God's countenance; now according to the truth   1050
To which you, Justice, refer,
If you do not allow mankind this
Then neither the will nor the great power
Of his creator will be accomplished
Because he did not, as I said before,   1055
Make man to let him be lost.
If he wanted to create him for glory,
Man must experience his creator's will,
And no one can gainsay that,
Unless God's will would fail.

JUSTICE   Listen to my warning,   1060
Sister Mercy: what you say
Sounds strange, for according to you,
Mankind's misdeeds would
Remain unpunished, and through mercy
He would be acquitted of his sins.   1065
So man would with impunity do good or evil.
That's no real argument, sister, as you know,
That proposal of yours.

ONTFERMICHEIT   Neen, suster, bekinde ghijt,
                   Dan hebbic u niet te voren geleit;
                   Maer de wise meester die seit   1070
                   In sinen boeke, nu hort na mi,
                   Dat God vele geringere si
                   Den mensce tontfermen, sijt seker des,
                   Dan hine te verdoemen es.
                   Want sijn grote ontfermicheit besneden   1075
                   Es meerder dan smenscen quaetheden.
                   Ende om dat dit prueflic ende claer es,
                   Soe eest noet, temelic, dat waer es,
                   Dat de mensce van sinen bedrive
                   Verlost si, dan hi verloren blive   1080
                   Ewelic, suster. Hier mede ic slute
                   Ende begeers recht.
GHERECHTICHEIT   En heb noch niet ute!
                   Hier op willic antwoorde geven.
                   Segt doch: waer vondi noit gescreven,
                   Wie dat mesdede, om cleer verstaen,   1085
                   Hi en moeste bi Rechte correxie ontfaen?
                   Dus Adam es mesdadich vonden,
                   Dies moet hi aernen dan sijn sonden
                   Ewelic, geduerich, sonder fijn,
                   Want alle die leven of selen sijn,   1090
                   En souden na groetheit des heren
                   De sonden gebeteren na der leren
                   Vander ewiger scrifturen.
                   Dus moet hise ewelic besueren,
                   Hi en sijn geslachte me.   1095
                   Dit seggic als Gerechtiche.
DE WAERHEIT   Heer vader, ic bid u om een woert
                   Ten besten te sprekene. Ic heb gehoert,
                   Dat mijn susteren in gescille
                   Gevallen sijn om des menscen wille,   1100
                   Dat qualic vuecht, here, mocht [ict] gelien,
                   Dat si dus jegen elc anderen strien.
                   Dus soudicse als Waerheit geerne versamen
                   Ende enegen, here; maer na dbetamen
                   Van mi, Waerheit, en van hem beyen,   1105
                   Dat si in dit gedinge voerseyen,
                   Soe waert wel noet, datmen dan vonde
                   Yemen, die beterde tsmenscen sonde
                   Metter doot ende dat uut trouwen,

MERCY	No, sister, you must admit
	That is not what I put before you;
	But the wise master who said 1070
	In his books — mark my words —
	That God is much quicker
	To pardon mankind, be sure of that,
	Rather than to condemn him.
	For his great and perfect mercy 1075
	Is greater than all mankind's sins.
	And because this can be proven beyond doubt,
	It's necessary, clearly, this is true,
	That mankind is pardoned
	For his sins, rather than that he remain lost 1080
	For ever, sister. With this I rest my case,
	And I require justice.
JUSTICE	I haven't finished yet!
	I want to answer that.
	Tell me: where did you ever find it written
	That whoever sinned, get this clear, 1085
	Would not have to receive punishment from Justice?
	Since Adam has been found guilty,
	He must atone for his sins
	For ever, and continuously without end.
	For all people now and in the future 1090
	Cannot atone for their sins
	As eternal scripture teaches
	In accordance with the greatness of the lord.
	So therefore Adam must suffer forever,
	He and his descendants as well. 1095
	This I, Justice, declare.
TRUTH	Lord father, may I also venture
	To intervene. I have heard,
	That my sisters have come
	In conflict for mankind's sake. 1100
	It's hardly proper, lord, if I may say so,
	That they are thus at odds with each other.
	So I, as Truth, would like to unite
	And reconcile them, lord: but according to me,
	Truth, and to both of them, 1105
	What they allege in this dispute
	Makes it necessary that we should find
	Someone who would atone for man's sin
	With his death and do it from love,

Die inde sonde niet en waer gehouwen,   1110
Die Yeve ende Adam bedreef.
Dus, vondemen yemen, die suver bleef
Ende ombesmet, ende claer van desen,
Die soude tgeslechte al mogen genesen.
Ende anders so en maecht niet gescien   1115
Bi mi als Waerheit.

ONTFERMICHEIT   Dan onder ons drien
Soe laet ons met begeerten groet
Besueken, of yemen der ewiger doot
Vanden sonden Adaems bedreven
Onsculdich en onbesmet es bleven.   1120
Wat segdi dies, Gerechticheit?

GHERECHTICHEIT   Neent, sustere, want tscrifture seit
Inden latine, claer becondicht:
Wi hebben alle in Adam gesondicht;
Oec en es niemen, na Davids leere,   1125
Si en hebben gesondicht jegen den here.

DE WAERHEIT   Susteren, om u te besceidene
Als Waerheit, gelieft mi u te leidene
Ten chore der ingelen, verstaet den fijn.
Want daer noch enege ingele in sijn,   1130
Die noyt noch en mesdaden in sonden
En ongehouden sijn en ontbonden
Van Adams mesdaet, dit es waer.
Dies gawi onder ons drien tot daer;
Ic hope, wy wordender bi gevraemt.   1135
Siet, sustere, daer steeter veel versaemt;
Als Ontfermicheit doet de relacien!

ONTFERMICHEIT   O heilege ingele van hoger nacien,
Sonder blamacien
Sidi bi Waerheiden, miere suster, vonden,   1140
Regnerende in jubilacien.
Sonder falacien
Biddic geerne, hoert mijn orconden:
Soude yemen die sonden
Afdoen willen van Adame,   1145
Ende tenegen stonden
Sterven willen om smenscen vrame?
Dat waer mi uterlic seer bequame.
Als Ontfermicheit doe ics bede,
Die vor u knielt in smenscen stede.   1150

EEN INGEL   Vrou Ontfermicheit, u tale besneden

	Someone not tainted by the sin	1110
	Committed by Adam and Eve.	
	So, if someone were found who has remained pure	
	And immaculate, and innocent,	
	He could then rescue all mankind.	
	There is no alternative to this,	1115
	According to me, Truth.	
MERCY	Amongst the three of us	
	Let us with firm intention	
	Try, whether anyone has remained	
	Innocent, and untainted by	
	The sins committed by Adam.	1120
	What say you, Justice?	
JUSTICE	No sister, for scripture says	
	In Latin, clearly stated:	
	We have all sinned with Adam;	
	And there is no one, according to David's teaching	1125
	Who has not sinned against the lord.	
TRUTH	Sisters, in order to judge between you	
	As Truth, let me lead you,	
	Understand my purpose, to the choirs of angels.	
	For there must still be some angels,	1130
	Who have never been tainted by sin,	
	And are free and not bound by	
	Adam's misdeed, that's the truth of it.	
	Let us go there, the three of us;	
	I hope we will gain by it.	1135
	Look sisters, many are gathered there;	
	You Mercy, speak for us!	
MERCY	Holy angels of exalted rank,	
	You have been found	
	To be without blemish by my sister Truth,	1140
	Reigning in glory.	
	Without deceit	
	I'd like to ask you, listen to my message:	
	Is there anyone at all	
	Who could atone for Adam's sin,	1145
	And at any time	
	Would die for mankind's sake?	
	That would satisfy me greatly.	
	As Mercy I do make this plea,	
	And kneel before you in mankind's stead.	1150
AN ANGEL	Lady Mercy, we have heard	

Hebben wi gehoert ende tuwer beden
Souden wi ons vuegen als van dien.
Wies der heileger drievuldicheden
Ghelieft van desen, sijt dies te vreden,   1155
Dat moet wel van ons gescien.
Hier en es niemen int oversien,
Die den natuerliken doot verdriet,
Eest God begerende tot ons lien.
Wy willen alle geerne plien,   1160
Wies dat de here aen ons gebiet.
Dus werdet u, vrouwe, van ons bediet.

ONTFERMICHEIT   Lof hebt ghi, ingele! Mijn susteren beie,
Laet ons vor den here dan gaen,
Want, soe mi die ingel seye,   1165
Soe doen sijt, wilt hijt hebben gedaen.

GHERECHTICHEIT   Neen suster, dat hebdi qualic verstaen;
Ghi sout mi so mijns rechts verdringen.
Si moestent minlic selve aengaen,
De here en machser niet toe dwingen!   1170
De sake die soude mi dus ontspringen
En fortse so worde gerekent dat feit.
De doot en mach hem niet verlingen,
Diet doen sal; dats verloren geseit.

DE WAERHEIT   Nu dan, ghi ingele, ic als Waerheit   1175
Die spreke u toe, wilt mi verzinnen.
Heeft yemen ten mensce selc onst geleyt,
Datti de doot wilt sterven uut minnen,
So mogense dewige vroude gewinnen
Ende inden hemel besitten dees ste.   1180
Doet mi daer af u jonst bekinnen,
Des biddic u, ingele, als de Waerhe.

Hier swigen sy alle.

Si swigen gemeyn op alle be!
Anderwerf vragic, of ghi wilt sterven
Om den mensce ten ewigen vree   1185

Your elegant tale and would like
To grant your plea in this respect.
That which pleases the Holy Trinity
In this matter, be assured,   1155
Must be carried out by us.
All considered, there's no one here
Who grieves about natural death,
That being what God desires of us.
We will all willingly comply   1160
With whatever the Lord bids us.
We offer this answer, lady, with respect.

MERCY   Praise be, Angel! My sisters both,
Let us go before the Lord,
For, as the angel tells me,   1165
They will act in accordance with his will.

JUSTICE   No, sister, you are severely mistaken;
You would suppress my rights in that way.
They would have to do this out of love;
The Lord cannot force them to it!   1170
If that were to happen I would be slighted
And it would be an abuse of power.
Death should not be repugnant to the one,
Who must endure it; that would indeed be unnatural.

TRUTH   Now then, angels, I as Truth   1175
Will speak to you: mark my meaning.
If anyone loves mankind so much
That he would endure death out of love
He will achieve eternal joy,
And occupy this place in heaven.   1180
Favour me with your compliance,
That's what I ask, as Truth, angels.

Here they are all silent.

They are all silent on this!
I ask again, whether you will die
To bring eternal peace to man.   1185

                  Te bringene? Noch vragicx u derdewerven,
                  Och niemen en antwert tonser bederven?
ONTFERMICHEIT   O laes, den troest, die wi hier vinden
                  Es cranc! Latet ons gaen ontbinden
                  Gode, den almechtegen here.   1190
                  Hi sal ons beraden, hopic sere,
                  Of de mensce blijft onverloest,
                  En crigen wi anders genen troest.
                  Dies gaic als vriendinne getrouwe
                  Tot Gode den vader met groten rouwe.   1195
                  Here vader, onder der ingele scare
                  En es nu niement int oppenbare,
                  Die hem uyt minnen wilt laten ontliven,
                  Noch oec ter werelt dies werdich ware,
                  Om te verlossen den armen sondare.   1200
                  Sal hi dan dus verloren bliven?
                  Ghi moecht doch alle leet verdriven!
                  Ic bids u, staet hem nu in staden,
                  Als u Ontfermicheit.
GOD   Wilt mi beraden
                  Suete sone, ende hoert mijn woerde.   1205
                  U susteren drie sijn buten trade
                  Gevallen ende sere van discoerde.
                  Gherechticheit als die gestoerde
                  Begeert, dat Adam blive in weene;
                  Ontfermicheit wilten te minen acoerde   1210
                  Bringen en sijn geslachte gemeene.
                  Hoe salict maken, en stoerder eene?
                  Want alle beide moeticker plegen.
                  Dadict niet, sone, hoert wies ic meene:
                  Ic ginge miere hoger godheit tegen.   1215
                  Dies wilt mi tesen avise gewegen.
DE SOEN GODS   O vader, uwen wille van dien,
                  Soet Recht begeert, moet wel gescien.
                  Wi en mogen niet bat, noch ghi noch icke,
                  Dan trecht in hout van desen sticke.   1220
                  Dus salmen Recht ende Waerheit vragen,
                  Wats hem van desen best sal behagen.
                  Dat dunct mi goet, eest soe u wille.
DE HEILEGE GEEST   O vader, laet zwichten dit gescille,
                  Dies biddic u, als Heilich Geest,   1225
                  In u als wortele ende keest
                  Eenwillich, volmaect ende onversceyen.

	For the third time I ask you	
	Is anyone going to meet our plea?	
MERCY	Alas, whatever the help to be found here	
	It's too small! Let's go and set this	
	Before God, the Lord Almighty.	1190

For the third time I ask you
Is anyone going to meet our plea?
MERCY   Alas, whatever the help to be found here
It's too small! Let's go and set this
Before God, the Lord Almighty. 1190
I hope dearly that he will guide us,
Or mankind will remain bound
And we will not have peace of mind.
So I, as loyal friend, will go
In great distress to God the Father. 1195
Lord Father, among the host of angels
There is no one, it would appear,
Who will suffer death out of love,
Nor anyone in the world sufficiently worthy
To liberate the poor sinner. 1200
Will he then have to remain bound?
You have the power to drive out all misery!
I, as your Mercy, beg you,
Stand by him now.
GOD   Listen to my words,
My sweet son, and give me advice. 1205
Your three sisters are at a loss,
And in great discord.
Justice, who feels slighted,
Desires that Adam remains in sorrow;
Mercy wants to reconcile 1210
Me with him and all his kind.
How shall I do this impartially?
For I must reckon with both of them.
You will understand, my son, if I did not
I would deny my own divinity. 1215
Therefore advise me in this dilemma.
THE SON OF GOD O Father, your will in this
Must be done, in accordance with Justice.
We cannot do better, neither you nor I,
Than follow what Justice requires here. 1220
Therefore we must ask Justice and Truth
What would please them best in this.
That seems good to me, if it pleases you.
THE HOLY SPIRIT O Father, let this conflict be settled.
I, as Holy Spirit, beg you, 1225
The root and kernel of the godhead,
Being of one will with you, perfect and indivisible.

	Wes u behaecht, gelieft ons beyen,	
	Als u ende mi, sonder mestermen;	
	Want doch ons proper es ontfermen.	1230
	Wat ghi begeert, dats oec mijn raet.	
DE VREDE	Ic als Vree, here, na dat staet,	
	Bid der Waerheit ende u om hulpe.	
	Die gaf den raet, dat hi dit stulpe.	
	Ghi sijt genadich in allen keere.	1235
DE WAERHEIT	Soe seggic dan als Waerheit, heere,	
	Yegelijcs saken wel oversien:	
	Sal den mensce sorcoers gescien,	
	Dat wort bi rechte van uwen sone;	
	Ende dat bi redenen, om dat gone	1240
	Elken in recht sta ende ombegrepen.	
	Bi hem was ierst de mensce gescepen.	
	Oec es gescreven, alsoe ic las,	
	Dat alle dinc bi hem gescepen was.	
	Dies laet ons sire wijsheit dan duer oetmoet	1245
	Bidden om sijn hulpe soet	
	Siere vrienden, die sijn in bitteren weene.	
ONTFERMICHEIT	O sone des vaders, in duechden reene,	
	Ic, vrou Ontfermicheit, bid met seere	
	Vor u vriende, groet en cleene,	1250
	Die bliven verloren emmermeere	
	Ten si, bi uwer sueter leere,	
	Dat ghi hens duegdelic wilt ontfermen.	
	Dan u genadicheyt op hen keere	
	Ende wilt gedincken haer bitter kermen.	1255
	Niemen dan ghi en machse beschermen!	
GOD	Mi, sone, na dat gewarich toe bringen	
	Van miere dochter Ontfermicheden,	
	Soe es mi zwaer ende groet verlingen,	
	Dat si daer sitten in onvreden,	1260
	Die mi dicwile in tiden voerleden	
	Hebben gedaen eere ende vrame:	
	Patriarken ende propheten besneden	
	Ende meest de af comst van Adame.	
	Dus dan, het waer mi seer bequame,	1265
	Haddi de minne tot hem so groet,	

What pleases you, pleases both of us:
All three of us, without conflict;
Because it behoves us to be merciful. 1230
What you desire is also my will.

PEACE   I as Peace, Lord, as it stands,
Beg Truth and you for help.
Having advised us, now give us a remedy.
You are merciful in every respect. 1235

TRUTH   This is what I as Truth say, my Lord,
Having weighed all these arguments:
If mankind is to be helped
By rights it should be by your son;
And the reason is that he 1240
Is the judge of all and incorruptible.
He it was who first created man.
Also it's written, as I have read,
That he created all things.
So let us beg his wisdom 1245
To grant his sweet help benevolently
To his friends, who are in bitter grief.

MERCY   Son of the Father, pure in virtues,
I, Lady Mercy, beg you fervently
On behalf of your friends, old and young, 1250
Who will be lost forever
Unless, according to your sweet teaching,
You strive vigorously to rescue them.
Please show your mercy towards them
And pay heed to their bitter lament. 1255
No one but you can protect them!

GOD   I, my son, after this convincing appeal
From my daughter, Mercy,
Am very burdened with great sorrow
That they dwell there in adversity, 1260
Those who have often in times past
Shown me honour and respect:
Holy patriarchs and prophets,
And most of Adam's descendants.
Therefore it would please me greatly 1265
If you felt so much love for them

<pre>
                  Woudise met uwen sueten name
                  Verlossen ende sterven de bitter doot.
DE SOEN GODS   O vader, twi eest, dat recht geboot,
                  Dat ic sal moeten boeten de sake   1270
                  Ende ontsluten, dat Adam sloet,
                  Met pinen ende met ongemake
                  Meer dan hi soude? Versint mijn sprake,
                  Heilege Geest, dat vragic dy,
                  Die alsoe mechtich es als wy.   1275
GOD   Mijn lieve sone, de sake aen hoert:
                  Ic ben soe uterlic gestoert
                  Op den mensce, ie segt u naect,
                  Dat mi leet es, dat icken heb gemaect.
                  Ende tusscen den ingelen, ic seg u mee,   1280
                  Ende den mensce, es oec een vee.
                  Ende ghi sijt middel persoen int weesen,
                  Mi ende tsheilichs Geests in desen.
                  Soe sidi sculdich, verstaet int cleere,
                  Hier af te sine een middeleere,   1285
                  Om te peysene tuwen wensche
                  De vete tusscen mi ende den mensche
                  Ende tusscen die ingelen, die in gescille
                  Oec liggen; aldus soe es mijn wille,
                  Dat ghi, sone, de sake aen gaet   1290
                  Ende sijts een middeleere.
DE WAERHEIT   Voert mede verstaet,
                  Wies dat ic uut des vaders monde,
                  Sone Gods, als die Waerheit orconde:
                  Ghi hebt de cracht ende macht warachtich
                  Van uwen vader ontfaen almechtich;   1295
                  Oec hebdi sijn wijsheit groet sonder getal;
                  Ende wie dees sake aenveerden sal,
                  Moet doen bi also wisen zecrete,
                  Datter de viant niet af en weete.
                  Want, here, geraecte hijt te verhorne,   1300
                  Hi soude hem pinen u doot te storne
                  Ende te beletten smenscen profijt.
                  Dus dan, ghi die de wijsheit sijt,
                  Selt best de sake al oversien
                  Tes menscen vrame ende doense gescien   1305
                  Ten siensten; dit slutic als Waerheit,
                  Dat u behoert.
GHERECHTICHEIT   Dats wel gheseit,
</pre>

	That you would liberate them, with your sweet name	
	And then yourself suffer bitter death.	
THE SON OF GOD	Father, why is it that Justice commands	
	That I shall have to pay a greater penalty than Adam	1270
	With my own torments and pain,	
	To unlock that which Adam locked?	
	Listen carefully to what I say,	
	Holy Spirit, I ask this of you	
	Who is as powerful as we are.	1275
GOD	My dear son, listen to this:	
	I am so greatly angered	
	Towards mankind, I tell you bluntly,	
	That I regret that ever I created him.	
	And furthermore there is also a feud	1280
	Between the angels and mankind,	
	And you are the core of the divine being	
	Between me and the Holy Spirit.	
	Therefore you are obliged, make no mistake,	
	To be in this a mediator,	1285
	To make peace, as you desire,	
	In the feud between me and mankind,	
	And the angels who are also	
	In this conflict. Thus it is my will,	
	That you, my son, take this upon you,	1290
	And be a mediator.	
TRUTH	You must also understand	
	That which as Truth I announce,	
	Son of God, coming from the Father's mouth:	
	You have the strength and the absolute power	
	Received from your Father almighty;	1295
	Also you have his infinite wisdom;	
	And whoever will undertake this matter	
	Must do so wisely in secret,	
	So that the enemy will not get to know it.	
	For, my lord, if he were to hear it,	1300
	He would try to nullify your death	
	So as to prevent any benefit to mankind.	
	Therefore you, who are wisdom,	
	Must best bring things about	
	To the advantage of mankind and ensure	1305
	The best outcome. This I, Truth, conclude	
	Is what you alone can do.	
JUSTICE	That is well said	

Bi redenen, die ic, als Recht, sal gheven.
Bi wijsheiden ontfinc de mensce sijn leven
Ende was van eerden, alsoe ic thoone,   1310
Bi u geordineert als de soone.
Dus es hi u bi enegen saken
Ontrocken, so moettien weder maken.
Ende bat behoert u, sone, nu merc,
Te volcomen uws selves werc,   1315
Die[t] mi recht te gronde besochte,
Dan dat u een ander vol wrochte.
Alsus soe lidic onbevreest,
Dat God u vader noch Heilich Geest
En betaemt den mensce, hoe dat si,   1320
Te verlossene, sone, tegen di,
Want ghijt voer hen sijt sculdich te doene.

GOD   Ghi wet doch wel mijn stercheit, sone;
              Die hebdi oec in u bedwanc.
              Ende die mensce es teeder en cranc.   1325
              Het es van node, diet wel verdacht,
              Dat hi bi u ontfa dan cracht.
              Aldus soe seggic ende es mijn raet,
              Dat ghi des menscen bederve bestaet
              In minnen, reyn ende onbevreest.   1330
              Het hoert u bat dan den Heilegen Geest,
              Soe ghi wel wet, sone, ocht dan mi.

DE SONE   Heer vader, al dat u wille sy
              Dat moet in mi altoes gescien.
              Uwer hoger begeerten so blivic bi,   1335
              Minlic soe willic mi voegen te dien.
              Die doot en willic niet ontsien;
              Sterven willic in rechter minnen.
              Met minen bloede salic haers plien,
              Die nu sijn ter hellen binnen.   1340
              Hen willic vriendelic doen bekinnen,
              Dat mi Ontfermicheit heeft ontstaect,
              Vierich dorscoten mijn hert, mijn sinnen,
              Ende metten strale van minnen geraect.
              Dies wort van mi de doot gesmaect.   1345

De Vrede sal Gerechticheit
cussen ende segghen dit:

For reasons which I, Justice, will explain.
Mankind received his life through wisdom
And was created, as I affirm,   1310
From clay by you, the Son.
If he is in any way cut off from you
You will have to restore him.
And it better behoves you, the Son, to pay heed,
When all is said and done,   1315
To perfect your own work,
Than that another should complete it for you.
So I declare without fear
That it is not fitting for God your Father,
Nor the Holy Spirit in any way   1320
To save mankind, Son, in your stead,
Because you owe it to him to do this.

GOD   My Son, you do know my strength quite well;
You too possess that,
And Mankind is weak and fragile.   1325
It is necessary, if you think about it,
That he will receive strength through you.
Thus I say and counsel
That you comply with man's need
Out of pure and fearless love.   1330
It behoves you better than the Holy Spirit
Or me, as you well know, my Son.

THE SON   Lord Father, all that is your will
Must be brought about through me.
I will acquiesce in your greatest desire,   1335
Out of love I will comply with this.
I will not evade death;
I will die out of righteous love.
With my blood I will care for them,
Who are now captive in hell.   1340
I will tenderly go and show them
That Mercy has kindled my emotions
And shot through my heart like fire
And struck me with the arrows of love.
That is why I will suffer death.   1345

Peace will kiss Justice and say this:

DE VREDE	O Gerechticheit, hebt danc van desen	
	Ende alle die hier toe hulpich wesen.	
ONTFERMICHEIT	Lof, werdich Gods sone gebenedijt!	
	Als Ontfermherticheit Gods togic mijn quale,	
	Daer ghi een medicijn af sijt	1350
	Ende een triacle int generale.	
	Aensiet, hoe ic met desen strale	
	Ben dorscoten om die onvrame,	
	Dat smenscen geslachte altemale	
	Moet liden die over zwaer mesquame.	1355
	Seert der beeten van Adame,	
	Soe heeft dees wonde ye sint gebloet.	
	Soet mi Ontfermherticheit betame,	
	Vindic u, Gods sone, nu gemoet.	
	U suete minne so in mi gloet,	1360
	Dat mi de quetse van desen gescichte	
	In u herte mijns seers verlichte.	
GHERECHTICHEIT	Lof, sone des vaders, tot mi genegen!	
	Als Gerechticheit Gods gevic orconde,	
	Dat ghi de balance van mi gedregen	1365
	Hebt effen geladen te deser stonde.	
	Want bi uwen rechtverdegen vonde	
	So wert de mensce sijns drux verloest.	
	Dies rise u lof uut elken monde,	
	Dat ghi de uwe aldus vertroest!	1370
DE WAERHEIT	Lof, sone des vaders, van dat ons noest	
	Sijn wi bi uwen eygenen wille	
	Als susteren, ja, diet wel geloest,	
	Verenicht van onsen zwaren gescille.	
	Bi Waerheiden ende Rechte verstoert de hille.	1375
ONTFERMICHEIT	Lof specie, edel vruchtbarich tac,	
	Sonder nommer soe es u weerde!	
GHERECHTICHEIT	Lof bloyende rijs, dat Adam brac,	
	Lof specie, edel vruchtbarich tac!	
DE WAERHEIT	U vruchten sijn reyn ende sonder lac;	1380
	Noyt edelre vrucht en wies op eerde.	

PEACE	Justice, you must be thanked	
	And all who have helped in this.	
MERCY	Praise be, blessed worthy Son of God!	
	I, as God's Mercy, show my illness,	
	For which you are a medicine	1350
	And a cure for everybody.	
	Look, how with this arrow	
	I am shot through with this pain	
	Because all of mankind's race	
	Must suffer this very heavy misfortune.	1355
	Since Adam bit into the apple	
	That wound has ever bled.	
	As is fitting for me, Mercy,	
	So I find you, Son of God, alike disposed.	
	Your sweet love glows in me so much	1360
	That the injury from this arrow	
	In your heart assuages my pain.	
JUSTICE	Praise be, Son of the Father, well disposed to me!	
	As God's Justice, I do declare	
	That you at this hour have balanced	1365
	The scales which I carry.	
	For your righteous solution	
	Will free mankind from his bonds.	
	So your praise will well up from every mouth	
	That you thus rescue your people!	1370
TRUTH	Praise be, Son of the Father, from all our troubles	
	We have been freed by your own will,	
	And, if you explain it properly, we as sisters	
	Have now been reconciled in our grave dispute.	
	Through Truth and Justice hell is negated.	1375
MERCY	Praise be, noble stem, fruitful branch,	
	Inestimable is your worth!	
JUSTICE	Praise be, flowering shoot which Adam broke,	
	Praise be, noble stem, fruitful branch!	
TRUTH	Your fruits are pure and without blemish;	1380
	No nobler fruit ever grew on earth.	

ONTFERMICHEIT   Lof specie, edel vruchtbarich tac,
                 Sonder nommer soe es u weerde!
GHERECHTICHEIT   Ghi wert gebloeit uut Yessen geerde,
                 Also ons Balam heeft vorsproken.   1385
DE WAERHEIT   Ende ons inder scrifturen vercleerde,
                 Werdi gebloyt uut Yessen geerde.
ONTFERMICHEIT   Gheen edelre bloeme noch soe vermeerde
                 En stont ter werelt noit ontploken.
GHERECHTICHEIT   Ghi wert gebloeyt uut Yessen geerde,   1390
                 Alsoe ons Balam heeft vorsproken.
DE WAERHEIT   Bi u soe wert de helle te broken!
                 Voetsel van vramen leit in u keerne.
ONTFERMICHEIT   U grote genaden staen wide ontploken,
                 Bi u soe wert de helle te broken!   1395
GHERECHTICHEIT   Ghi sult sorcoersen met uwen roeken
                 U vrienden, Lucifer te deerne!
DE WAERHEIT   Bi u soe wert de helle te broken!
                 Voetsel van vramen leit in u keerne.
                 Al onduecht steet tot uwen beweerne!   1400

                                                      Selete.

JOACHEM   O makere ende stichtere van alder stichtinge,
                 Ic bidde uwen heilegen weerdegen name,
                 Dat mijn offerande ende mijn beghichtinge
                 Inden tempel van duechden mach sijn bequame.
                 Ic sie de priesters; God geefs my vrame,   1405
                 Als dat haer mijn onvruchtbaricheit
                 Onversteken moet wesen, alsoet betame,
                 Inden tempel vol duechdeliker claerheit.
                 Met bescaemder herten, met groter zwaerheit,
                 Salic hier mijn offerande bewisen.   1410
                 Vrame van duechden moeter uut rijsen.   *Pause.*
                 O pyleren des tempels gesticht in vreden,
                 Ontfaet hier in onderhoricheden
                 Mijn offerande ter Gods eeren.
                 Al wordic out ende zwaer van leden,   1415
                 Van alder vruchtbaricheit af gesneden,
                 En wiltse mi niet blamelijc wederkeren!
                 Woude God mijn generacie vermeeren,
                 Hi soude mi wel doer sijn hoge weerde

MERCY	Praise be, noble stem, fruitful branch,	
	Inestimable is your worth!	
JUSTICE	You have flowered from Jesse's tree,	
	As Balaam has prophesied.	1385
TRUTH	As scripture has explained,	
	You have blossomed out of Jesse's tree.	
MERCY	No nobler flower ever blossomed,	
	Or ever unfolded in the world.	
JUSTICE	You have flowered from Jesse's tree,	1390
	As Balaam has prophesied.	
TRUTH	Through you hell will be broken!	
	In your kernel lies blessed food.	
MERCY	Your great mercies have opened wide;	
	Through you hell will be broken!	1395
JUSTICE	Your fragrance will give succour	
	To your friends, to Lucifer's detriment.	
TRUTH	Through you hell will be broken!	
	In your kernel lies blessed food.	
	All evil will be defeated by you!	1400

[Exeunt]
Selete.
[Joachim, two priests and a Bishop come out.]

JOACHIM	O maker and founder of all that is created,	
	I pray to your holy, worthy name	
	That my sacrifice and my gift	
	May be pleasing in the temple of virtue.	
	There are the priests; may God give me his blessing	1405
	That my barrenness may not	
	Be repugnant to them, as might be expected,	
	In this temple, so full of heavenly light.	
	With a heart full of shame, greatly burdened,	
	I will offer my sacrifice.	1410
	May good things come from it.	

Pausa.

You pillars of the temple, founded upon peace,
Receive here my humble sacrifice
With which I honour God.
Though I be old and heavy of limb,   1415
Cut off from all fruitfulness,
Do not disgrace me by rejecting my sacrifice!
If God desired to bless me with offspring
He would then, from his great power,

	Natuerlike kinderen verleenen op eerde.	1420
	Dus nemtse int goe.	
i PRIESTER	Gaet uwer veerde!	
	U offerande die es seer onbequame.	
ij PRIESTER	Ghi sijt onvruchtbarich, tes scande en blame.	
	Ghi moet emmers verwaten sijn van Gode.	
BISSCOP	Ghi doet enichsins tegen Gods gebode,	1425
	Dat ghi dus onvruchtbarich blijft.	
i PRIESTER	Tes uws levens scult, dat ghi bedrijft,	
	Anders en dorfdijs niemen op tygen.	
JOACHEM	Ten es, oft God wilt.	
BISSCOP	Ghi moegt wel swigen!	
	Dat u God geen vruchtbaricheit toe en sint,	1430
	Dats een teeken, dat hi u niet en kint;	
	Ende en kint u God niet in u werken van minnen,	
	Twaer onredene, souden wi u dan kinnen	
	Inden tempel van duechden, verchiert met eeren,	
	Hier sittende inde stad des heren,	1435
	Als die alle onduegden werpen ter nedere.	

ij PRIESTER	Hout daer u offerande!	
JOACHEM	Ic en begheerse niet wedere.	
i PRIESTER	Neen, dats om niet,	
	Want diemen onvruchtbarich siet,	
	Tes een teeken van quaden exemple.	1440
ij PRIESTER	Heft u van hier!	
BISSCOP	Gaet uten temple!	
	Wi refuseeren u nu dijn offerande.	
	Hout. Worptse hem na!	
JOACHEM	Och, noyt meerder scande	
	En gescie my, lacen, noch sulken confuse	
	Binnen minen geslachte.	
i PRIESTER	Nu, elc verhuse	1445
	Uten temple metter spoet	
	En volgen wi den bisscop opten voet.	
JOACHEM	Och God, en hoe my de ogen leeken	
	Van drucke dor dese grote blaemte!	
	Men saels mi ewelijc scande spreken	1450
	Ende minen geslechte, noyt selken onvraemte!	
	O God, here, aensiet mijn grote scaemte,	
	Hoe ic inden tempel nu ben vercleent,	
	Om dat ghi my na der natueren betaemte	
	Gheen vrucht op erterike en verleent.	1455

	Grant me natural children here on earth.	1420
	Receive this with grace.	
FIRST PRIEST	Get out of here!	
	Your sacrifice is out of place.	
SECOND PRIEST	You are barren, a shame and a disgrace;	
	You must surely be accursed of God.	
BISHOP	In some way you must have offended God's command	1425
	To have remained barren.	
FIRST PRIEST	The cause is your way of life;	
	No one else is to blame.	
JOACHIM	As God knows, I'm not at fault.	
BISHOP	How dare you say that!	
	That God does not grant you fruitfulness	1430
	Is a sign that he does not acknowledge you.	
	And if God does not know you	
	And bless your love,	
	It would be unreasonable to expect us to recognise you	
	In this most holy temple, the seat of honour,	
	Situated in the town of the Lord.	1435
	Obviously it is our task to oppose all evil.	
SECOND PRIEST	So take away your sacrifice!	
JOACHIM	I don't want to take it back.	
FIRST PRIEST	No, that's no good,	
	For if someone is shown to be barren	
	That is a sign of something wrong.	1440
SECOND PRIEST	Get up and go!	
BISHOP	Out of the temple!	
	We do reject your sacrifice.	
	Take it. Throw it after him!	[*Exit*]
JOACHIM	Alas, never greater shame	
	Nor such disgrace has ever come upon me	
	Or my family.	
FIRST PRIEST	Now, let's quickly	1445
	Leave the temple	
	And follow the bishop closely.	[*Exeunt* Priests.]
JOACHIM	O God, how my tears spring up	
	With grief at this great disgrace!	
	People will talk scandal about me for ever	1450
	And about my family, a terrible fate!	
	O God, my Lord, look upon my great shame,	
	How I am now humiliated in the temple,	
	Because you have not seen fit, in the way of nature,	
	To grant me offspring here on earth.	1455

Waer magics verdient hebben En weet wat meent.
Noyt en was mijn herte soe seere ontstelt.
Al suchtende met natten ogen beweent
Willic mijn beestkens gaen wachten opt velt
Ende bevelen mi der godliker gewelt.   1460

Hier singen ende spelen inden trone.
God sal seggen totten ingel:

GOD   Nu willic recht, het dunct mi tijt,
                Mijn Ontfermicheit suet van seden
                Gansen, die lange gehadt heeft strijt
                Jegen mine Rechtverdicheden.
                Dus vliecht, mijn yngel, tot daer beneden   1465
                Aen enen, Joachemme genaemt,
                Die es bevaen met zeericheden.
                Om sijn onvruchtbaerheit es hi geblaemt.
                Segt hem, dat hi niet bescaemt
                En si, noch en draghe geen verlingen,   1470
                Want Anna sijn wijf, alsoet betaemt,
                Die sal een salege vrucht voort bringen,
                Soe salich, dat alle die lesen oft singen
                Haer salicheit niet en souden gegronden.
                Ghi sulten vinden nu ten stonden   1475
                Bi sinen beesten, daer hi mi claecht
                Seere bitterlijc, om waer orconden,
                Dat Anna sijn wijf geen kint en draecht.
DINGEL   O Here, na dat ghijt hebt gewaecht,
                Soe salt gescien, sijt dies te binnen.   1480
                Ic sal hem blide ende onversaecht
                U hoge bederven laten bekinnen.
JOACHEM   O God, here, met bedructen sinnen
                Soe clagic u mijn bitter vernoysele.
                O Anna, vercorne bloeme vol minnen,   1485
                U vruchtbarich boem en draegt geen groysele.
                O here, sint ons een overvloysele
                Van uwer minliker gracien soet,
                Dat den boem der natueren mach crigen bloysele,
                Daer ons salige vrucht uut groyen moet.   1490
                Alsoe waerlijc als ghi uut rechter oetmoet
                Uter droger roetsen daet water springen,
                Ende naemt al dysraelsche in u behoet,

I do not understand how I have deserved this.
My heart was never in such turmoil.
Sighing, with my eyes wet with tears,
I want to go and watch over my animals in the field,
And commend myself to God's power. 1460

Here they sing and play in heaven.
God will say to the angel.

GOD Now it is right, now it is time,
For my sweet-natured Mercy
To be healed, she who long has struggled
Against my Justice.
So fly, my angel, down to earth 1465
To one called Joachim,
Who is burdened with grief.
He is blamed for his barrenness.
Tell him that he should not be ashamed
Nor burdened by any sadness, 1470
For Anna his wife will, as is fitting,
Bring forth a blessed child,
So blessed, that all those who read or sing
Could not grasp her blessedness.
You will find him at this time 1475
Among his animals, where he laments
Very bitterly to me, to tell the truth,
Because Anna is childless.
THE ANGEL Lord, just as you have decreed
So shall it be, as you know. 1480
I will make known to him
Gladly and without fear your noble purpose.
JOACHIM Lord God, greatly oppressed,
I lament my bitter grief to you.
O Anna, excellent flower, full of love, 1485
Your blossoming tree bears no fruit.
O Lord send us an abundance
Of your loving sweet grace
So that the tree of nature may flower
And bring us blessed fruit. 1490
Just as you from true benevolence
Make water flow from dry rocks
And take all Israelites into your protection

Soe wilt ons met uwer gracien mingen,
Dat Anna een vrucht ter werelt mach bringen.   1495

DINGEL   Joachem, u seit God, ons here,
Dat ghi u selven te vreden stelt
Ende en truert noch en droeft niet meere,
Want uwen druc wert haest bevelt.
Aldus dan u niet meer en quelt   1500
En gaet thuus. Hoert wies ic meyne:
God seit, dat ghi gecrigen selt
Een vrucht, van allen vruchten greyne.
Vol duechden wort si een fonteyne;
Elc sondaer sal in haer genaden   1505
Hem mogen suveren van allen weyne;
Derfsonde die wert bi haer ontladen.
Ten tekene dat u God sal gestaden,
Soe sal u comen te gemoete
U wijf, bevreed van allen quaden,   1510
Ende sal u bieden hoefsche groete
Ter guldender porten om stwifels boete.

JOACHEM   Lof, here, en danc soe hebt van dien,
Dat ghi den uwen aldus versiet!
Den ewigen lof moet u gescien   1515
Altoes dat ghi der uwer pliet!
Des willic, also mi es bediet,
Thuus keren ende stellen mi te vreden;
In hem, die mi dit weten liet,
Soe settic mijn ellendicheden.   1520
Lof hebbe sijn gracie groet besneden,
Want ic ter guldender porten mach scouwen
(Dies danckic Gode met sueter beden)
Annen, mijnre geminder vrouwen.
Vor waer soe magict nu wel behouwen,   1525
Dat mi seide die ingel soete!
Dies willic haer bieden huessche groete.

Pause lutter.

	So endow us with your grace	
	That Anna may bring a child into the world.	1495
THE ANGEL	Joachim, God our Lord says to you	
	That you should be content	
	And not sad or grieved any longer,	
	For your misery is nearly over.	
	So do not continue to torment yourself,	1500
	And return home. Hear my message:	
	God decrees that you will receive	
	A child, blessed above all children.	
	She will be a fountain full of grace;	
	Each sinner will through her mercy	1505
	Be relieved of all wretchedness;	
	Original sin will be removed through her.	
	The sign that God will grant you this	
	Will be that you will be met	
	By your wife, freed of all burdens,	1510
	And she will offer you loving greetings	
	At the Golden Gate and take away all doubt.	
JOACHIM	Praise Lord, and thanks be to you	
	That you have thus come to our aid!	
	Eternal praise must be yours	1515
	Because you always look after your servants!	
	Now I will, as I am told,	
	Go home and be content;	
	On him who let me have this knowledge	
	I place all my burdens.	1520
	Praise be his perfect heavenly grace,	
	For I can see at the Golden Gate	
	(And I thank God with sweet prayers)	
	Anna, my beloved wife.	
	Truly I now can behold,	1525
	That which the sweet angel told me!	
	I shall now offer her loving greetings.	

Pausa parva.

God gruetu, Anne, suete vercorne!
Los benic van allen torne,
Want mi dingel heeft verhuecht.   1530
Dies gae wi te vreden, suver juecht!
Hi heeft mi bracht seer goede mare,
Dies benic vroe.

ANNE   In groten vare
Wasic om u, vercorne man.
Om dies ic u te volgen began   1535
Ende bid u vriendelic, hoert mijn vercleeren,
Dat ghi u emmer in Gods begeeren
Niet en verslaet, want waert sijn wille,
Wi cregen wel vrucht.

JOACHEM   Vrouwe, zwijcht al stille:
Daeraf so es mijn clagen gedaen!   1540
Dies laet ons beide te vreden gaen,
Gode biddende als van dien,
Datter ons salicheit in moet gescien,
Soe ic ben hopende vanden sticke.
Dies gawi te vreden, ghi en icke.   1545

Sanc; spel opt lanxste.

EEN VANDEN GEBUEREN   En hoorde mijn dage noyt vremder abuus!
Wat seitmen van Joachem?

ij GEBUER   Hi es weder thuus,
Alsoe ic corts heb horen verclaren;
Ende oec en was hi in .vij. jaren
Soe vrolijc noch soe blide van moede,   1550
Ja van gelate.

i GEBUER   Na dat ic bevroede,
Soe en waest niet goet, datmen hem dede
Ja alsulken onwerde ende confusichede
Ende vor alle tvolc alsoe bescaemde.

ij GEBUER   Mi docht, dat alsoe niet en betaemde,   1555
Ja, mochtment seggen int openbaer!

i GEBUER   Thoet es thoet, dat latic daer.
Laet ons van onsen woerden stillen.
Dese papen makent, alsoe si willen;
Ic hebs meer gehoort, ic en segge niet hoe.   1560

God greets you, Anna, sweet beloved!
I am freed of all torment,
For the angel has brought me joy. 1530
So let us go in contentment, purest wife!
He has brought very good tidings,
And so I am full of joy.

ANNA Great fear
I felt for you, beloved husband.
And therefore I began to follow you, 1535
And I ask you lovingly, understand me well,
That you will not be downhearted
About God's will because if he wanted it
We should certainly have a child.

JOACHIM Lady, say no more:
All my laments about that are over! 1540
Let us go in peace together,
Praying to God in this respect
That blessedness may come to us,
As I hope in this case.
Let's go contentedly, you and I. 1545

Singing and playing for a long time.

ONE OF THE NEIGHBOURS
I never heard of such a strange thing in all my days!
What are they saying about Joachim?

SECOND NEIGHBOUR He's at home again,
As I have heard just now;
And also in the past seven years he has never been
In such a cheerful or happy mood, 1550
As you can tell in his behaviour.

FIRST NEIGHBOUR As far as I understand
It was not good that he was treated
Indeed, in such a scandalous and shameful way,
And also disgraced in front of everyone.

SECOND NEIGHBOUR And I thought that it wasn't right at all 1555
If I may speak plainly.

FIRST NEIGHBOUR Oh well, it's not for us meddle with the high-ups.
Let's keep our mouths shut.
These priests do just as they like;
I've often heard that, I won't say how. 1560

ij GEBUER	Het en hoert ons oec niet wel toe
	Daerin te sprekene; dats anders nochtan.
i GEBUER	Wilt ment hem witen?
ij GEBUER	Wat maechs de man?
	Oft hem God geen vrucht en verleent,
	Eest dan sijn scout?
i GEBUER	Wat? trouwen eer neent! 1565
	Hi creechse wel, waren si aen hem versien.
ij GEBUER	Gods gracie die moeter inne gescien
	Ende oec in onser alder leven,
	Tsi hier oft eldere.
i GEBUER	Dat moet God geven
	En wil den bescaemden sijn scaemte so lijen, 1570
	Datti na dese scaemte vor sijn scaemte noch moet verblien!

Selete

ANNA	O godlijc licht vol gracien claer,
	U scijnte es blickende altoes eenpaer!
	Op den uwen ghi hittelijc laeyt;
	U grote gewichte es openbaer 1575
	In hemel, in erde, grondeloes zwaer.
	U vonc invierich altoes raeyt!
	Lof hebt der vrucht, die ghi gesaeyt
	Hebt in minen besondegen lichame.
	Mijn man, die teersten was ontpaeyt, 1580
	Sal nu des drux, here, sijn verfraeyt;
	Ghebenedijt si dies u name!
	Want seer bequame
	Soe wert mijn vrucht, ic heb[t] bevonden;
	Dies rise u lof, heere, tallen stonden! 1585

Pause: sanc of spel.

SECOND NEIGHBOUR   It's really not up to us
        To say anything about that; but that's another story.
FIRST NEIGHBOUR   Do they hold it against him?
SECOND NEIGHBOUR   What can the poor man do?
        If God doesn't grant him a child
        Is it his fault?
FIRST NEIGHBOUR   What! No, of course it isn't!   1565
        He would have children, if that was meant.
SECOND NEIGHBOUR   God's grace is needed in this
        As it is in all our lives,
        Be it here or elsewhere.
FIRST NEIGHBOUR   May God grant that
        He who is disgraced may endure it in such a way   1570
        That once the shame is over, he will value it.

Selete.

ANNA   O heavenly light, clear and full of grace,
        Your radiance shines without cease or change;
        You burn fiercely in front of your people;
        Your great might is revealed   1575
        In heaven, on earth without limit.
        Your intense light shines always!
        Praise be for the child, which you have granted
        In my sinful body.
        My husband, who was so terribly sad,   1580
        Will now, Lord, be released from his burden;
        Blessed therefore be your name!
        For very lovely
        Will my child be, I know that;
        So may your praise, Lord, increase at all times.   1585

Pausa: singing or playing.

JOACHEM   Noyt blider man en was op eerde,
                     Want Anna, mijn wijf, soet God begeerde,
                     Die heeft, also mi es verclaert,
                     Een suete dochter nu gebaert.
                     Soe edel, soe reyn, soe scoen van live   1590
                     En was ter werelt noyt van wive
                     Geboren! Lof hebt dies, hemelsche vader,
                     Want ghi mijn troest sijt en berader;
                     Dies sijt geloeft in ewegen tie!

EEN PRIESTER   Joachem, ghi scijnt seer blie.   1595
                     Vercorne vrient, wats u gesciet?
                     Segt ons de sake.
JOACHEM   En soudic niet,
                     Ghi heren? Ic ben soe wel gepaeit!
                     God heeft sijn gracie op mi gespraeit
                     Soe overvloedich, ja, diet wel vaet.   1600
                     Ic, hopic, nemmeer en werd versmaet
                     Inden tempel, des ben ic vro,
                     Om mijn onvruchtbaerheit.
DANDER PRIESTER   Keren lieve, hoe soo?
                     Joachem, dats ons lief om horen!
JOACHEM   Noyt scoender kint en was geboren   1605
                     — Ghi heren, dat si u wel verclaert -
                     Dan Anna .j. dochter heeft gebaert,
                     Mijn lieve wijf. Dies soudic begeeren
                     Aen u beiden, om cort vercleeren,
                     Dat ghi mi enen sueten name   1610
                     Wout condegen, soet haer best betame
                     Na haer scoenheit ende behoerte.
EEN PRIESTER   Welc tijt was des kints geboerte?
                     Joachem, vrient, doets ons gewach.
                     Dit horen wy gheerne.
JOACHEM   Den .viij. dach   1615
                     Van september dat kint lofsam
                     Van harer moeder ter werelt quam
                     Ende daer om spoet u sonder beyen.
                     Ic wil gaen thuus en doen bereyen
                     Mijn dingen, alsoe daer toe behoert,   1620
                     Ende wilt mi volgen rechtevoert.

JOACHIM   There was never a happier man on earth,
For Anna, my wife, as God willed,
Has, as has been explained to me,
Borne me a sweet daughter.
So noble, so pure, so beautiful a child   1590
Never was born of woman
On earth! Praise be to you, heavenly father,
For you are my consolation and helper;
You shall be praised for evermore!

[Enter Priests.]

A PRIEST   Joachim, you seem very happy,   1595
Dear friend, what has happened you?
You must tell us everything.
JOACHIM   How can I not be happy,
You lords? I am so comforted!
God has poured his grace out upon me
So abundantly, yes, as anyone would agree.   1600
I will never again be disgraced, I hope,
In the temple, for my barrenness —
That's why I am so happy.
ANOTHER PRIEST   Joachim, that's good to hear.
But, dear friend, tell us more.
JOACHIM   A more beautiful child was never born —   1605
You lords mark this well —
The daughter that Anna, my dear wife,
Has borne. Therefore I would like
To ask you both, in short,
That you would give me a sweet name   1610
Which would suit her best
According to her beauty, as it befitting.
A PRIEST   At what time was the child born?
Joachim, my friend, tell us that.
We would be glad to know.
JOACHIM   On the eighth day   1615
Of September that precious child
Was brought into this world by her mother:
So please come quickly without delay.
I will go home and prepare
My things, as is fitting,   1620
And you can follow after.

       Dies biddic u, tes meer dan tijt,
       Scep hem den name.
DANDER PRIESTER   Ghebenedijt
       Moet sijn de vrucht om ons verhogen.
       Maer hoe selen wijt heeten mogen,   1625
       Dit kint? Geselle, wilt mi beraen,
       Ic bens te weets.
DEERSTE PAPE   Bidt vol genaen
       Den oversten here met goeden avise,
       Datti ons enen naem bewise,
       Als sijn heilege wille si.   1630
       Bidt dies met nernste.   *Hier bidden si.*

DINGEL   Soe hoert na mi,
       Wies dat ic u nu sal vercleeren:
       Noemse Maria: dit seit hi di,
       Die hoechste here; tes sijn begeren.
       Den wreeden viant te sijnder deeren   1635
       Ende alle den hemelscen heere ter vrame
       Makic te binnen u deser meeren,
       Dat Maria wert haren name.
       Si wort den here alsoe betame,
       Dat noyt haer weerde en was volscreven,   1640
       Hoe hoge, hoe groet ende hoe bequame
       Dat si daer boven sal sijn verheven.
       Den staet der inglen sal haer aencleven.
EEN PRIESTER   Lof, salich kint, gebenedijt
       Van Gode, die ons dees boetscap brachte!   1645
DANDER PAPE   In uwer moeder lichame gewijt,
       Lof, salich kint, gebenedijt!
EEN PRIESTER   Ghespruyt, geboren dat ghi sijt
       Uut Yesse, den edelen gheslachte.
DANDER PAPE   Lof, salijch kint, gebenedijt   1650
       Van Gode, die ons dees bootscap brachte!
       Van groter crachte, hoge inde[n] here,
       Soe sijn u machte onsprekelic seere.
       Dies vloye u lof toe emmermeere.

             Selete; wech.

I beg you, it's high time
That you came up with a name.

THE OTHER PRIEST   Blessed
May be the child who brings us joy.
But what shall we call it,   1625
This child? My friend, give me some advice
Because I'm at a loss.

FIRST CLERIC   Pray earnestly
To the highest Lord who is full of grace
That he might give us a name
According to his sacred will.   1630
Pray for this with all your heart.

Here they pray.

ANGEL   Listen to me,
And do what I shall now explain to you:
Call her Maria. This is decreed by him,
The highest Lord: it's his desire.
To the detriment of the cruel fiend,   1635
And to the advantage of all heavenly hosts,
I will convey this message to you,
That her name shall be Maria.
She will be so pleasing to the Lord
That her worth can never be expressed: 1640
How high, how great and how pleasing,
She will be elevated above all.
She will be ranked with the angels.

A PRIEST   Praise, holy child, be blessed,
By God who brought us this message!   1645

SECOND CLERIC   Sanctified in your mother's womb,
Praise, holy child, be blessed.

A PRIEST   Come forth, born as you are
From the noble line of Jesse.

SECOND CLERIC   Praise, holy child, be blessed,   1650
By God who brought us this message!
Of great strength, and close to the Lord
Your powers are inexpressibly great.
May praise flow to you always!

Selete; they go out.

ANNA	Lof, here, en danc in allen tien! —	1655

ANNA   Lof, here, en danc in allen tien! —   1655
Vercorne man, wilt u verblien:
Al es ons kint seer jonc van dagen,
Soet blijct, het es na Gods behagen
Seer wijs van sinne, suptijl en vroet,
Scoen, bequame. vol der oetmoet.   1660
Nochtan en eest — God hebs gewout —
Nu recht omtrent maer .iij. jaer out.
Dus, waert u wille, ic sout wel raen,
Dat wise inden tempel daen,
Want si hevet mi gewaecht.   1665
Wat segdier af, dochter?
JOACHEM   Mijn suver maecht,
Uwe begeerte als van dien,
Lief kint, die sal u wel gescien.
Dies segt mi — gaet mi me of tegen —
U wille sal sijn.
ONS VROUWE, *i. jonc kint*
          Vader, ic ben genegen   1670
Altijt te doene na u bevelen
Ende Gode te dienene.
ANNA   Dees vier gespeelen,
Maria, dochter, wilt met u leyen:
Wijsheit en laet van u niet sceyen,
Oetmoedicheit es den anderen name,   1675
Suverheit, de derde, die geeft vrame,
Ghehorsamheit om duecht verstiven.
Dese selen altoes met u bliven.
Nu kinder, tert op, weest onversaecht.
Heere, ontfaet dees suver maecht   1680
Met haren gespeelen, dies biddic dy,
En nemtse in hoeden.
BISSCOP   In Gods namen sy!
Nu ga wy, dochter, onder u viven.
Dat ghi eendrechtich tsamen moet bliven,
Alsoe ic hope, na recht bekin,   1685
Dat sal volcomen.
JOACHIM   Nu, kinder, tert in.
Dat alden hemelschen heere soet
U reyn bestaen bequaem sijn moet!
Wi sceiden van u nu; als in desen
Gods gracie wil altijt bi u wesen.   1690

ANNA | Praise, Lord, and thanks be at all times!   1655
Beloved husband, be happy now:
Even if our child is still young
It is clear that it is according to God's pleasure
That she is sensitive, clever and wise,
Beautiful, perceptive and full of humility.   1660
Nevertheless she is—by God's grace —
Just now barely three years old.
If you agree, I would advise
That we present her in the temple
Because she has asked me to.   1665
Isn't that so, daughter?

JOACHIM   My pure little girl,
Your desire in this matter,
Sweet child, will certainly be fulfilled.
So tell me—whether I agree or not —
What is your wish?

OUR LADY, *a young child*
                              Father, I am prepared   1670
Always to act at your command
And serve God.

ANNA   These four playmates,
Maria, daughter, you should take with you:
Do not be separated from Wisdom,
The other is called Humility,   1675
Purity the third, which brings great benefit,
Obedience strengthens virtue.
These must always stay with you.
Now, children, climb up, don't be afraid.
Lord receive this pure virgin   1680
With her playmates, as I pray you,
And take them into your protection.

BISHOP   May it be so, in God's name!
Now let us go, daughter, all five of you.
I hope that you may always stay together
In harmony; if I judge right   1685
That's how it will be.

JOACHIM   Now children, go in.
May your pure lives be pleasing
To all the sweet heavenly hosts!
Now we shall leave you; as it is now
God's grace will be with you forever.   1690

BISSCOP	Lief kint, hoe es den name dijn?
MARIA	Maria.
BISSCOP	Wel moetti comen sijn!

In duechden wil u God gesterken.
Ghi selt nayen, stofferen en werken
De orlementen des tempels en voort   1695
Seldi u oefenen, alsoet behoort,
Ten geboden Gods in allen tyen.
Ter leeringen ende ter prophecien
Pijnt u te volgen in allen keere.
Seldi, Maria?

MARIA	Jaic geerne, heere! 1700
ANNA	Nu ga wi, Joachim, vercorne man,

Maria es inden tempel bleven.

JOACHIM	God wilse met duechden verlichten voort an.
ANNA	Nu ga wi, Joachim, vercorne man.
JOACHIM	Die hemel ende erde heeft int gespan, 1705

Die wille haer salegen voortganc geven.

ANNA	Nu ga wi, Joachim, vercorne man,

Maria es inden tempel bleven.

JOACHIM	Haer onsprekelike wijsheit, haer duegdelijc leven,

Die sal noch, hopic, naer Gods gehingen,   1710
Alle menscen salicheit in bringen.
Want na de wijsheit, die in haer gesticht es,
Si metten heilegen geest verlicht es.
Hoe soude haer joncheit anders beseffen
Den keest van duechden?

ANNA	God wiltse verheffen 1715

In duechden als alder weertste geminde,
Datter elc gracie ende troest aen vinde!   *Selete.*

BISSCOP	Ghi heren, mi wondert alte sere,

En dede de gracie vanden here,
Hoe dat Maria, dese suete maegt,   1720
Dus jonc haer soe suptijlec draegt.
In allen dingen, dats openbaer,
Es si soe duegdelijc.

EEN PRIESTER	Dats seker waer,

Her bisscop. Wi en hebben noyt vernomen
Selc maegt hier inden tempel comen,   1725
Van bedene, van werkene soe wijs, soe vroet,

BISHOP	Dear child, what is your name?
MARIA	Maria.
BISHOP	You are most welcome!
	May God strengthen you in virtue.
	You will sew, adorn and embroider
	The treasures of the temple, and also 1695
	You will learn, as it fitting,
	The commands of God at all times.
	Try and pay attention in all ways
	To the scriptures and to the prophets.
	Will you do that, Maria?
MARIA	I will gladly, my lord! 1700
ANNA	Now, Joachim, beloved husband, we must go;
	Maria will stay in the temple.
JOACHIM	May God grace her with virtues henceforth.
ANNA	Now, Joachim, beloved husband, we must go.
JOACHIM	He who has heaven and earth in his hand 1705
	May give her future blessings.
ANNA	Now, Joachim, beloved husband, we must go;
	Maria will stay in the temple.
JOACHIM	Her limitless wisdom, her virtuous life
	Will, as I hope, if God allows it, 1710
	Bring salvation to all mankind.
	I'm sure that because she is so wise,
	The light of the Holy Spirit must be upon her.
	How else would one so young know
	The core of virtue?
ANNA	May God raise her 1715
	In virtues to be the most beloved,
	So that all may find grace and comfort in her.

Selete.

BISHOP	My lords, I wonder very much
	How, unless through the grace of God,
	Maria, this sweet girl, 1720
	Behaves so sensitively, though so young.
	In all things, that is evident,
	She is so virtuous.
A PRIEST	That is true,
	Lord bishop. We have never before
	Had such a girl come into the temple, 1725
	So perceptive, so wise in prayers and in works,

	Soe scoen, soe lieflijc en vol der oetmoet.	
	Ic en can gepeynsen, hoe dat sy	
	Na haer joncheit.	
BISSCOP	Wat raeddy my,	
	Ghi heren? Wi moeten den gebode	1730
	Gehoorsam wesen, al sceiden wi noode	
	Van deser maegt, om cort verclaren.	
	Si es seer nakende hueren jaren.	
	Onsprekelijc eest, datmen soude rueren	
	Van enegen jongen creatueren,	1735
	Dat sy mocht hebben alsulken sin,	
	En hadsi den heilegen geest niet in.	
	Want si es een vorme der reynicheit	
	Ende der oetmoet.	
DANDER PRIESTER	Vor waer geseyt,	
	Si es de sorchfuldichste ende de bequaemlijxste,	1740
	De gehorsamste ende de tamelijxste	
	In allen dingen, soet es beseven.	
	Si leit bat yngelen - dan menscenleven;	
	Si es volmaect ende onbevlect.	
BISSCOP	Maecht fijn, daer Salamon af sprect	1745
	In sinen cantiken, soe ic verzinne:	
	'Ghi sijt met allen scoen, mijn vriendinne!	
	In u en es geen smette gesticht.	
	Scoender dan de zonne ende boven dlicht	
	Der sterren duytnemenste, ongebreckelijxste	1750
	Fonteine vloyende inder gracien, de reckelijxste	
	Die noyt ter werelt ontfinc wesen.'	
	Wat saels gescien?	
DEEN PRIESTER	Nu, als te desen	
	Wille ons de here verlenen spoet,	
	Dat tonser salicheit wesen moet.	1755

Selete. Dan sal Ons Vrouwe groot sijn.

JOACHIM	Anna, vercorne geminde vrouwe,	
	Daer ic in duegden mi toe betrouwe,	
	Eest wonder, dat mi therte verhuecht es,	
	Als Maria, de duegdelike kersouwe,	
	Besprayt es metten hemelscen douwe	1760
	Van gracien, daer elkerlijc in verhuecht es.	
	Want si tverchiersele van alder duecht es,	

So beautiful, so sweet and full of humility.
I cannot think how that can be
In one so young.

BISHOP   What is your advice
My lords? We must obey   1730
The law, even though we are reluctant
To part from this girl, to be brief.
She has nearly reached marriageable age.
It is unthinkable that one should say
Of any such young creature   1735
That she would have such a disposition
If it were not for the Holy Spirit.
She is a paragon of purity
And of humility.

SECOND PRIEST   It's very true that
She is the most careful and the loveliest,   1740
The most obedient and the most pure
In all things, as is well known.
She leads more an angelic than a human life;
She is perfect and immaculate.

BISHOP   Noble maid, of whom Solomon says   1745
In his canticles, as I remember:
'You are beautiful in all things, my beloved!
You are without blemish, more beautiful than the sun
And a brighter light
Than all the stars, the most incomparable   1750
Fountain flowing from grace, the most excellent
Ever created in the world.'
What should we do?

FIRST PRIEST   Well, may the Lord
In this grant us joy,
That it may bring our salvation.   1755

Selete.
Then will Our Lady be grown up.

JOACHIM   Anna, my excellent, beloved wife,
In whose virtue I trust
Is it to be wondered that my heart is joyous,
Since Maria, that most virtuous cherry tree,
Is besprinkled with the heavenly dew   1760
Of grace, in which everyone rejoices?
For she is the treasure of all virtue,

                              Oetmoedelijc inden tempel des heren
                              Boven alle meechden, dwelc ons een vruecht es.

	Salicheit moeter by vermeeren.	1765
ANNA	Joachim, geminde man vol eren,	
	Si en salder niet lange in mogen bliven.	
JOACHIM	Soe machse haer tot huwelike state keren,	
	Oft in suverheden haer selven bescriven.	
ANNA	Gods gracie die wil in haer becliven	1770
	Want si scier hubaer wesen sal,	
	Reyn, duegdelijc boven alle wiven.	
	Dies lovic den oversten here van al.	
JOACHIM	Hi, die hemel ende erde, berch ende dal	
	Gemaect heeft, die laetse voort regieren;	1775
	Hi salse best hueden voor ongeval	
	Ende duegdelijc tsijnder gelieften bestieren.	
ANNA	Nu laet ons met herten goedertieren	
	Loven den here, tes meer dan tijt,	
	Dat Maria soe duegdelijc es van manieren	1780
	Dor de gracie des heren gebenedijt.	
JOACHIM	Lof, goddelijc wesen, diet al verblijt,	
	Ingelen, menscen, hemel ende erde.	
ANNA	Lof, specie vol duechden, der yngelen jolijt.	
JOACHIM	Lof, goddelijc wesen gebenedijt.	1785
ANNA	Lof, die fonteyne van gracien sijt;	
	Onsprekelic es u hoge weerde.	
JOACHIM	Lof, godlijc wesen, diet al verblijt,	
	Ingelen, menscen, hemel ende erde.	
	Dat Maria, die meegdelike geerde,	1790
	Met uwer gracien dus es versien,	
	Dies moet u ewigen lof gescien.	
BISSCOP	Na Gods gebod moet u verclaert sijn:	
	Alle meegden, die verjaert sijn,	
	Die trecken thuus bi vader ende moedere	1795
	Ende nemen man als haren behoedere.	
	Dit benic gebiedende sonder respijt.	
	Maria, ghij hebt oec uwen tijt,	
	Die daer toe steet; reyn, suver geerde,	
	Ghi moet oec huwen.	

	Humble in the temple of the Lord	
	Above all other maids, which is a joy to us.	
	Our blessings are the greater for this.	1765
ANNA	Joachim, honourable and beloved husband,	
	She will not be able to remain there for long.	
JOACHIM	Yes, she could choose to be married,	
	Or decide to remain in maidenly virtue.	
ANNA	God's grace will grow inside her,	1770
	For she will soon be of marriageable age,	
	Pure, excellent above all women,	
	And for that I praise the greatest Lord of all.	
JOACHIM	He who has made heaven and earth,	
	Mountain and valley, may guide her future;	1775
	He will know how best to guard her from misfortune,	
	And steer her into virtuous ways according to his will.	
ANNA	Now let us praise the Lord	
	With joyful hearts, — it's more than time—	
	That Maria is so virtuous in her life,	1780
	And blessed by the grace of the Lord.	
JOACHIM	Praise, divine being, who brings joy to all,	
	Angels, humans, heaven and earth.	
ANNA	Praise, an example of great goodness, the delight of	
	the angels.	
JOACHIM	Praise, divine and blessed being.	1785
ANNA	Praise, you who are a fountain of grace;	
	Your great worth is ineffable.	
JOACHIM	Praise, divine being, who brings joy to all,	
	Angels, humans, heaven and earth.	
	That Maria, that maidenly garden,	1790
	Is so adorned by your grace,	
	For which eternal praise is meet.	
BISHOP	It must be clear that, according to God's command,	
	All maidens who have come of age	
	Go home to their fathers and mothers	1795
	And take a husband as their protector.	
	This is my command for all.	
	Maria, you too have come to the time,	
	Which is ordained for it; pure and virtuous garden,	
	You too must marry.	

MARIA	By uwer weerde,	1800
	Eerwerdich vadere, ic hebbe in my	
	Genomen, op dat Gods wille sy,	
	Dat ic mijn reinicheit ende mijn trouwe	
	Gode almechtich offeren souwe.	
	Dus soudic geerne houden Gode	1805
	Mijn opset van dien, ende den gebode	
	Niet contrarie en ware van dien.	
BISSCOP	Maria, dat en mach niet gescien	
	Na mijn verstaen; ic en weets hoe keren.	
	Almechtich God, here alder heren,	1810
	Wilt ons verlichten met saleger leeren	
	In duegden tot onser sielen bate:	
	Oft Maria, wiens duegden altijt vermeeren,	
	Hier bliven sal inden tempel des heren	
	Oft haer voegen tot huwelijken state.	1815
i PRIESTER	Balseme van gracien, suet honich rate,	
	Wilt u grote genadicheit hier bewisen.	
ij PRIESTER	Verwerft ons in glorien de hemelsce sate,	
	Daer men de sielen mach ewich spisen.	
BISSCOP	Soe datter elc confoort van duechden in vate,	1820
	Balseme van gracien, reyn honichrate.	
ij PRIESTER	Verwerft ons inder glorien de hemelsce gesate,	
	Daer men de sielen mach ewich spisen.	
BISSCOP	Balseme van duechden, reyn honichrate,	
	Wilt u grote genadicheit haer bewisen,	1825
	Wiens lof dat niemen en can volprisen.	
DINGELE	Her bisscop, hoort de redene mijn:	
	Alle, die van Davits geslachte sijn,	
	Die bringen droege roeden sonder vernoyen;	
	Ende de wiens dat daer sal bloyen,	1830
	Sal Marien hebben in hoeden	
	Te huwelike; wilt u hier met spoeden.	
BISSCOP	Lof, cracht, des alle crachten cracht hebben,	
	Dat ghi u vrienden aldus versiet.	
i PRIESTER	Wel hem, die u in haer gedacht hebben.	1835
	Lof, cracht, des alle crachten cracht hebben.	

MARIA	By your leave,	1800
	Honoured father, I do intend,	
	If it is God's will	
	That I should offer my purity	
	And my trust to God almighty.	
	So I would gladly like to keep to my plan	1805
	To be near God if this were not	
	Contrary to his command.	
BISHOP	Maria, as far as I can see	
	That is not possible; I do not know what to do.	
	Almighty God, Lord of all Lords,	1810
	Please enlighten us, with blessed knowledge	
	To benefit our souls:	
	Whether Maria, whose virtues ever increase,	
	Should remain here in the temple of the Lord,	
	Or acquiesce in the state or marriage.	1815
FIRST PRIEST	Balm of grace, sweet honeycomb,	
	Show us please your great benevolence.	
SECOND PRIEST	Gain for us in glory the heavenly place,	
	Where the souls will be eternally nourished.	
BISHOP	So that each will gain great solace of virtue	1820
	Balm of grace, pure honeycomb,	
SECOND PRIEST	Gain for us in glory the heavenly place,	
	Where the souls will be eternally nourished.	
BISHOP	Balm of virtue, pure honeycomb,	
	Show us please your great benevolence,	1825
	Which can never be praised enough.	
THE ANGEL	Lord bishop, hear my words:	
	All who are of David's line,	
	Will joyfully bring dry rods;	
	And he whose wand shall flower	1830
	Shall take Maria into his protection	
	And marry her: let this come to pass without delay.	
BISHOP	Praise be to that power which empowers all powers,	
	That so you watch over your friends.	
FIRST PRIEST	Bless them who keep you in their thoughts.	1835
	Praise be to that power which empowers all powers.	

BISSCOP	Wat dat wi, menscen, in duechden gewracht hebben,
	Bi uwer duecht soe en eest al niet.
ij PRIESTER	Lof, cracht, des alle crachten cracht hebben,
	Dat ghi u vrienden aldus versiet.	1840
BISSCOP	Nu salic sonder te letten yet
	Alle dat van [Davits] geslechte es
	Ende tot huweliken state bequaeme int wesen es,
	Gaen doen versamen met groter spoede.
	Laet sien, wie Marien, vol der oetmoede,	1845
	Sal vallen te goede; si es soe duegdelijc.
i PRIESTER	Elc mach int herte wel wesen vruegdelijc,
	Al Davits geslechte mach wel verblien!
	Tert voort, ghi heren, in allen sien.
i JONGELINC	Gods werken sijn wonderlijc te verstane.	1850
ij JONGELINC	Wie sal sijn wijsheit dan gronderen?
iij JONGELINC	Het gaet verre buten minen vermane.
i JONGELINC	Gods werken sijn wonderlijc te verstane.
iij JONGELINC	Nu pinen wi na sbisscops bevel te gane
	Ten temple, daer elc mach veryubileren.	1855
i JONGELINC	Gods werken zijn wonderlijc te verstane.
ij JONGELINC	Wie sal sijn wijsheit dan gronderen?
iij JONGELINC	Die hem in wijsheden met wijsheden fonderen,
	Doent sonder vaer.
ij JONGELINC	Die wise dolen meest.
i JONGELINC	Dats emmers waer!	1860
iij JONGELINC	Te beter hebben sijt, die goet clerc sijn.
i JONGELINC	Ja, wat segdijs? Moet niet een wonderlic werc sijn,
	Dat Maria, de maegt, reyn van gedachte,
	Bi Gods bevelene uut Davids geslachte
	Enen man sal trouwen, geseit vor al,	1865
	Niet wetende, wie dat hi wesen sal,
	Dan si in Gods begeerte te vreden es?
ij JONGELINC	Menich maecht, die opten dach van heden es,
	En soude soe lichte niet gepayt sijn.
iij JONGELINC	Die haer gecrigen sal, mach wel verfrayt sijn,	1870
	Want haer minlijc opsien es soe sedelijc.
i JONGELINC	Ende Maria, die oetmoedege maecht seer vredelijc,
	Sal op Gods betrouwen, soet jonst huer riet,
	Enen man gaen trouwen, al en kint sijs niet.
ij JONGELINC	Wie hoerde noit wonderliker dingen?	1875
iij JONGELINC	Die sijn rijsken bloyende sal bringen,
	Sal de maegt trouwen, dats openbaer.

BISHOP	Whatever good we people have achieved
	Compared to your greatness it is nothing.
SECOND PRIEST	Praise be to that power which empowers all powers,
	That so you watch over your friends. 1840
BISHOP	Now I will, without further ado,
	Join together with great speed
	All those who have arisen from David's House
	And are ready, fit for the married state.
	Now let us see to whom Maria, full of grace, 1845
	Will be given; she is so excellent.
FIRST PRIEST	Now everyone has reason to be glad,
	All of David's line may well rejoice!
	Come forth, you lords, from all sides.

FIRST YOUNG MAN   God's works are a mystery to comprehend. 1850

SECOND YOUNG MAN   Who will then plumb his wisdom?

THIRD YOUNG MAN   It's far beyond my grasp.

FIRST YOUNG MAN   God's works are a mystery to comprehend.

THIRD YOUNG MAN   Now we must strive according to the bishop's command

To go to the temple where all can rejoice. 1855

FIRST YOUNG MAN   God's works are a mystery to comprehend.

SECOND YOUNG MAN   How can anybody then plumb his wisdom?

THIRD YOUNG MAN   Those who apply themselvesto wisdom with wisdom,

Do it without fear.

SECOND YOUNG MAN   But the wise err most.

FIRST YOUNG MAN   That's surely true! 1860

THIRD YOUNG MAN   The truly learned succeed the best.

FIRST YOUNG MAN   So, what are you saying? Is it not a mysterious thing

That Maria, the Virgin, pure in thought,

Will marry a man, by God's command,

From the house of David as ordained 1865

Not knowing who he will be,

But only that she should be content with God's will.

SECOND YOUNG MAN   Many a maiden amongst those now living

Would not be persuaded so easily.

THIRD YOUNG MAN   Whoever will gain her may well be elated, 1870

Because she is demure and lovely to behold.

FIRST YOUNG MAN   And Maria, that gracious and serene maiden,

Will trust in God, as his grace advises,

And marry a man even though she does not know him.

SECOND YOUNG MAN   Whoever heard more mysterious things? 1875

THIRD YOUNG MAN   He who brings a flowering branch

Will marry the maiden for sure.

i JONGELINC	Dat teeken sal groot sijn.	
ij JONGELINC	Dats emmers waer!	
	Men sach sulc wonder noyt gevallen.	
iij JONGELINC	Diense geburen sal van ons allen,	1880
	Es van Gode seer uutvercoren.	
i JONGELINC	Op eerde en was noit scoender geboren.	
	Haer scoenheit verlicht al tscijn der sonnen.	
ij JONGELINC	Haren meegdeliken lichaem es soe dor ronnen	
	Met minnen tot duegdeliker ingloedicheit!	1885
iij JONGELINC	Si es soe vol der oetmoedicheit;	
	Elker herten geeft si goet exempele.	
i JONGELINC	Hets de vorsienichste vanden tempele,	
	De wijste, de oetmoedichste ende de reynste,	
	De gehorsamste den here ende de serteynste,	1890
	Die noyt op groyende was in duechden.	
ij JONGELINC	Dat esse warechtich.	
iij JONGELINC	Si es soe vol vruechden,	
	Dat noyt op eerde en quam haers gelike,	
	Alsoet wel blijct.	
i JONGELINC	Ic ben mechtich ende rike,	
	Maer mocht mi de scoen maegt geburen,	1895
	Ic dancte Gode der goeder aventuren.	
	Ende ic wilder herte ende sin toe leggen	
	Huer te beminnene.	
ij JONGELINC	Alsoe mochten wi oec seggen:	
	Hier en es niement, vaet mijn vercleren,	
	Hi en soudse te huwelike wel begeren,	1900
	Marien, die een bescut vor toren es.	
iij JONGELINC	Hi salse wel crigen, diere toe geboren es.	
	Ic meynder noch sulc es, diere na lesen sal.	
i JONGELINC	Sijn roede sal bloyen, die brudegoem wesen sal.	
	Ga wi ten temple de maecht aenscouwen.	1905
ij JONGELINC	Tes messelic, wie ons meskief genesen sal.	
	Sijn roede sal bloyen, die brudegoem wesen sal.	
iij JONGELINC	Sijn aventuere es groet, die in desen sal	
	Gode behagen ende de maget trouwen.	
i JONGELINC	Sijn roede sal bloyen, die brudegoem wesen sal.	1910
	Ga wi ten temple de maegt aenscouwen.	
	God wil ons met siere gracien bedouwen!	
BISSCOP	Inden name des heren, hoort alle, die sijt	
	Van Davids geslechte sonder verwijt	
	Te huwene: brinct elc een roe	1915

FIRST YOUNG MAN   That will be a great sign!
SECOND YOUNG MAN   That's quite true!
             No one has ever seen such a miracle.
THIRD YOUNG MAN   Of all of us he to whom this happens   1880
             Will be greatly preferred by God.
FIRST YOUNG MAN   There never was a more beautiful girl born on earth.
             Her beauty outshines the rays of the sun.
SECOND YOUNG MAN   Her maidenly body is suffused
             With a passionate love of virtue!   1885
THIRD YOUNG MAN   She is so full of grace;
             She is an example for everyone.
FIRST YOUNG MAN   She is the most loving in the temple,
             The wisest, the purest and the most gracious,
             The most obedient to the Lord and the most faithful, 1890
             Who ever grew up in virtue.
SECOND YOUNG MAN   She is that indeed.
THIRD YOUNG MAN   She is so full of joy,
             She has no equal on earth,
             As is made clear.
FIRST YOUNG MAN   I am powerful and wealthy,
             But if I might win this beautiful maiden   1895
             I would thank God for my good fortune.
             And I would strive with all my heart and mind
             To love her.
SECOND YOUNG MAN   And we may say that too:
             There is no one here, take my word for it,
             Who would not desire to marry her,   1900
             Maria, who is a protection against evil.
THIRD YOUNG MAN   He who is destined for her will gain her.
             I think there will be many who would pray for it.
FIRST YOUNG MAN   Whoever will be the bridegroom his rod will flower.
             Let's go into the temple to see the maiden.   1905
SECOND YOUNG MAN   It's uncertain who will cure our misfortune.
             Whoever will be the bridegroom his rod will flower.
THIRD YOUNG MAN   Great blessing will befall him
             Who will please God and marry the maiden.
FIRST YOUNG MAN   Whoever will be the bridegroom his rod will flower. 1910
             Let's go into the temple to see the maiden.
             May God bestow his grace upon us!
BISHOP   In the name of the Lord, listen all
             Of the house of David who are blameless
             And fit to marry: each shall bring a dry rod   1915

	Droege, dat God sijn gracie doe	
	Tot onser salicheit, hoe dat geet.	
i VAN DAVIDS GESLECHTE	Her bisscop, wi sijn alle bereet	
	Naer u gebod, soet redene si.	
	Joseph tert voort.	
JOSEPH	Wat hanct aen my?	1920
	Ghi heren, wilt mi dies verdragen.	
	Ic bens onwerdich.	
BISSCOP	Hoort mi gewagen:	
	Wiens roede dat bloyt, mach wel verblien,	
	Want hi sal trouwen der maegt Marien,	
	Joachems dochter, na Gods bevel.	1925
	Stect op u roeden! — O God Emanuel,	
	Hoe mach dit wesen? Dits vremt bediet:	
	Hier en bloyt een ynckel roede niet.	
	Nochtan seide dingle int openbaer,	
	Dat soude gescien.	
i PRIESTER	Joseph, comt naer,	1930
	Weest onderhorich naer dbetamen.	
	Stect op u roede, en wilt u niet scamen;	
	Wat God begeert, dat moet gescien.	
JOSEPH	Ghi heren, dat kennic, maer al in dien	
	Benic bereet in alder maten;	1935
	Maer dees soe mochti mi wel verlaten.	
BISSCOP	Lof, here, die niement en can geliken!	
	Hier doedy openbaerlijc bliken,	
	Dat alle dinc es in u vermogen.	
	Joseph, ghi moecht u wel verhogen,	1940
	Want God die heeft u uutvercoren	
	Boven al dandere; nu na dbehoren,	
	Josep, soe moetti trouwen te wive	
	Marien reyn, suver, bequame van live,	
	Alsoet de overste here begeert.	1945
JOSEPH	Her bisscop, dat en wert u niet geweert.	
BISSCOP	Nu, Joseph, in onderhoricheden	
	Soe geloefdy den here, dat ghi met vreden	
	Ende met getrouwicheden, in werken van minnen,	
	Marien, vol der oetmoedeger sinnen,	1950
	Volstandich bi bliven selt emmermeere	
	Sonder af sceiden?	
JOSEPH	Dat gelovic haer ende Gode den here	
	Vor u, her bisscop, als man van trouwen.	
BISSCOP	Dat geloefdy oec, Maria?	

	That God may bestow his grace	
	For our salvation, whatever may befall.	
ONE OF DAVID'S HOUSE	Lord bishop, we are all prepared	
	To do your command as we should.	
	Joseph, come forward.	
JOSEPH	Why me?	1920
	You lords, please absolve me from this,	
	I am not worthy.	
BISHOP	Listen to my words:	
	He whose rod will flower, may well rejoice,	
	For he will marry Maria, the maiden,	
	Joachim's daughter, as God ordains.	1925
	Hold up your rods!—O God Emmanuel,	
	How can this be? This is a strange thing:	
	Not a single rod flowers.	
	And yet the angel said quite clearly	
	That it should happen.	
FIRST PRIEST	Joseph, come closer,	1930
	Be obedient as is befitting.	
	Hold up your rod and don't be ashamed:	
	Whatever God desires that must come to pass.	
JOSEPH	My lords I know that, and in all this	
	I am ready in every way;	1935
	But please let this pass me by.	
BISHOP	Praise be to the Lord who has no equal!	
	Here you show for all to see	
	That you can accomplish everything.	
	Joseph, you may well rejoice,	1940
	For God has chosen you,	
	Above all others; now it is right,	
	Joseph, that you must take as your wife	
	Maria, pure, chaste and beautiful,	
	As the Lord of all Lords desires.	1945
JOSEPH	Lord bishop, that I cannot refuse you.	
BISHOP	Now, Joseph, will you promise the Lord	
	In obedience that you in peace	
	And with loyalty, and with love,	
	Will be faithful for ever more	1950
	To Maria, full of grace	
	Unceasingly.	
JOSEPH	I promise her and God, the Lord,	
	Before you, lord bishop, as a man of my word.	
BISHOP	Do you promise too, Maria?	

MARIA	Jaic, here.
BISSCOP	God laet u wel houwen!

Nu, Joseph, vrient, wilt u bereiden   1955
Thuus wert te treckene sonder beiden.
Maria, dochter, ende Joseph, ghi,
Weest onderhorich.

JOSEPH   In Gods namen si. —
Maria, laet ons gaen gereetscap maken,
Soet ons betaemt, van alle saken: 1960
Ic wil gaen trecken ongelet
Te Bethleem wert.

MARIA   Ende ic te Nazareth.
Gods gracie wil ons alsoe gewegen,
Datter sinen lof in sy gelegen.

GOD   Gabriel, hoert: wilt u bereyen;   1965
Sijt snel en wil niet langer beyen.
Ic wil aen nemen menscen natuere,
Volcomen dat die propheten seyen
Van mire hoger gebuertelicheyen
Aen een meechdelike figure,   1970
Om te verlossen, die daer int sure
Lange bedruct hebben geseten;
Die willic nu als creature
Bringen, daer ewelic geduere
Mijn grote bliscap ongemeten.   1975
Gabriel, ic doet u weten,
Dat ghi selt trecken te Nazaret.
Daer seldi vinden in secreten
Maria, die maget onbesmet.
Haer seldi seggen ongelet   1980
Van minen wegen in corter spacien:
'God gruetu sonder wee, vol gracien!'
Dat segt haer vanden monde Gods.

GABRIEL   O here, behouden uws geboods,
Mi wondert, hoet u gelieven souwe   1985
Menscheit te nemen aen een vrouwe,
Al es si suver, ic segt u bloet,
En sterven natuerlic dan de doot,
Ende ghi onsterfelic sijt, soet claer es.
Want de mensce, soet oppenbaer es,   1990
Met sonden ontreint es en besmet,
Contrarie sgebods en uwer wet.
Dits hoech verstaen, ic segt u vrilic.

MARIA	I do, my lord.
BISHOP	May God keep you!

Now Joseph, my friend, prepare yourself   1955
To travel back home without delay.
Maria, my daughter, and Joseph, you too,
Be obedient.

JOSEPH	As God wills it. —

Maria, let us go and prepare
Everything, as we should do: 1960
I want to travel immediately
To Bethlehem.

MARIA	And I to Nazareth.

May God's grace guide us in such a way,
That we praise him in our deeds.

GOD	Gabriel, listen: prepare yourself. 1965

Be quick and do not linger.
I wish to take on human form,
Fulfil that which the prophets foretold
Of my elevated birth
From a maidenly person   1970
In order to free those who in wretchedness
Have long been oppressed;
In my human form
I want to bring for all eternity
My great joy which shall be endless.   1975
Gabriel, I want you to know
That you should go to Nazareth.
There you shall find in seclusion
Maria, the maiden immaculate.
To her you will say beyond all doubt   1980
What I intend to do at once:
'Fear not, God greets you who are full of grace!'
Tell her that is God's message.

GABRIEL	My Lord, of course I'll do your bidding.

But I wonder why it would please you   1985
To take on human form through a woman;
Even if she is pure—I speak plainly —
You would die a natural death,
But you are immortal, without doubt.
For mankind, as is quite clear,   1990
Is tainted and marked with sins,
Contrary to your command and your law.
To be frank, I don't quite understand.

GOD

Gabriel, dees maecht heeft mi so blilic
Gedanct, geloeft, als haren verminden,   1995
Ghi en selter blame noch smette in vinden.
Dies es mijn herte in haren bedwange.
Gescreven staet in Salamoens sange:
Mijn liefste vriendinne eest, hoe dat si,
Want si es geheilicht in my.   2000
Ende op wien sal rusten Gods geest,
Dan opten oetmoedegen alder meest?
Dus segt haer voert sonder respijt:
'De here es met di, gebenedijt
Soe sidi boven alle vrouwen!'   2005

GABRIEL

O claerheit, die niemen en mach dorscouwen,
Hets meer dan tijt, ic lide verwonnen
Grondeloes sijn u hoge connen
Ende u genaden onbesneden
Uut uwer hoger godlicheden.   2010
Om, here, te quitene die nu sterven,
Soe werdic nernstich ter bederven.

Pause cort.
Gabriel knielt vor Marien, ende si
leit en leest in haer camere, haer
hande te Gode wert hebbende.

GABRIEL

Van Gods wegen, suver vercorne,
Los van allen smetten, reyne,
Soe comic tu, in tsviants toorne: 2015
Ghi selt verlossen die verloorne!
Hi wilt hem rusten in uwen pleyne
Ende wilt vertroesten vor die veleyne,
Die liggen inder duvele tra.
Ave, gracia plena!   2020

Hier verscricse haer.

Maria, vrouwe, sijt onversaecht!
Natuerlic seldi baren een kint
Ende werden moeder ende bliven maecht.
Die gracie des heren heeft u vermint;
Jhesus saelt heten, mi wel versint,   2025
De hoechste van deser werelt wijt.
Ghi sijt, soemen gescreven vint,

GOD	Gabriel, this maiden has so joyously	
	Thanked me, praised me as her beloved,	1995
	And you will find neither blame nor taint in her.	
	Therefore my heart is in her power.	
	It is written in Solomon's Song:	
	She is most beloved to me, however it be,	
	For she is made holy in me.	2000
	And on whom will rest God's spirit,	
	If not on the most gracious of all?	
	So go and tell her immediately:	
	'The Lord is with you, blessed	
	You are above all women.'	2005
GABRIEL	Radiant light, which no one can comprehend,	
	It's more than time, I am persuaded.	
	Fathomless is your great knowledge	
	And your mercy without end	
	From your supreme divinity.	2010
	To free, Lord, those who now are dying	
	I will at once do your bidding.	

Short Pause.
Gabriel kneels before Maria and she lies and prays in
her chamber, with her hands towards God.

GABRIEL	I've come from God, chosen virgin,	
	Free from all taints and pure,	
	I come to you, despite the Devil's wrath:	2015
	You will set free those who are lost.	
	God will come to rest in your womb	
	And will console those who are wretched,	
	Who are captured in the Devil's pool.	
	Ave, gracia plena.	2020

She is sore afraid.

	Maria, lady, be not afeard!	
	You bear a child according to Nature,	
	And will become a mother and remain a virgin.	
	The Lord's grace and love are upon you.	
	Jesus, he will be called, hear my words,	2025
	The most exalted in all the world.	
	You are, as one finds written,	

	Vor alle vrouwen gebenedijt!	
MARIA	Her ingel, die hier dus comen sijt,	
	Seer verwondert mi van dien;	2030
	En kinde noyt man ter werelt wijt,	
	In wat manieren saelt dan gescien?	
DINGEL	Suver maecht, sijts onbevreest!	
	Gods gracie heeft u daer toe bereit.	
	Ghescien saelt biden heilegen geest	2035
	Mids uwer groter oetmoedicheit.	
	Ten tekene van dien, vor waer geseit,	
	Heeft Elizabeth, u nichte, ongewaent	
	Enen sone ontfaen in haer outheit	
	En es nu in haer seste maent,	2040
	Nochtan datsi onvruchtbaer sy,	
	Ten dae Gods gracie.	
MARIA	Her ingel, soe ghi	
	Mi seit, soe moet met mi verkeren.	
	In Gods genaden soe keeric my:	
	Siet hier de deerne Gods ons heren!	2045
GABRIEL	Reyn maecht vol eren, suete Marie,	
	Die gracie Gods heeft u om vaen.	
	Een godlike hemelsce tresorie	
	Seldi voort bliven sonder vergaen.	
	Orlof, ic keere ten hemel saen.	2050

Selete.

DE NAPROLOGHE

O Alder hoechste, gebenedie,
Godlike, hemelsce trezorie,
Laet u ons slechtheit sijn bequame,
Dat wi hier minlic, sonder envye
Hebben vertoecht. In weder sye   2055
Ter eren van uwen soeten name
Dor uwen oetmoet huetse vor blame,
Diet duegdelic hebben willen verzinnen
Ende hier sijn comen tot onsen verzame.
Gheeft hem te harer sielen vrame,   2060
Dat si die ewige vruecht gewynnen.
Wy doen u duegdelic bekinnen,
Dat wi, en God wilt, tander jare
U dander bliscap selen beginnen
Ende vort van jaer te jare met minnen   2065

	Blessed above all other women.	
MARIA	Lord Angel, who has come to me,	
	I wonder greatly about these things;	2030
	I have never known a man in this world.	
	In what manner, then, will this come about?	
ANGEL	Pure maiden, do not be afraid!	
	God's grace has prepared you for this.	
	It will happen through the Holy Spirit	2035
	And because of your great virtue.	
	And as a sign of this, let me make it clear,	
	Your cousin Elizabeth has unexpectedly	
	Conceived a son in her age,	
	And now she is in her sixth month,	2040
	Though she would have remained barren,	
	Were it not for God's grace.	
MARIA	Lord angel, just as you say	
	So it will be with me.	
	I entrust myself to God's mercy:	
	See here the handmaid of the Lord!	2045
GABRIEL	Pure maiden, full of honour, sweet Maria,	
	The grace of God has embraced you.	
	From now on you will forever remain	
	A divine and heavenly treasure.	
	Farewell, I must quickly return to heaven.	2050

Selete.

THE EPILOGUE

O most powerful and blessed,
Divine and heavenly treasure,
Let our simple play please you
Which we with love and good intent
Have performed. On the other hand   2055
In honour of your sweet name,
Through your grace protect from harm
Those who have meant it to be virtuous
And who have come here for our benefit.
Give to them comfort for their souls,   2060
So that they will gain eternal joy.
And we would like to tell you honestly
That, if God allows, next year
We will bring another *Bliscap*,
And so on, year after year, with love   2065

Oec dander bringen int oppenbare.
Tot sevene lanc, verstaet int clare,
Salmen u achter volgende vertogen
Ter eren der weerdicheit van hare,
Die veel meerere eren werdich ware   2070
Dan wy van haere vercleren mogen.
Dies bidt der lampten sonder verdrogen,
Dat si ons allen moet bevrien
Ende dat wi ons te haren dienste so pogen,
Dat wi in vreden ende in hogen   2075
Met salicheien den tijt gebyen.
Bidt dies der sueter maecht Marien
Gemeynlic, die hier sitten of staen.
Orlof geminde, hets nu gedaen.
Tot tander jaer, soet es vorseit.   2080
Ic beveel u der drievuldicheit!

We will perform the others as well.
Seven in all, let me make that clear,
Will be shown to you in sequence
In honour of the excellence of her
Who is worth far more honour   2070
Than we could ever show you.
So pray to the lamp which will never dry out,
That she may protect us all
And that we endeavour to serve her so much
That we in peace and in joy   2075
Spend our time on earth here in blessedness.
Ask this of the sweet virgin Maria
All of you who sit or stand here.
Farewell my friends, it's finished now.
Until next year, as we said.   2080
I commend you to the Trinity.

DIE SEVENSTE BLYSCAP VAN ONSER VROUWEN

DIERSTE PROLOGE

Maria vol gracien, die moecht gebien
Dat hemelsce, eertsce ende helsce knien
U moeten bugen, wyken ende eren, —
Want alle dat God nye liet gescien,
Oft noit met ogen oec wort gesien,   5
Daer moet na recht dijn lof bi meeren, —
Ik biddu, moeder ende bruut des Heren,
Tabernacle Gods, fonteyne der duecht,
Dijn rayen van gracien laet altijt keren
Op alle sondaren, want ghijt vermuecht;   10
Oetmoedege, suete, suver juecht,
Hout alle tkersten gelove in vreden
Doer dere dien ghi soe minlic suecht,
Onsen prince, princersse, haer slote en steden;
Dies biddic u met ynneger beden   15
Tees nu recht leden omtrent een jaer,
Dat wi hier speelden int openbaer
De seste bliscap van Onser Vrouwen.
Tverhael van dien dat latic daer,
Wi volgen der materien naer;   20
Ic meent de selke wel heeft onthouwen.
Op dat sier bi verlichten souwen,
Gods moeder ende sine jongeren meest,
Soe sant hi hem in rechter trouwen,
In viereger minnen den Heilegen Geest.   25
Van desen smaect wel der keerne keest,
Dit wort de sevenste ende de leste.
Al staet op enen slichten leest,
Eest leec oft clerc, elc neemt int beste,
Al waert soe datter yemen in meste.   30
Int oeste int weste biddic vor vre,
Voer al in Bruesel, die suete ste.
Voort gruetic u allen, die hier versaemt sijt,

THE SEVENTH JOY OF OUR LADY

THE FIRST PROLOGUE

Maria, full of grace who can command
That all those in heaven, on earth and in hell
Must kneel to you, in submission and honour—
For everything that God ever brought about,
Or that ever has been seen by mortal eyes,   5
Rightfully should increase your praise—
I pray you, mother and bride of the Lord,
Tabernacle of God, fountain of virtue,
May your rays of grace always turn
Towards all sinners, such is your power.   10
Gracious, sweet and purest virgin,
Protect all Christendom in peace
For the Lord, whom you suckled so tenderly,
Also protect our prince and princess, their castles and towns.
This I beg you, with passionate prayer.   15
It is now exactly a year ago,
Since we performed here in public
The Sixth Joy of Our Lady.
The story of that I won't repeat,
But we will now continue the tale;   20
I think many people will still remember it.
Because they were in need of consolation,
God's mother and most of his disciples,
God sent to them the Holy Spirit
According to his promise, and from great love.   25
Do understand the essence of this play:
This will be the seventh, and also the last.
Even though it's built on a simple foundation
Be they lay or cleric, all should take it as best they can,
Even though it may have some shortcomings.   30
I pray for peace in the east and the west,
And especially in Brussels, that sweet town.
Then I greet you all who are here together,

Dat elc gesonde ende saliche
Moet hebben, ende dewige leven me   35
Na deser tijt, hoe ghi genaemt sijt.
Dus, eerbaer notabele, die onbefaemt sijt,
Siet gunst vor cunst in onsen werke.
Ic hope de meester dan ongeblaemt blijt,
Op datmens niet te nauwe en merke.   40
Thout meest scriftuere, som scrivent clerke
Met sconen redenen geapprobeert,
Maer waermen tkersten gelove bi sterke.
Hi es onwijs, diet lichte batteert
Soe verre alst redene consenteert.   45
Dus dan cesseert, om cort vermaen,
Als van gescille, en wilt verstaen
Den sin der hoger materien soet.
Wat vrouden Maria heeft ontfaen
Doen hier haer leven wert gedaen,   50
Geen sin en mocht dies wesen vroet.
Hoe slecht mer hier bewijs af doet,
Noijt meerder vruecht haer en gescie.
Elc seg haer dan des yngels groet,
Dat si elc droef herte verblie.   55
Ende nyemen en scympe noch en benye
Ons sympels wercs: wi doent uut minnen,
Ter eeren der stat en sonder envye,
U allen ter liefden, dat wilt versinnen.
Hoort alle en swijt, wi gaen beginnen.   60

SINT JAN   O hoge, eerwerdege, gebenedie
Maget vrye,
Tresoer, daer alder werelt scat
In lach besloten na claren belye;
Want, suete Marie,   65
Wi cochten daer met de hemelsce stat;
Den dau van gracien es in u nat,

. . . .

Des hemels ende der erden gevloyt;
Die heeft ons in u suver bat,   70
Der specien vat,
Gedwegen ende met genaden bespoyt.
Oetmoedege Vrouwe, u niet en vernoyt
Dat ic ghemoyt
Dus worde u minen troest te gevene;   75
Want ic ontfinc, invierich gegloyt

May all of you be healthy and blessed
And also attain eternal life 35
After this time, whoever you are.
So, worshipful citizens of good repute,
Accept our good intention if our art falls short.
I hope that the writer will not be blamed
And that you won't be too critical. 40
We follow mostly scripture and some learned clerks,
And it is supported with eloquent speech:
All of which strengthens the Christian faith.
He is unwise, who would make light of it,
Since it is grounded upon truth. 45
So please refrain, in short,
From all dissent and please understand
The true meaning of this sweet and momentous story.
Whatever joys Maria received
When her life on earth was finished 50
Is beyond human comprehension.
However artlessly we show this here,
No greater joy ever befell her.
Let everyone now give her the angel's salutation
So that she may lighten every sad heart. 55
And let no one mock or take amiss
Our simple work: we do it out of love,
For the honour of the city and with good intent,
For the love of all of you, be sure of that.
Now be quiet all and listen: we will now begin. 60

SAINT JOHN   O mighty, praiseworthy, blessed,
Noble virgin,
Tabernacle in which all the treasure of the world
Lay enclosed, as is manifest;
For, sweet Maria, 65
We gained with that the city of God;
The dew of grace is in your essence
. . . . . .
Which streams in heaven and earth;
This dew has washed us in your sweet bath, 70
In your vessel of fragrant spice,
And sprinkled us with mercy.
Benevolent lady, do not be dismayed
That I am thus enjoined
To offer you my consolation; 75
For I received, with burning love,

	Ende hittich dorbroyt,	

Ende hittich dorbroyt,
Den last, geminde, van uwen aenclevene.
Dies blivic voort in minen levene,
Hoge verhevene,   80
In u hoede, soet u betame,
U biddende dat u si bequame.

MARIA Jan, geminde vrient vercoren,
Lacen! ghi wet hoet met my steet:
Gods jongeren hebbic alle verloren.   85
Die mi te troesten plagen te voren,
Achermen! die sijn my ongereet.
Si sijn getrocken, verre ende breet,
Dwoort Gods tot sinen bevele bedien.
Alsoe hi selve den orboer weet,   90
Tot sijnder begeerten, tsi cout of heet,
Moet sinen wille altoes gescien.
Dus, Jan, vercorne vrient, in dien
Dat ic my selven nu vinde alleene,
Soe biddic u, wilt de woerde aensien   95
Die mijn kint sprac tot ons lien,
Daer ic stont in bitteren weene.
Hi gaf mij u hoede, ende el negheene.
Hi seide: "Wijf, sich daer u kint.
Jan, dits dijn moeder." Hoort, wes ic meene.   100
Dus blijft mi bi, in duegden reene,
Want hi u vor dandere hoechst heeft gemint.

JAN O Vrouwe, daer te voren noch sint
Dat de werelt heeft gestaen,
Seggic vor waer, en loegens twint,   105
En was soe ermen wissel gedaen,
Want, Vrouwe, ghi moestet daer ontfaen
Eens visschers sone, cleyn van geslachte,
Voer hem, die, na sijn vermaen,
Hemel, ende erde van nyeute wrachte.   110
Niet min, eerwerdege, de hoge van machte
Deet om een beter, des sijt te vreden.
Al sidi gestelt tot mijnder wachte,
Ic en kynne mi niet werdich genoech om treden
Den wech, die ghi voer mi waert leden.   115

MARIA Jan, vrient, laet u dies genuegen,
In alsoe velen alst God begeert;
Sijt dies gevreet, hi saelt wel vuegen,
En daer op niet en murmereert.

	And inspired by diligence	
	The burden, beloved, of staying close to you.	
	So I will remain with you for the rest of my life,	
	Greatly beloved,	80
	In your service, if it pleases you,	
	That it may give you joy.	
MARIA	My beloved, excellent friend John,	
	Alas, you know how it is with me:	
	I have lost all God's disciples.	85
	Those who used to console me,	
	Alas, they are beyond my reach.	
	They have travelled far and wide,	
	To spread God's word as he commanded.	
	Since he himself knows what is good	90
	His will must always be fulfilled,	
	As he desired, whatsoever it is.	
	So, John, beloved friend, because	
	I find myself now quite alone,	
	I implore you, remember the words	95
	Which my child spoke to us both	
	Where I stood in bitter sorrow.	
	He gave me into your protection, and in none other.	
	He said, 'Lady, see there your child.	
	John, this is your mother.' Hear what I say.	100
	So stay with me, in pure virtue	
	For he has loved you above all others.	
JOHN	O lady, never before, nor since	
	The world was created,	
	This is the truth and I do not deny it,	105
	Was there ever was such a poor exchange,	
	For, lady, you had to accept there	
	The son of a fisherman, of humble descent,	
	Rather than him who, as he said,	
	Created heaven out of the void.	110
	However, honoured lady, that powerful being	
	Did this for the best, so be content.	
	Even though you were placed in my keeping,	
	I am not worthy enough to follow	
	The road you travelled before me.	115
MARIA	John, my friend, let this content you	
	In every respect as God desired;	
	Make your peace with this, he will help,	
	And do not resist.	

SINT JAN	Ic dancke u, suete maget weert,	120
	Dat ghi mijns te vreden sijt.	
	De gracie Gods heeft u vercleert	
	Daer mede, dat ghi geheilicht blijt.	
	Dus, weerde bloeme gebenedijt,	
	Een huusken hebbic noch staende hier bi,	125
	Daer moegdi in leiden uwen tijt,	
	Eest u gelieflic, maget vri.	
	Hier onder den berch, verstaet wel mi,	
	Van Syon, suete ende oec bequame,	
	Soe steet dit huus. Alsulc alst si,	130
	Soe ghevict u, Vrouwe, ent u betame.	
MARIA	Jan, dat es my seere gename,	
	Want wel ter goeder plaetsen steet	
	Om visenteren sonder blame	
	De steden, daer God sijn passie leet.	135
	Die willic dagelijcs, daer icse weet,	
	Visenteren tot sijnder eeren,	
	Tsi daermen doopte oft besneet,	
	Gheeselde oft cruuste om sijn verseren.	
	Daer willic mi ynnechlijc toe keeren	140
	Om te besuekene met wille goet,	
	Uut rechter devocien sijns loofs vermeeren,	
	Dat hi daer stortte sijn heilege bloet.	
SINT JAN	O suete moeder ende maget soet,	
	Als ghi daer sijt, tot elker stede,	145
	Soe biddic u vriendelijc, dor oetmoet,	
	Dat ghi my doet in uwen gebede,	
	Want sijn gracie die es u mede,	
	Hi en sal u nemmermeer verhoren.	
	Wat si, ghi bringet in Gods vrede,	150
	Dat weet ic wel, biddier hem voren.	
MARIA	Jan, mijn goede vrient vercoren,	
	Mijn hulpe en weert u niet ontseit,	
	Noch nyemens die na sijn hulde sporen	
	En hopen aen sine genadicheit;	155
	In haren troeste wordic bereit.	
JAN	Nu, gawy met anderen voort in minnen,	
	Tot Gode gelieft dat hi ons hale.	
MARIA	Sijn heilege gracie laet hi ons kinnen,	
	Gawy met anderen voort in minnen.	160
JAN	Sijn godheit doe ons genade gewinnen,	
	Dat wi ontvlien der helscer quale.	

SAINT JOHN	I thank you, sweet and worthy virgin,	120
	That you are content with me.	
	The grace of God has shone upon you	
	So that your life is holy.	
	So worthy, blessed flower,	
	I have a little house nearby,	125
	Where you may pass your days,	
	If it should please you, noble virgin.	
	Here at the foot of the mountain of Syon	
	Which is, you understand, sweet and suitable,	
	Stands this House. Such as it is	130
	I give it to you lady, if it pleases you.	
MARIA	John, that pleases me greatly	
	For it stands in a very good place	
	To visit without giving offence	
	The places where God suffered his Passion.	135
	I would like to visit those daily	
	Those that I know of, in his honour	
	Whether he was baptised there, or circumcised	
	Scourged to torment him, or crucified.	
	I will devote myself to that with passion	140
	To visit those places with good intent,	
	And by honest devotion magnify his praise,	
	Where he shed his holy blood.	
SAINT JOHN	O sweet mother and sweet virgin,	
	When you are there in each of these places	145
	I ask you humbly and warmly	
	That you include me in your prayer,	
	For his grace is also in you	
	And he will never reject your prayer.	
	Whatever may happen, if you ask for God's peace,	150
	I know for sure it will be granted.	
MARIA	John, my good and beloved friend	
	My help will not be denied to you,	
	Nor to anyone who tries to be pleasing to him	
	And hopes for his compassion;	155
	I am prepared to help them find consolation.	
JOHN	Now let us go forward together in love;	
	May it please God to gather us in.	
MARIA	He makes us aware of his holy grace	
	Let us go forward together in love.	160
JOHN	His divinity will bring us grace,	
	So that we escape the pains of hell.	

MARIA	Nu gawi met anderen voort in minnen,
	Tot Gode gelieft dat hi ons hale
	Uut desen ellindegen eerdscen dale. 165

Selete cort. Die wile besuect si
de steden, ende si gaen wech.

i JODE	Claer, dese temptacie van desen wive
	Es quaet te lidene, selc van bedrive,
	Want, dat luttel es gesien,
	Si popelt, si leest, si buecht haer knien,
	Si weent, si carmt, nu hier, nu daer, 170
	In allen plaetsen.
ij JODE	Dat doetse voer waer.
	Ic siet soe node, mi dunct ic splite.
	Si makes oec te vele.
i JODE	Tes recht tenen spite
	Van ons, ende onser wet eest blamelic
	En diese regeren.
ij JODE	Tes onbetamelic, 175
	Dus openbaerlic dat si gaet stupen,
	Cnielen, wagebaerden en crupen
	In allen steden, daer haer kint leet
	Enege scoffieringe.
i JODE	Tes onbesceet.
	Daedsijt doch heymelic, ondertiden 180
	Dat tfolc niet en mercte!
ij JODE	Soe mochtment liden;
	Maer nu maect si selken geveert,
	Recht al waert der pinen weert,
	Als quansus hi ware een coninc der Joden.
i JODE	Si heeft hem eren genoech geboden, 185
	Al waer hi een heildom oft een sant.
	Maer thout al elder: wi worden gescant,
	Worden si, diet taenscouwene plegen,
	Bekeert ende te harer secten genegen.
	Oec wasser menich, alsoe wi merken, 190
	Die hem na gingen.
ij JODE	Ende alle haer werken
	Sachmen soe duegdelic daer si geet;
	Maer tes al geveyst.

MARIA	Now let us go forward together in love,
	May it please God to gather us in
	Away from this wretched earthly vale. 165

Short selete. Meanwhile she visits the places and then
they go away.

FIRST JEW	Clearly, this woman's provocation
	Is hard to bear in the way she goes on,
	For— and this shouldn't be seen—
	She mutters, she reads her prayers, she kneels,
	She weeps, she laments, now here, now there, 170
	All over the place.
SECOND JEW	Yes, so she does.
	I hate seeing it, I'm bursting with anger.
	She makes such a fuss.
FIRST JEW	It's surely done to spite us
	Bringing our law into disrepute,
	And those using it.
SECOND JEW	It's outrageous, 175
	The way she goes about bending,
	Kneeling, lamenting and creeping
	In all those places where her child suffered
	Degradation.
FIRST JEW	It's unbearable.
	If only she did it in secret, now and then, 180
	So that people didn't notice!
SECOND JEW	Then you could put up with it;
	But now she makes such a display,
	Just as though it were merited,
	As if he really was a King of the Jews.
FIRST JEW	She's offered him enough honour, 185
	As if he were a relic or a saint.
	But there's something else: we will be shamed
	If they, who observe all this,
	Are converted and drawn into her sect.
	And there were quite a few, as we see, 190
	Who used to follow him.
SECOND JEW	And all her devotions
	Seem to be so virtuous wherever she went;
	But it's all a sham.

i JODE   Vor waer, en weet,
    Maer docht u goet, ic wist ons raet
    Om dit te beletten.
ii JODE   Hoe?
i JODE   Den potestaet   195
    Selen wijt opt corte gaen vercleren,
    Ende dan, men later hem met geberen.
    Hi saelt haer, sonder veel gescals,
    Wel doen laten.
ij JODE   Vele ongevals
    Worder af nakende onser wet,   200
    Ja, wort niet in tijts belet
    En strangelic genomen metten tanden
    Van dies macht hebben.
i JODE   Noyt soe veel scanden
    En hadden de Joden van haren kinde,
    Als si hier af wel mochten ten inde,   205
    Waert so datmens niet en vermaende
    Vor den rechter.
ij JODE   Hi comt hier gaende.
    Dits yuust, wi willen hem spreken an
    Van deser saken.
i JODE   Aenveertten dan
    Op tcorte, eer dat hi ons ontgae.   210
ij JODE   Here, geliefdet uwer genae,
    Wi souden u geerne in corter sprake
    Wat nyeus vercleren.
POTESTAET   Ja? wats de sake?
    Ghi scijnt gestoort, wat hebdi vernomen?
    Eest yet lastichs?
i JODE   Jaet; wi sijn comen   215
    Tot u met nernste versuekende raet
    Op dese Maria, die hier gaet;
    Het scijnt si gect, en weet hoet si,
    Met onser wet.
POTESTAET   Ja? waer by?
    Bedrijfse oft doetse yet onreens   220
    Ons in contrarien?
ij JODE   Jaes, here, en neens.
    Ic sal u seggen van haren bestiere.
    Sie toent ons dagelics selken maniere
    Van vremden geveerten int openbare,
    Als oft haer kint een heilichdom ware;   225

FIRST JEW	Well, I don't know,
	But if you agree, I know a way
	To put a stop to it.
SECOND JEW	How?
FIRST JEW	We should shortly 195
	Go and explain this to the Hugh Priest,
	And we'll let him deal with it.
	He will, without a fanfare,
	Make her stop.
SECOND JEW	Our law
	Would be greatly damaged by this, 200
	If this is not scotched in time
	And forcefully dealt with
	By those in power.
FIRST JEW	The Jews have never endured
	So much scandal by one of their own,
	As will now come upon them 205
	If steps are not taken to bring it
	Before the judge.
SECOND JEW	Here he comes.
	That's useful, we'll talk to him
	About these matters.
FIRST JEW	Go on then
	Speak to him before he disappears. 210
SECOND JEW	Lord, if it pleases your grace,
	We would like to talk to you at once
	About something that's just happened.
HIGH PRIEST	Well, what's the matter?
	You seem upset: what have you heard?
	Is it urgent?
FIRST JEW	Oh yes, we've come 215
	To seek your advice about something serious
	About this Maria who goes around here:
	It would seem that she heaps mockery, I don't know why,
	Upon our law.
HIGH PRIEST	Yes? In what way?
	Does she say or do anything improper 220
	Against us?
SECOND JEW	Yes and no, Lord.
	I shall tell you what she does.
	Every day she shows us in public
	Such a strange way of behaving
	As if her child were a relic 225

Soe nijchse, soe stuypse in allen steden,
Daer haer sone sijn passie heeft leden.
Ghi en saecht noit wijf so overlijc drabben
Over en weder.

i JODE   Si sal de steene uut scrabben,   230
Soet scijnt bi wilen, daer haer kint leet
Tsiere doot weert.

ii JODE   Waer dat si weet,
Dat haren sone gesciet confuse,
TAnnas oft in Pylatus huse,
Ende tanderen steden, daer loopse dagelijc
Bidden en lesen.

i JODE   Tes ons meshagelijc,   235
Gemerct si mochte met selker nacien
Enege bringen in murmeracien,
Slechte, onnosele, dies niet en gevroen
Haer quade secte.

DOUWERE   Wat salmen haer doen
Daer bi? na recht, secreet gesproken,   240
Wi hebben ons hoech genoech gewroken
Aen Jhesum, dien wi dleven namen,
Al en bringen wi de moeder oec niet in blamen.
Om datse met rouwe haer kint beweent,
Salmense daer om dooden?

POTESTAET   Met rechte neent,   245
Want elc moederlijc herte die mint
Bi rechter natueren geerne haer kint.
Maer waerse hem vremde, ent haer gesciet,
Soe en soudemens haer gedogen niet.
Men mocht haer dan met rechte aen spreken   250
Van ongelove, ende dat soe wreken
Aen hare, met pinen int openbare,
Dat yegeliken exemple ware
Om een castien telker ure,
Diet hoerde vermonden.

DOUWERE   Dit wijst natuere,   255
Dat dit wijf dese minne bestaet.
Waer bi? ten was noyt kint soe quaet,
Die moeder en sout met rechte minnen.
Aldus dan, wildijt wel versinnen,
Soe en eest der moeder niet mesprijst,   260
Dat si natuerlike minne bewijst

Because she bows, she kneels in all those places
Where her son has suffered his passion.
You never saw a woman going about so restlessly
Here, there and everywhere.

FIRST JEW   She'll dig up the stones,
So it seems sometimes, where her child went   230
Towards his death.

SECOND JEW   Wherever she knows
Her son to have been humiliated
At Annas' or in Pilate's house,
Or in other places, she daily walks around
Praying and reading.

FIRST JEW   We really hate it,   235
Since with such behaviour,
She could make innocent people discontented,
Because they do not see through
Her evil sect.

THE ELDER   What should one do
To her? Frankly, between you and me,   240
We have avenged ourselves enough
On Jesus, whose life we took.
Even though we don't bring the mother to shame,
Because she mourns and weeps for her child,
Should she be killed for that?

HIGH PRIEST   In all justice, no.   245
For each motherly heart loves
Her child deeply as is natural.
But if she were not his kin, and behaved like this
Then one wouldn't permit this.
Then one could then rightly accuse her   250
Of bad faith, and punish her in such a way
With public retribution,
That it would be an example to all
And a lasting warning
To whoever heard it.

THE ELDER   It's due to Nature   255
That this woman feels such love.
And why? There was never a child so evil
But the mother would love it fully.
So then, mark my words,
You can't criticize the mother,   260
That she shows natural love

	Tot haren kinde; om wel verstaen,	
	Mesdoet si luttel.	
ij JODE	Daer hanct meer aen,	
	Dat ic u niet en hore solveren,	
	Op dwelke ic nu wille ergueren	265
	Tot uwer correctien, na datse bedrijft	
	Met harer devocien. Als si doot blijft,	
	Wat meyndi, wat mochter af gescien	
	Met haren lichame? Tes vremder gesien.	
	Ja, mochten sine onder hen gewinnen,	270
	Haer vriende, die noch Jhesum minnen,	
	Si soudender reliquien willen af maken,	
	Tot onsen spite.	
i JODE	Dat sijn de saken;	
	Daer soudense den duvel met allen af brouwen	
	En tfolc bekeren.	
DOUWERE	Dies weetic ons mouwen;	275
	Sijt dies te vreden, dat salic verwerren.	
	Waerse doot, men salse verberren	
	In cleynen pulvere, my wel versint,	
	En sayen de asschen tegen den wint	
	Alsoe dunne, dat si wech wayen	280
	Elc versceiden.	
ij JODE	Soe mochti ons payen;	
	Maer seker, twaer anders groet verlies,	
	Dat mense gaen liete.	
POTESTAET	Neen, wacht u dies	
	Kinder, al haddi noch geswegen,	
	Tes langen tijt over een gedregen.	285
	Wi weten oec wat, alst comt aent nypen;	
	Laet elken gewerden. Maer tsijn al pypen,	
	Wie hem wilt sporren tegen de gaert:	
	Tswaerste verweecht.	
i JODE	Tes goet verwaert.	
	Men sal den viant altoes ontsien,	290
	Hoe cranc hi es. Maecht soe gescien	
	Alsoe ghi ons nu hier vertrect,	
	Soe worden de jongeren wel begect,	
	Want si hopense, als domme dwase,	
	Hoge te verheffene.	
DOUWERE	Ic seg u jase,	295
	Maer de contrarie sal hem gebueren.	
ij JODE	Wi sijns gepaeyt.	

	To her child; when all is said and done	
	She's not behaving badly.	
SECOND JEW	There's more to it	
	And that I don't hear you solve.	
	Which I will now start tackling	265
	To put you right about all that she does	
	With her devout actions. When she dies	
	What could happen	
	With her body? Stranger things have happened	
	And if any amongst her friends who still love Jesus	270
	Were able to get hold of her body	
	They would want to make relics out of it	
	To our disadvantage.	
FIRST JEW	You're quite right;	
	That would be one in the eye for the devil	
	As well as converting the people.	
THE ELDER	I can fix that;	275
	Don't you worry about it, I'll put a spoke in that wheel.	
	Once she's dead she should be burned	
	To fine ashes, if you follow me,	
	And then the ashes thrown into the wind	
	So thinly, that they blow away	280
	As in tiny particles.	
SECOND JEW	Yes, that would cheer us up;	
	And for sure it would be a great loss	
	If she escaped us.	
HIGH PRIEST	No, no, be sure not to do that,	
	My children; even if you kept silent	
	It was decreed long ago.	285
	We know a thing or two when it comes down to it;	
	Let everyone hold back. But it's all in vain,	
	It is no good resisting the spur:	
	There's no point.	
FIRST JEW	You've got that right.	
	You must always reckon with your foe,	290
	However weak he is. If it happens	
	As you have explained to us	
	Then the disciples will be completely deceived	
	For they hope, stupid fools as they are,	
	To put her on a pedestal.	
THE ELDER	That's as may be,	295
	But the reverse will occur.	
SECOND JEW	We're quite happy with that.	

DOUWERE   En sorchter niet vueren,
Maer hout u vrilic aen ons woort,
Al in secreet; en of ghi yet hoort
Van dien eer wy, om cort vermaen,   300
Dat laet ons weeten.

i JODE   Twort gedaen,
Daer aen en derf u twivelen niet.
Adien, myn heren.

POTESTAET   Ghebrect u yet
Des wi vermogen, ter waerheden,
Getroest u des; elc ga in vreden.   305

Selete. Maria leit in haer gebede in haer camere.

MARIA   O laes! God Here! Wat salic bestaen?
Salic van troeste dus bliven versteken?
Mijn herte mocht my in drucke ontgaen.
Ay laes! God Here! Wat salic bestaen?
Ic ben in sulken rouwe bevaen,   310
Mi dunct al soude mi therte breken.
O laes! God Here! Wat salic bestaen?
Salic van troeste dus bliven versteken?
En can van drucke nauwe gespreken,
Dat hi my laet, mijn liefste geminde!   315
Ic en was vertroest van deser weken,
Des blivic beswaert in groter alinde.
Dagelijcs datti my versinde,
Daer hi met bluschte mijn verdriet;
Altoes soe hoordic van minen kinde   320
By sinen yngel doch emmer yet;
Nu en wasic in drie dagen niet
Vertroest. Elaes! Wat maecht bedien?
Waer es mi dese mesquame gesciet,
Datti my laet dus onversien?   325
En weet te clagene hoe noch wien!

*Selete. Die wile salmen den
hemel op doen, daer God sit,
ende seggen toten ingel Gabriel:*

GOD   Nu willic recht, het dunct mi tijt,
Mijnder suver moeder gebenedijt
In mijnder glorien hier ontbien;

THE ELDER   Don't worry about it,
        But put your trust in our words,
        But in secret; and if you hear something
        About it before we do, then in short   300
        Come and tell us.
FIRST JEW   That'll be done,
        Don't have any doubts about it.
        Adieu, my lords.
HIGH PRIEST   If you need anything
        That we can do, in truth
        Just let us know; and now let all go in peace.   305

Selete. Maria kneels in prayer in her room.

MARIA   Alas, Lord God! What shall I do?
        Shall I be denied all consolation?
        My heart will give way in misery.
        Alas, Lord God! What shall I do?
        I am so overcome with sorrow   310
        It feels as if my heart would break.
        Alas, Lord God! What shall I do?
        Shall I be denied all consolation?
        I can barely speak for grief
        That he has left me, my dear beloved!   315
        This week I had no consolation,
        And I remain oppressed by sorrow.
        Every day when he thought of me
        It lessened my grief;
        I always heard from my child   320
        Something at least via his angel;
        But now three days have passed without
        Consolation. Alas! What does it mean?
        Why am I struck with this misfortune,
        That he has left me so alone?   325
        How, or to whom shall I complain?

Selete.
Meanwhile they will open the heaven where God sits
and says to the Angel Gabriel:

GOD   Now, as is right, and I think it's time
        To ask my blessed unblemished mother
        To come and share my glory here;

Den ertscen druc willic haer quijt   330
Maken, ende bringense int hoge jolijt,
Daer haer niet en mach messcien.
Soe ict bi redenen hebbe versien,
Soe es sijs weert, ende el negheene,
Dat haer mijn gracie sal gescien.   335
Grotelic boven al anderen lien
Sal si de upperste sijn alleene.
Ic hebse daer lange gelaten in weene,
Daer si volstentich in es bleven,
En vast geduerich gelijc den steene   340
Es therte te myweert bleven reene;
Dus wert si hoechst der hoechster verheven.
Gabriel, bode, haest, sonder sneven
Moetti mijn hoge gebod volbringen.

GABRIEL   Hets redelic, Here, want u aencleven   345
               Es juecht en voetsel van allen dingen.
               Ghi hebbet al in u beringen,
               Boven ende onder, hoghe verlichtere.
               Tsi stuer of wreet, ghi connet bedwingen;
               Van allen erge sidi een swichtere;   350
               Ghi wert uut ouden een nuwe stichtere,
               Ende nyemen en mach u werc volsinnen;
               Duegdelic sidi een medeplichtere
               Tot hen die uwe genade bekinnen;
               Dies maect my uwer begeerten te binnen.   355

GOD   Gabriel, dat icse minne es redelic.
               Die mi vor al selve heeft vercoren,
               Die willic bi mi doen eren vredelic,
               Want ic van haer wou sijn geboren.
               Die suverste ende reynste verre te voren   360
               Es si voer alle die ic weet.
               Die seldi, sonder enich verstoren,
               Vor my hier halen; doet mijn beheet.
               Ghi selt te dragene oec sijn bereet
               Een palmrijs uten paradyse;   365
               Daer bi seldi haer doen besceet
               Haer doot, ende segt haer bi avise,
               Dat icse ontbie, die hoge van prise,
               Te mijnder vruecht, reyn van behage,
               Want siere in vriendeliker wise   370
               Sal wesen binnen derden dage.

	From earthly pain I want to make her	330

              From earthly pain I want to make her   330
              Free and bring her to that great delight,
              In which no grief can touch her.
              As I have planned with reason good,
              She is most worthy, and no one else,
              To have my grace alight upon her.   335
              Splendidly above all others
              She alone will be most blessed.
              I have left her long in sorrow
              In which she has remained steadfast,
              And always firmly as a rock   340
              Her heart has stayed faithful to me;
              She will be raised highest amongst the high.
              Gabriel, my messenger, make haste; without delay
              You'll have to accomplish my command.

GABRIEL   That is just, Lord, for to cleave to you   345
              Is strength and nourishment for all things.
              You have it all within your power,
              Heaven and earth, comfort supreme.
              Harshness or cruelty, you can contain it;
              Of all evils are you the healer;   350
              From the old you create a new covenant,
              And none can comprehend your work;
              You are the greatest of all helpers
              For those who realise your grace;
              Show forth to me your dear intent.   355

GOD   Gabriel, it is just that I should love her.
              I myself would want to honour with peace
              My mother who has chosen me above all,
              For I wanted to be born of her.
              She is far and above the most chaste and most pure   360
              Amongst all that I know.
              You must bring her to me here
              In a perfectly peaceful way; do as I bid.
              You must also be prepared to carry
              A palm branch from paradise;   365
              And besides you will announce to her
              Her death, and tell her considerately
              That I bid her, worthy of great praise
              To come to my joy which is gracefully pure,
              For she will in a pleasing manner   370
              Be here with me within three days.

GABRIEL   Eerwerdich Sceppere, en ben niet trage
              Tot uwer bederven; die en mach niet bliven.
              Hets recht dat ic haer bliscap drage,
              Want si es bloeme van allen wiven.   375
              Dies willic, om haer lof verstiven,
              Mi spoeden om tpalmrijs bequame,
              Datmen eerbarlic int bedriven
              Sal dragen vor haren soeten lichame.
              Gebenedijt si haren name,   380
              Die in haer duecht es suver bleven,
              Soe datter noyt no smette no blame
              In haren lichame en was beseven.
              Dies wort si hoge bi u verheven.

              Verhuecht u, gebenedide Vrouwe,   385
              Suver kersouwe,
              U lieve kint heet my orconden,
              Datti u met des hemels douwe,
              Al vri van rouwe,
              Wilt besprayen tot ewigen stonden.   390
              Salich der saliger sidi vonden.
              Na Gods vermonden
              Soe seldi u tot hem bereyen;
              Want ghi seere hoechlic sonder gronden
              Ende los van sonden,   395
              Binnen derden dage selt sceyen
              Uut deser broesscher keytivicheyen,
              Daer na u beyen
              Marteleers, maegden ende confessoren,
              Die u hoechlijc selen geleyen   400
              Met weerdicheyen
              Daer boven inder yngelen coren,
              Ter vruecht, Vrouwe, na u toebehoren.
MARIA   Suet ingel, dat es mi seere bequame.
              En hadde noyt geen meerder vruecht.   405
              Dies biddic u, oft u tseggen betame,
              Hoe es u name,
              Die mi dus uterlic seere verhuecht?
              Segt mij dat, oft ghijt seggen muecht.
GABRIEL   Jaic, Vrouwe, ic saelt u geerne belien: 410
              Ic quam u yerst gebenedien

GABRIEL   Noble Creator, I won't be slow
To carry out your wish; and that is as it should be.
It's just that I will bring her joy,
For she is the flower amongst all women.   375
And so in order to increase her praise
I'll haste to get that lovely palm branch,
Which will be carried with great honour
In front of her sweet body.
Blessed be her name,   380
Who has remained so pure in virtue
So that no stain nor blemish
Was ever found in her body.
That's why she will be exalted.

[Gabriel goes to Maria.]

     Rejoice, you blessed lady,   385
Sweet daisy,
Your beloved child asked me to tell you
He would like to bless you forever
With dew of heaven
That is without any grief.   390
Blessed amongst the blessed are you judged.
According to God's message
You will have to prepare to go to him;
For you will depart, full of immeasurable joy
And wholly free of sin,   395
And on the third day you will leave
This fragile captivity,
To where there will await you
Martyrs, virgins and confessors
Who will conduct you solemnly   400
And with great display of honour
High up into the hosts of angels
To the joy, lady, which by right is yours.

MARIA   Sweet angel, that is very pleasing.
I never felt a greater joy.   405
So may I ask, if you don't mind,
What is your name,
You who bring me such unbounded joy?
Tell me that, if you are allowed to say.

GABRIEL   Yes, my lady, I'll gladly tell you: 410
'Twas I who blessed you first of all

Metter Gods gracien groet van crachte;
Ic waest die u, sonder vermyen,
Den mogenden, hogen, eerwerdegen, vrien,
Saligen, Heilegen Geest in brachte;   415
Gabriel heetic, reyne van gedachte,
Ende bring u die benedixie bloet,
Die God de Here, groet van machte,
Tot salicheden suet en sachte
Jacoppe, sinen vrient, ontboet.   420
Dit palmrijs, eerwerdege Vrouwe minyoet,
Bringic u uten paradise,
Om datmen dit, Vrouwe, na u doot
Dragen sal uut minnen devoet
Vor uwen fiertel van hogen prise.   425
Als mennen in oetmoedeger wise
Ter erden sal dragen, suver geminde,
Salmen u vor gaen met desen rise
Na sijn bevel, diet al versinde.

MARIA   Dies lovic minen eerwerdegen kinde,   430
Dat my dese eere aldus gesciet,
Datti minlijc dus in mijn ynde
Bi sijnder genaden soe wel versiet.
Maer, suete yngel, doet my bediet,
Oftic den viant sal moeten scouwen   435
Eer ic sterve; om dat verdriet
Soe es my therte bevaen met rouwen.
Woude hi mijn ogen beloken houwen,
Dat ic den viant niet en sage.
Gabriel, lieve vrient, vol trouwen,   440
Bidt Gode datti mi dies verdrage.

GABRIEL   O Vrouwe, en sijt in ghenen versage
Voer hem, maer stelt u des te vreden.
Ghi hebt den viant beraden plage
Met uwer groter oetmoedicheden,   445
Ende hebten soe onder voet getreden,
Datti hem ewelic sal ververen
Van uwen sueten, suveren seden;
Want nyemen dan ghi en mag hem deren
Naest Gode. Ghi selten ewelic weeren,   450
Waer datti comt, na u gebien,
Ende oec, vor wien ghijt sult begeren
Mids uwer gracien, daer sal hi vlien.
Van hem en mach u niet messcien.

	With God's grace, so powerful;	
	'Twas I who brought you,	
	The mighty, noble, supreme, exalted	
	Blessed Holy Spirit, in truth;	415
	Lady, pure of thought, I tell you I am Gabriel	
	And I bring you now the selfsame grace	
	Which the Lord God, great and mighty,	
	Gave to Jacob who was his friend,	
	With blessings mild and sweet.	420
	This palm branch, noble, lovely lady,	
	I bring to you from paradise	
	Because after your death, my lady,	
	People will carry this with great devotion	
	Before your honoured bier.	425
	When with great deference, people	
	Will commit your body to earth, blessed beloved,	
	They will go before you with this branch,	
	As he commanded who created all.	
MARIA	For this I praise my noble child,	430
	That such an honour thus befalls me,	
	That he, so lovingly, out of his mercy,	
	Looks after me so well.	
	But, sweet angel, do explain:	
	Will I have to see the fiend	435
	Before I die? Because that horror	
	Makes my heart heavy with grief.	
	I wish I might keep my eyes closed,	
	So that I may not see the fiend.	
	Gabriel, my dear and faithful friend,	440
	Pray God to save me from that sight.	
GABRIEL	My lady, don't be afraid of him	
	And be reassured of that.	
	You have so damaged the foul fiend	
	With your greatness of heart,	445
	And you have crushed him underfoot	
	So that he will forever be afraid	
	Of your sweet and purest nature;	
	For no one but you can damage him	
	Except God. You will forever exclude him,	450
	Wherever he comes, if you so wish,	
	And also whomever you desire to guard	
	With your grace, from them he must flee.	
	Him you do not need to fear at all.	

MARIA	Lof u gescie, almechtich Heere, 455

MARIA   Lof u gescie, almechtich Heere,   455
Die my met gracien dus versiert
Ende my, erme, bewijst dees eere
Met uwen yngel wel gemaniert.
Dies biddic u vort, dat ghijt bestiert,
Dat u apostelen, mijn broeders gemeene,   460
Versamen mogen ongescoffiert
Ende wesen te miere uutvaert reene,
Op dat ic doch niet en sterve allene;
Want de Joden onbequame
Souden sturberen groot en cleene,   465
Hadden sijs macht, minen lichame.
Dus dan, dor uwen sueten name,
Mijn lieve sone, nemt dies ware,
Ende dat ic scouwen mach sonder blame
U jongeren, der apostelen scare,   470
Ende orlof nemen int openbare
Aen hen, die u met herten minnen.
En sachse in soe menegen jare;
Laat mi noch troest van hen gewinnen.
GABRIEL   Maria Vrouwe, sijt dies te binnen,   475
Al sijnse verre, tes in sijn machte,
Die Daniele, wilt wel versinnen,
Voetsel toesant met sijnre crachte;
Want Abecuc, die hem teten brachte,
Was menich hondert milen versceeden;   480
Nochtan God sijnre vriende gedachte
Ende dedene tot Daniele leeden.
Al heefti dapostelen oec willen breeden
In verren lande, wide geseten,
Gelievet sijnre genadicheden,   485
Ghi selter haest tidinge af weten.
Een vat vol gracien, ongespleten,
Sidi volmaect, gebenedijt
Boven alle andere hoechst ongemeten,
En bliven selt in ewiger tijt.   490
Adieu, dits wech, in vreden blijt:
Na minen woerden sal u gescien,
De gracie Gods heeft u versien.
MARIA   Lof deser bliscap, in mi gemaect
Bi des yngels sueten ingevene!   495
Nu benic met alder vruecht onstaect.
Lof deser bliscap in my gemaect!

MARIA	Praise be to you, almighty Lord,	455
	Who adorns me thus with grace	
	And who bestows on me, though unworthy,	
	This honour through your decorous angel.	
	I also ask you that you allow	
	That your apostles who are all my brothers	460
	May come together unmolested	
	And be with me at my peaceful deathbed,	
	So that I do not die alone;	
	For the malicious Jews,	
	Would, if they could, utterly	465
	Violate my body.	
	Now then, in your sweet name,	
	My dear son, take care of this,	
	So that I may behold blamelessly	
	Your disciples, all the apostles	470
	And take my leave quite openly	
	Of them who love you with all their hearts.	
	I haven't seen them for so many years;	
	Let me at last be consoled by them.	
GABRIEL	Maria, lady, be reassured	475
	Even if they are far away, it's in his power,	
	He who to Daniel, remember,	
	Sent nourishment by his strength;	
	For Habakuk, who brought him food,	
	Was many hundreds of miles away;	480
	But God remembered his friends	
	And caused him to be led to Daniel.	
	Even if he wanted to dispose the apostles	
	In foreign countries far apart,	
	If it pleases his benevolence	485
	You will soon have tidings of them.	
	You are perfect and also blessed	
	A vessel full of grace, without a flaw	
	Supremely reckoned above all others,	
	And so you shall remain forever.	490
	Adieu, I must go, remain in peace:	
	As I have said so it shall happen,	
	The grace of God will keep you.	
MARIA	Praise for this joy wrought in me	
	By the angel's sweet address!	495
	Now am I refulgent with all joy.	
	Praise for this joy wrought in me!	

Lof hebt, die mi ontbiet dus naect,
Dat ic sal comen ten ewigen levene!
Lof deser bliscap, in my gemaect   505
Bi des yngels sueten ingevene.
Los van snevene,
Getroest, van alder noot bevrijt,
Salic aenscouwen als die verhevene
Minen lieven sone gebenedijt.   505
Lof hem gescie in ewiger tijt!

*Selete: Hier sal Jan staen
predeken den volke inder stat
van Ephesen.*

SINT JAN   Tot uwer vramen, meerder en mindere,
Die hier sijt comen om aenhoren
Dat woert Gods, mijn weerde kindere,
Ic biddu, en willet niet verstoren.   510
Saeyt men u yet, laet niet verloren
Tsaet daer voetsel bi gesciet.
Suvert u herte en weert den doren,
Daer tsaet bi te verdwinen pliet.
Want dicker vele dan gers en griet   515
Soe sayt doncruut de lede viant,
Daer hi de goede vruchten siet
Becloven in goet winnende lant.
Al sidi gevallen, biet hem de hant,
Die u mach hulpen uten onreenen.   520
Ontcnoept van ongelove den bant;
Of neen, u siele saelt noch beweenen.
En laet u herte soe niet versteenen,
Ghi en leert den hoechsten Scepper kinnen,
Die u de gracie wilde verlenen,   525
Datti u sciep uut rechter minnen.
De doot wildi om u gewinnen;
Aenden cruce storti sijn bloet,
Om datti u, met viereger sinnen,
Woude lossen uter helscer gloet.   530
Daer bi hier penitencie doet
Ende wilt dat kerstendom ontfaen,
En vreest de doot, soe sidi vroet.
Ghi sult in dewige bliscap gaen.
Want dese werelt heeft God doen staen   535

Praise be to him who shows me clearly
That I will ascend to eternal life!
Praise for this joy wrought in me   500
By the angel's sweet address!
Free from dying,
Consoled, and liberated from all pain,
I will behold as one exalted
My dear and blessed son.   505
Praise be to him for ever more.

Selete. Here John will stand and preach to the people in the
town of Ephesus.

SAINT JOHN   I ask you, one and all,
Who've come here be told
The word of God, my worthy children,
Not to reject it; 'twill be for your benefit.   510
Let not go to waste what's sown for you
The seed from which nourishment grows.
Purify your hearts and push away the thorns,
In which the seed tends to be lost.
For far more often than grass and corn   515
The evil fiend sows weeds,
Wherever he sees good crops
Growing in fertile soil.
Even if you've fallen, let him take your hand
Who can help you out of error.   520
Loosen the bonds of disbelief;
If not, your soul will always rue it.
Don't let your hearts turn into stone,
Or you won't know the great creator,
Who will bestow upon you this grace,   525
That he created you from perfect love.
For you he wanted to suffer death;
On the cross he shed his blood,
So that with heartfelt passion
He could free you from the fires of hell.   530
For the sake of this you must do penance
And enter into the kingdom of God;
And if you are wise you will fear death.
You will arrive at eternal bliss.
For God has made this very world   535

Soe ghise siet, reyn van aenscouwe,
Om datti u inder vruechden baen
Bi sinen yngelen stellen souwe.
Peinst niet, ghi kindere, waert datti wouwe
Dees werelt ontmaken, die ghi hier siet,   540
Ende dit nyeuwe verkeren int ouwe,
Sijn vroude en bleefs te minder niet;
Want eer dat uut hem selven [ghesciet],
Datti de werelt van nyeute wrachte,
Soe was sijn godheit sonder verdriet   545
Soe wel als nu, diet wel bedachte;
Maer om u menscelic geslachte
Bi hem te bringen in sijn vruecht,
Soe dede hi bliken sijn grote machte
Ende stelde dees werelt dus in haer yuecht,   550
Des ghi hem niet voldancken en muecht.
Sijn wonderlic werc es sonder gronden,
Want hi mids sijnre heileger duecht
Om uwer salicheit hem liet wonden.
Dies laet ons dan in allen stonden   555
Hem dancken, minnen ende ontsien,
En vreesen de doot, en scuwen de sonden;
Want nyemen en can der doot ontvlien.
Ten mach geen dinc soe haest gescien,
In hemel, in eerde, ten es hem cont,   560
Ende alle datti wilt gebien,
Dat moet gescien in corter stont.
Vaet dit in dijnre herten gront,
Des biddic u allen met ynneger beden,
Hoe Ihesus Christus was dor wont   565
Ende dor u allen de doot heeft leden.
Inden name der Drievuldicheden,
Den Vader, den Sone, den Heilegen Geest,
Sceedic van u, blijft alle in vreden,
Maer smaect wel miere woerden keest,   570
Ende dat ghi dinen Scepper vreest.

Hier selen comen twee ingle met
enen cleede ende omslaen Sint
Janne ende tcleet sal scinen als
een wolke. Ende soe bedect selen
sine voeren vor Marien dore, oft
anderssins, soet best es.

As you now see it, pure to behold,
So that he may place you
Amidst his angels on the path of joy.
Don't think, my children, if he desired
To undo this world which you see here   540
And change this new world into the old one,
His joy would not at all be less;
For before he himself
Made the world out of nothing
His godhead was without any sorrow   545
Just as it is now, think on that.
But to bring you, human kind,
Close to him in his joy
He made apparent his very great might
And set this world in all her splendour: 550
You cannot thank him enough for that.
His miraculous work cannot be fathomed,
For he out of his holy virtue
Accepted wounds for your salvation.
So let us at every moment   555
Thank him, love him, and yet fear him.
And fear death too, and shun all sins;
For no one can escape from death.
There is no thing that does occur
In heaven or earth which he knows not,   560
And all that he wants to command,
That should come to pass at once.
This you must grasp, deep in your heart—
I ask you that with passionate prayer,—
How Jesus Christ was sorely wounded   565
And suffered death for all of you.
And in the name of the Trinity,
The Father, the Son and the Holy Spirit,
I depart from you: remain in peace,
But savour well the core of my words,   570
And be sure to fear your Creator.

Here two angels will come with a cloth and wrap it around
Saint John and the cloth will shine like a cloud. And so
covered, they will transport him to Maria's door or in another
way, as it seems best.

De ghene die saten te predecacien
inde stat van Ephesen:

i GEBUER	Wat ou! en siedi niet, ghi lie?
ij GEBUER	Wat, ghebuer?
i GEBUER	Mi dunct ic sie

Een overwonderlic werc hier baren
Aan desen predecare.

iij GEBUERINNE	Ic sachen henen varen	575

In een wolke, alsoe my dochte,
Deeddi niet?

i GEBUER	En weet wat wesen mochte.

Het es seere wonderlic te verstane,
Aldus een wolke te omvane
Enen man, ende als een winken   580
Wech te vuerene.

ij GEBUER	Men saels gedincken

Hier binnen Ephesen, dat weetic clare,
Hierna noch over ij^c jare;
Want, in presencien van ons gemeene,
Eest niet seer vremde?

iij GEBUERINNE	Ten es niet cleene	585

Te gronderene, wat sal bedien.

i GEBUER	Wonderlike werken selen gescien,

Es te duchtene, teneger steden.

ij GEBUER	God wille al ons vriende bevreden!	
	Elc es hem sculdich te verveerne.	590

Twas een groet leerere.

iij GEBUER	Ic hoorden soe geerne,

Want alle sijn woerden gaven bediet,
Diese wel verstont. Hi en achtes niet,
Waest hoge of neder, wijf of man,
Hi gaf elken tsine.

i GEBUER	Dat doet de selke nochtan	595

Nu te vele plaetsen diemen vint,
Daermen de hoyke hanct tegen den wint;
Ja, geestelic en weerlic, mochtment wel seggen,
Elc int sine, diet scone omleggen
Vor hen die mechtich sijn van state,   600
Uut vreesen, om miede, om loen, om bate.
Nochtan, sal diepe wonde genesen,
Men moetse tyntelen.

Those who sat listening to the sermon
in the town of Ephesus:

FIRST NEIGHBOUR   Hey, you folks, didn't you see that?
SECOND NEIGHBOUR   What's that, neighbour?
FIRST NEIGHBOUR   I think I'm seeing
          A most miraculous thing happen here
          With this preacher.
THIRD NEIGHBOUR, A WOMAN   I saw him go away   575
          In a cloud, it seemed to me;
          Didn't he?
FIRST NEIGHBOUR   I don't know what it could have been,
          It's a very miraculous thing
          To see a cloud wrap around
          A man, and take him away   580
          In the twinkling of an eye.
SECOND NEIGHBOUR   This will be remembered
          Here in Ephesus, I'm sure of it,
          Over two hundred years from now;
          For, with us all looking on,
          Wasn't it very strange?
THIRD NEIGHBOUR   It's not exactly simple   585
          To understand what this will mean.
FIRST NEIGHBOUR   Miraculous works will happen,
          It's to be feared, in some place or other.
SECOND NEIGHBOUR   May God protect all our friends!
          Everyone must have some reason to fear.   590
          He was a great teacher.
THIRD NEIGHBOUR   I so liked listening to him,
          For all his words were full of meaning
          For those who did understand. And he didn't mind
          Whether noble or humble, woman or man:
          He gave something to all.
FIRST NEIGHBOUR   That's the same for many of those 595
          Whom you find in many different places,
          Where they trim the sails to the wind;
          Yes, in a spiritual or in a worldly manner, as you could say
          Everyone in his own way, those who pretend
          In front of those who are of high rank   600
          From fear, or for the sake of gifts, reward, profit.
          However if deep wounds are to be healed
          You'll have to probe them.

ij GEBUER   Het moet soe wesen.
Ic sie men vint nu officiere
Van vele officien, die de maniere   605
Recht maken met woerden en met gebare,
Als oft geen ander God en ware
Dan die si dienen, — sijn die niet sot? —
Ende doen hem meer eren dan haren God,
Om titelic goet, om weerlic eere;   610
Dit sietmen dagelijcs.

iij GEBUER   Die doolen seere.
Nochtan eest waer. Maer claer, van desen
Gelike en quam noyt binnen Ephesen
Van predecare, soe ict can gemerken,
Noch die bat volchde metten werken   615
Na sinen woerden, sonder omwympelen,
Dats goet exempel.

i GEBUER   Dat eest ons sympelen,
Mi ende andere, die niet en weten
Dan men ons seit.

ij GEBUER   En can niet vergeten,
Wat dit wonder sal mogen bedien;   620
Tes recht een mirakele.

iij GEBUER   Mocht doch gescien,
Datti hier weder tonser vrame
Dwoert Gods noch bedieden quame,
Soe waer ons allen wel gesciet.
Wat maecht meenen?

i GEBUER   Claer, anders niet   625
Dan biden werken Gods almechtich
So en eest toecomen. Het blijct warechtich
Datti wel es metten Here.
Dies rise hem lof toe emmermeere,
Ende laet tot onser alder vramen   630
Vergaen ten besten.

ii GEBUER   Elc segge dies amen,
Ende bidden Gode met genynde,
Dat hine ons cortelic weder sinde
Tot onser bederven, ende van mesvalle
Ons wille behueden.

iij GEBUER   Dies bidden wi alle   635
Neernstelic met inneger be.
Nu gawi tsamen in onsen vre,

SECOND	Well that's the way it has to be.

SECOND Well that's the way it has to be.
I'm aware that you can now find officials
In many positions who act as if   605
They can make things right with words and gestures
As if there weren't another God
Besides the one they serve — aren't they crazy? —
And give him more honour than the true God
For the sake of short-lived benefit, for worldly honour; 610
This you see every day.
THIRD   They err gravely.
However, it's true. But without doubt such a one
As this preacher never came before
To Ephesus, as far as I'm concerned,
Nor one who better matched his deeds   615
To his words, without embroidery,
And that sets a good example.
FIRST   That it is for us simple folk
For me and others who don't know anything else,
Than what we're told.
SECOND   I can't forget,
What this miracle might mean;   620
It really is a wonder.
THIRD   Well if it happened,
That he would come another time
To explain God's word to us for our benefit
That would be good for all of us.
What can it mean?
FIRST   Clearly in no other way   625
Than through the works of God almighty
Can this have happened. It's shows truly
That he is really with the Lord.
For that he should be praised forever.
And I hope it may continue to be   630
For our benefit.
SECOND   Let's all say Amen to that
And pray to God passionately
That he will soon send this man to us again
For our good, and may protect us
From misfortune.
THIRD   That we all pray   635
Very seriously with passionate intent.
Now let's go together in peace

	Ende loven den Here gebenedijt.	
	Adieu, dits wech, in vreden blijt.	
SINT JAN	O alre hoechste verlichtere des sijns,	640
	Der werelt behoudere, wat es nu mijns?	
	Waer benic aldus gevlogen — dits vri —	
	Met deser wolken? Heere, ontdect mi	
	U hoge begeerte, ende maect mi vroet	
	Wes u gelieft, Here; ende ontdoet	645
	Mijn ogen, dat ic worde versinnende	
	De redene van desen. Ic worde bekinnende,	
	Dunct mi, — eest waer, soe est abuus? —	
	Den berch van Syon en mijn huus,	
	Daer Maria, Gods moeder volmaect,	650
	In woent. Hoe benic nu hier geraect	
	Dus haest? Dit moet wat groets bedien;	
	Salicheit moeter ons bi gescien.	
	Ic wil gaen cloppen best aen de duere.	
	Ouseg, Maria.	
MARIA	Wie es daer vuere?	655
	Van Gods wegen, vrient, wildi inne,	
	Segt wie ghi sijt.	
JAN	Ic bent, vriendinne,	
	Jan, u sone, reyn suver maecht,	
	Ic biddu, dat ghi u niet en versaecht	
	Mi in te latene; gebenedijt	660
	Soe seldi bliven.	
MARIA	Ach, Jan, sidijt,	
	Vercorne vrient? Lof Gode van al,	
	Dat ic u nu aenscouwen sal	
	Vor mijn doot! segt, hoet u geet	
	En wanen ghi comt.	
JAN	Seker en weet,	665
	Maria, Vrouwe, maer wilt gevroen:	
	Ic stont en predicte een sermoen	
	Binnen Ephesen. Soe vremden dinc	
	Es selden gesciet, want mi omvinc	
	Een wolke, ende bracht mi sonder verdriet	670
	Hier voer dit huus, soe ghi my siet,	
	Recht in een swerc. Dits vremde sake,	
	Ic en weet niet hoe ic hier gerake,	
	Noch oec waer bi, want geen vermaen	
	En hebbic gehadt.	

	And praise the blessed Lord.	
	Adieu, let's go: remain in peace.	
SAINT JOHN	Highest Enlightener of existence,	640
	Keeper of the world, what's happening to me?	
	Where am I being flown to? — it's strange —	
	In this cloud. Lord, reveal to me	
	Your noble desire, and disclose to me	
	Your wish, Lord; and open	645
	My eyes so that I will understand	
	The reason for this. I think I'm seeing	
	It seems to me — is it true or am I wrong? —	
	The Mount of Syon and my house,	
	Where Maria, God's perfect mother,	650
	Lives. How did I get here	
	So quickly? This augurs something great;	
	This must give us blessedness.	
	I want to go and knock on the door.	
	Listen, Maria.	
MARIA	Who is that there?	655
	In God's name, friend, if you want to come in,	
	Tell me who you are.	
SAINT JOHN	It's me, my friend,	
	Beautiful, pure maiden; it's John, your son.	
	I hope that you're not too frightened	
	To let me in. Blessed	660
	You will remain.	
MARIA	O John, It's you,	
	Beloved friend? Praise be to God	
	That I now see you	
	Before I die. Tell me how you are	
	And from where you've come.	
SAINT JOHN	I'm not at all sure	665
	Maria, lady, but let me tell you:	
	I stood and preached a sermon	
	In Ephesus. Such a strange thing	
	Has rarely happened. For a cloud	
	Enveloped me and took me unhurt	670
	To this house, as you see	
	Completely in a cloud. It's a strange thing,	
	I don't know how I got here,	
	Nor by what means, because I didn't get	
	Any explanation.	

MARIA	Dies moetti ontfaen	675
	Ewegen lof ende sonder mincken,	
	Die dus siere vriende wilt gedincken	
	Ende aldinc can ten besten bringen.	
	Sijn wijsheyt gaet voer alle dingen,	
	Sinen godliken wille mach niemen keeren.	680
	Sijt willecome inden name des Heeren,	
	Jan, die u hier heeft gesonden.	
	Ic sal u de waeromme orconden,	
	Dat God dees grote sake bestoet	
	U hier te bringene.	
JAN	Och, Vrouwe, soe doet,	685
	Des biddic u, geminde vercorne,	
	Want my lancter na te hoorne	
	Wat dinge dat bedieden mochte,	
	Dat mi dees wolke tot hier dus brochte,	
	Ende watter Gode gelieflic is	690
	Bi te bewisene.	
MARIA	Hoort dan na my;	
	Jan, ten es sonder redene niet,	
	Dat u God hier comen liet	
	Tot mijnder begeerten, als vrient ter noot;	
	Want mi God biden yngel ontboet,	695
	Dat ic serteyn tot sinen behage	
	Soude sceiden binnen derden dage	
	Van deser broesscher menscelicheden.	
	Dies biddic u met devoter beden,	
	Gevoudender hande, met knien gebogen,	700
	Met druckeger herten, met natten ogen,	
	Dat ghi de suete woerden versint	
	Van uwen Meester, doen hi als kint	
	Mi u beval; sijt mijns behoeder.	
	Hi seide: "Siet daer uwe moeder".	705
	Tot mi soe seidi: "Dats dijn sone".	
	Gedinct dies nu—dat di God lone!—	
	Des daer gescie tusscen ons beyen,	
	Ende en wilt ter noet van my niet sceyen,	
	Want, claer, het naect seere minen ynde.	710
	Dus sijt mijn troest.	
JAN	Bidt niet, geminde,	
	Maer beveelt sonder verdrach	
	Al dat der moeder vanden kinde	
	Gescien mach; vri van meswinde	

MARIA	For that he deserves	675
	Eternal praise, without any doubt,	
	He who so cares for his friends in that way	
	And can bring all things to a good end.	
	His wisdom guides all things;	
	No one can deflect his divine will.	680
	Be welcome John in the name of the Lord,	
	Who has sent you to me.	
	I shall reveal to you the reason,	
	That God undertook this great act	
	Of bringing you here.	
JOHN	O Lady, please do,	685
	I implore you, my beloved friend,	
	For I long to hear	
	What this deed may signify,	
	That I was brought here by this cloud,	
	And what it is that it pleases God	690
	To prove by it.	
MARIA	So listen to me,	
	John: it is not without purpose	
	That God allowed you to come here	
	As a friend in need, as was my desire.	
	Through the angel God revealed to me	695
	That it was certain, as he wished,	
	That I would leave within three days	
	This fragile human existence.	
	So I implore you with tender prayer,	
	Hands folded and on bended knee,	700
	Oppressed of heart, eyes full of tears,	
	That you recall the sweet words	
	Of your master, when he entrusted you to me	
	As my child: be my protector.	
	He said 'See, there, your mother'.	705
	To me he said 'That is your son'.	
	Do you remember— may God reward you—	
	That which then happened between the two of us,	
	And do not forsake me in this need,	
	For clearly my end is very near.	710
	Please be my comfort.	
JOHN	Don't beg, beloved,	
	But command without delay	
	All that the mother of the child	
	May need; I will keep you	

Salic u hoeden soe ic best mach.   715
Maer, Vrouwe, mi wondert u geclach.
Souddi te rechte nu druckich wesen,
Ende u de yngel dede gewach,
Dat ghi sonder ommeslach
Hoge ten hemele selt sijn geresen   720
Bi uwen sueten kinde gepresen?
Hoe mach u enegen druc gederen?
Ghi sout te rechte werden genesen
Van allen seere, die uut ghelesen
Wort boven alle marteleren   725
In vruechden, na uus soens begeren.

MARIA   Jan, sone, verstaet wel wat ic meene.
Al eest, dat ict met ogen beweene
Dat sceiden van hier, my wel versint,
Mijn bliscap dat ic niet en vercleene;   730
Mijn herte dat es vol vruechden reene.
Mijns weenens en verdruevic twint.
Hoe dogen oetmoedelic doen bekint
Haer werc inder natuerlicheyen.
Die vruecht, die doghe int herte vint,   735
Es nuttelic dat si die ontbint;
Dus doet de bliscap dogen screyen
Den genen die na vruecht verbeyen.

JAN, *knielende*   O vader, der glorien werkere,
Der druckeger sinnen een verlichtere,   740
Tot allen duegden een versterkere,
Volmaect van allen erge een swichtere,
Sijt uwer sueter moeder meplichtere
Nu inde ure van harer doot.
Hulpt ons versamen, hoechste richtere,   745
Van uwen jongeren een conroot.
Soudsi versceeden aldus bloet
Van deser werelt, twaer onbetame;
Dies staet haer bi te harer noet
Doer uwen gebenediden name.   750

MARIA   Jan, die yngel Gods bequame
Seide, des willic wel betrouwen,
Dat icse alle tot mijnder vrame
Vor mijn doot bi mi sal scouwen.
Aldus so willen wiere ons aen houwen   755
Ende stellen ons te vreden van dien.
God saelt so wel te passe vouwen,

	As best I can, safe from hurt.	715
	But, lady, your complaint amazes me.	
	Why would you now be oppressed	
	Since the angel made it clear,	
	That you will ascend	
	Without further ado right up to heaven	720
	To you own sweet beloved child?	
	How could any sadness touch you?	
	You should by rights be cured	
	Of all grief, you who are raised up	
	Above all martyrs	725
	In joy, according to your son's desire.	
MARIA	John, my son, understand what I'm saying:	
	Even though my eyes are weeping	
	Over my leaving here, do realise,	
	My joy could not be greater.	730
	My heart is full of pure joys.	
	My tears do not sadden me at all,	
	However much my eyes may meekly fulfil	
	Their natural function.	
	The joy, which finds sadness in the heart,	735
	Usefully releases it;	
	So joy brings tears to the eyes	
	Of those who are striving for joy.	
JOHN, *kneeling*	O father, you who create glory,	
	You who console saddened hearts,	740
	You who strengthen all virtue,	
	A perfect scourge of all evil,	
	Be your sweet mother's helper	
	Now in the hour of her death.	
	Help us to bring together, highest judge,	745
	A host of your disciples.	
	If she were to depart thus lonely	
	From this world, that would be wrong;	
	So aid her in her hour of need,	
	This we ask through your blessed name.	750
MARIA	John, the blessed angel of God	
	Said, and I trust in that,	
	That I shall see all of them	
	To my joy before my death.	
	And so we want to trust in that	755
	And derive our peace from it.	
	God will no doubt arrange it so	

Selete, hier selen dapostelen
versamen met eender wolken
vor Marien duere, hem sere
verwonderende.

PETER	O Here, wilt uwer gracien plegen	760
	Aen mi! waer benic? waer wordic gedregen?	
	Slapic of wakic? wat eest van my?	
	Waer vindic mi selven noch? sie ic vry?	
	Beenic alleene hier? Mij dunct neen ic.	
	Lof Gode! ic sie hier oec, dat meenic,	765
	Van minen bruederen. God huede ons van plagen!	
	Wat wonder es dit? Ic wil hen vragen	
	Na dit bestier; dits vremt bediet.	
	Wanen comdi, mijn brueders?	
ANDRIES	Wi en wetens niet,	
	Wanen wi comen, noch hoe, noch waer	770
	Dat wi hier sijn.	
PETER	Hebt gheenen vaer,	
	Hoept inden Here gebenedijt,	
	Hi sal ons bestieren.	
PAUWELS	Hoo, Peter, sidijt?	
	Mijn lieve geselle, nu beenic te vreden.	
	Ic hope dat God dit wonder als heden	775
	Om een beter tot salicheyen	
	Ons heeft gedaen. Wi waren versceyen	
	Seere verre van een, dwoort Gods te leerne;	
	Nu heeft ons God gevuecht te keerne,	
	Ende hier versaemt op cort termijn.	780
	Heyl moets ons bueren.	
MATHIJS	Dat moet waer sijn,	
	Ende onsen tijt alsoe te besteene,	
	Dat hem gelieve ons te bevreene	
	Van alle blameliken werke,	
	Dat ons mocht nosen.	
ANDRIES	Ic sta en merke	785
	Dese plaetse. Mijn bruers, alsict versinne,	
	Dunct mi dat icker my aen bekinne,	
	Alsic oec doe, en twivels niet,	
	Dat es den berch van Syon, siet,	

That we shall shortly see them;
There can be no doubt of that.

Selete. Here the Apostles will gather together with a
cloud in front of Maria's door, greatly wondering.

PETER   O Lord, spread your mercy over me.   760
                 Where am I? Where am I being taken?
                 Am I asleep or awake? What's happening to me?
                 Where do I find myself now? Do I really see this?
                 Am I quite alone here? No, I think not.
                 Praise God! I see here also, I think,   765
                 Several of my brothers. May God protect us from evil!
                 What miracle is this? I'll go and ask them
                 What's happening; this is a strange thing.
                 Where have you come from, my brothers?

ANDREW   We have no idea
                 Where we've come from, nor how, nor where   770
                 We are now.

PETER   Don't be afraid,
                 Trust in the blessed Lord,
                 He will guide us.

PAUL   Ah, Peter, is that you?
                 My dear friend, now I am content.
                 I hope that God has today   775
                 Wrought this miracle for us
                 To our salvation. We were scattered
                 Far away from each other, to teach God's word;
                 Now it has pleased God to return us
                 And quickly bring us here together.   780
                 Good must come of it.

MATTHEW   That must be true,
                 And may our time be spent in such a way
                 That it would please him to protect us
                 From all wicked deeds
                 Which might bring us harm.

ANDREW   I think I know   785
                 This place. My brothers, when I think of it,
                 I think that I do recognise this,
                 And so I do, I don't doubt it,
                 That is the Mount of Syon, look,

               Daer ic dicke hebbe willen verkeren;   790
Dits thuus daer oec de moeder ons Heren
In woent. Lof Gode, nu weetict claer,
Wy sijnder vore.

PETER   Serteyn, tes waer.
Gheminde bruers, nu ben ic blie;
Ie salder gaen cloppen. O Vrouwe Marie,   795
Laet in u vriende, die tuwen gebie
Hem presenteren.

MARIA   Wie sijn die lie?
Jan, die scinen herde ruut,
Dat si soe cloppen.

JAN   Twas recht den luut
Van Peteren, Vrouwe, soe mij dochte.   800
Ic sal gaen weten wiet wesen mochte.
Hi wilt er emmer inne, soet scijnt.
Wie es daer vore?

PETER   U vriende sijnt,
Jan, Gods jongeren, die in corter spacien
Hier nu versaemt sijn.

JAN   Van deser gracien   805
Lovic Gode, dat ic u scouwe
Nu tonser noot. Maria Vrouwe,
Comt, hulpt ontfaen na haer betamen
Gods jongeren, die tot uwer vramen
Hier sijn versaemt in 't openbaer   810
Tot uwer eren.

MARIA   Ach! sidi daer,
Gods uutvercorne vriende gemeene?
Sijt willecome, in duegden reene,
Mijn herte verlicht my recht van dien,
Dat ic u mach te samen sien   815
Vergadert in duegden ende in minnen.
Hoe mochtic meerder vruecht gewinnen,
Dan daer my therte met es dorvluegen?
Hoe salic u bewisen muegen
Der groter gunst die ic u gan?   820
Van blijscapen dat ic nauwe en can
Gespreken, dat ic u aenscouwe
Voer mijn ynde.

PETER   Vercorne Vrouwe,
Wi seggen u danc in corter spacien
Van uwer volmaecter visentacien,   825

	Where I often have longed to be;	790
	This is the house where the mother of our Lord	
	Dwells. Praise God, I'm now quite clear	
	That is where we are.	
PETER	That must be true.	
	Beloved brothers, now I'm glad;	
	I'll knock on the door. O Lady Maria,	795
	Let your friends enter who at your command	
	Present themselves.	
MARIA	Who are those people?	
	John, it seems rather rude to me	
	To knock so loudly.	
JOHN	But that was the voice	
	Of Peter, Lady, I feel sure.	800
	I'll go and see who's there.	
	Someone does want to come in, it seems.	
	Who is out there?	
PETER	These are your friends	
	John, God's disciples, who have gathered here	
	In a very short time.	
JOHN	I praise God	805
	For this blessing, that I see you now	
	In our hour of need. Maria, Lady,	
	Come and welcome with me, as we should,	
	God's disciples, who for your sake	
	Are brought together here as you can see	810
	In honour of you.	
MARIA	Ah, is that you,	
	All God's beloved friends?	
	Be welcomed, in pure virtue,	
	My heart is lightened greatly thereupon,	
	That it is possible for me to see all of you	815
	Gathered in virtue and in love.	
	How could I gain any more joy	
	Than this, with which my heart is filled?	
	How could I possibly show you	
	The great affection which I cherish for you?	820
	I can barely speak	
	For joy, that I behold you	
	Before my end.	
PETER	Beloved lady,	
	And we in our turn now thank you	
	For your loving welcome	825

Die ghi ons tonsen willecome tuecht,
Ende bidden u voort, volmaecte yuecht,
Eest dat ghi yet aen ons begeert,
Dat ghi ons minlijc dat vercleert;
Want al ons vermogen, tsy na of breet, 830
Wes u gelieft, es u bereet
Van ons allen, meerder en mindere,
Tot uwer eeren.

MARIA Danc hebt, mijn kindere.
God laet mi sonder uwen noot
Aen u verdienen.

JAN Dits wonder groot, 835
Geminde bruers, dat dit gesciet,
Datmen u allen te samen siet
Vergadert nu te deser steden.
Ghi waert soe menege mile versceden
Dwoort Gods te leerne; hoe comt dit toe? 840
Segt ons dbediet.

BERTELMEEUS Wi en weten hoe,
Seker, Jan, dan bi Gods gracien;
Want wi in alte corter spacien
Hier quamen. Wi waren op geheven
Elc tsijnder plaetsen en sonder sneven 845
Bi een versaemt in corter tijt
Ende tot hier bracht. Gebenedijt
Moet sijn de Here, die alles macht heeft.

JAN Dat God dit wonder aen ons gewracht heeft
Ter eren sire moeder na dbetamen, 850
Ende oec den kerstene gelove tot vramen,
Des moet hi ewelic na desen
Van allen tongen gesalicht wesen,
Die ons met eenre ogen opslage
Hier dus versaemt.

PETER Jan, vrient, ic vrage 855
Bi orlove ende oft u gelieflic si,
Waer bi dat comt, tverwondert my,
Want wi hebben door Gods eere,
Menech jaer, lof heb de Heere,
Versceeden geweest, beyde achter en voort, 860
Om te vercleerne sijn salige woort,
Alsoe hi ons mondelinge beval.
Nu vinden wi ons te samen al,

Which you bestow on us,
And also beg you, lady of perfection,
If there is anything you would want from us,
Be so kind as to tell us;
For all our skills in every respect 830
Whatever you would like is at your service,
That goes for all of us, older and younger,
In your honour.

MARIA   I thank you, my children.
God allows me to enjoy your company
Without imposing on you.

JOHN   It is a great miracle, 835
Beloved brothers, that this has happened
That we see you all together
Gathered now in this same place.
You were scattered so many miles apart
While teaching God's word; how has this come about? 840
Please explain it.

BARTHOLOMEW   Well we don't quite know,
John, other than by God's grace;
For in fact we were conveyed here
Very rapidly. Each of us
Was lifted up from where he was and without delay 845
Collected together in a very short time
And brought here. Blessed
Must be the Lord, who is all powerful.

JOHN   Since God has wrought this miracle for us
In honour of his mother as is fitting, 850
And also to the advantage of the Christian faith
He must forever after this
Be blessed and praised by all tongues,
He who in the twinkle of an eye
Assembled us here together.

PETER   John, my friend, 855
I'd like to ask with your permission, if you please,
How this came about. I greatly wonder
For we have for many years
For the sake of God's honour, praised be the Lord
Been separated, hither and thither, 860
In order to proclaim the blessed gospel,
As he had expressly commanded us.
And now we find ourselves inexplicably all together;

Onwetens; dus lust ons wel te hoorne
Dit hoge bewijs.

MARIA   Salege vercoorne   865
Vriende, dat salic u bedien.
Het es gesciet in tsviants toorne,
Ende ter eeren van ons lien.
Mijn ogen die hadden u geerne gesien,
Eer ic van deser werelt moet;   870
Dus heeft my God dat laten gescien,
Soe mi die yngel maecte vroet;
Dus, lieve kinderen, elc nemt vor goet:
Uut mire begeerten soe eest geresen,
Dat my God dese eere dus doet.   875
Gebenedijt soe moet hi wesen!

PAUWELS   O bloem der bloemen, hoge gepresen,
Wiens roke den sieken geeft confortacie,
Ghi sijt een specie, die can genesen
Hen allen die hopen in uwer gracie.   880
Lof dat ic in mijns levens spacie
Sal mogen gebien ende sien ten claren,
Dat ghi sonder tribulacie
Met uwen kinde te hemel selt varen.

PETER   Lof sijns, die my hier wilde gesparen   885
Soe lange, dat ic oec sal gebien
Datti boven alle martelaren
Sijnder heileger moeder sal benedien.
Ic can geen meerder vruecht gelien
Dan ic dat metten ogen aensage,   890
Dat si ter hemelscer melodien
Sal trecken, na haers liefs kints behage.

BERTELMEUS   Mijn herte ontpluyct, dat ics gewaghe,
Dat de blusschersse van onsen sonden
Ende de verbiddersse van onsen mesdrage   895
Voer ons in dewige vruecht wort vonden.
Dies laet ons met reynen suveren gronden
Loven den Here in beden soet,
En datti ons nu en tallen stonden
In sire gracien gesterken moet.   900

JACOP   O Vrouwe, nemt ons int behoet,
Als ghi daer sijt in jubilacien;
Behuet ons vander hellen gloet,
Ende weert van ons al quade temptacien.

	So we would really like to know	
	How this can be explained.	
MARIA	Blessed, beloved	865
	Friends, I will explain that to you	

So we would really like to know
How this can be explained.

MARIA Blessed, beloved · 865
Friends, I will explain that to you
It all came about to spite the devil,
And in honour of us all.
My eyes would have liked to see you
Before I had to depart this world; · 870
So God has made that possible for me
As the angel came to tell me;
So, beloved children, you can be sure of this:
It has arisen from my desire
That God now honours me in this way. · 875
Blessed may he be!

PAUL Flower of flowers, exceedingly precious,
Whose scent gives comfort to the sick,
You are a herb which can cure
All those who hope for your grace. · 880
Praise be that I in my lifetime
Will be allowed to experience and clearly see
That you without any hindrance
Will ascend to heaven to your child.

PETER Praise be, who spared me here · 885
So long, that I too will experience
That he, above all martyrs,
Will bless his holy mother.
I can't imagine a greater joy
Than that I'll see with my own eyes · 890
That she will journey
Towards the heavenly music, as her sweet child desires.

BARTHOLOMEW My heart blossoms, when I reflect,
That she who quells our sins
And effects the forgiveness of our trespasses · 895
Will be set in eternal joy for our sakes.
Let us praise the Lord with sweet prayers
From the pure and chaste depths of our hearts
And that he may now and at all times
Strengthen us with his grace. · 900

JACOB Please lady, take us into your protection
When you are seated there with jubilation;
Guard us from the fires of hell,
Divert from us all evil temptations.

MATHIJS	Bescermt ons, Vrouwe, van desperacien	905
	Als ghi daer sidt bi uwen sone;	
	Laet druppen van uwer hoger gracien	
	Op ons hier neder uten trone.	
PHILIPS	Verhuecht u, Vrouwe, want uwe crone	
	Wert boven alle cronen verchiert;	910
	Soe groten bliscap noch soe scone	
	En was van herten noyt gevisiert.	
SYMON	U hoge inwesen wel gemaniert	
	Dat wert begaeft met selken gichten	
	Ende met soe groter wijsheit bestiert,	915
	Soe dat al erterike sal verlichten.	
MATHEUS	Den wreeden viant seldi swichten	
	Tot haren profite die u eeren;	
	Den wech des levens seldi ons slichten;	
	Dies moet u lof voort ewelic meeren.	920
ANDRIES	U vruecht mach nimmermeer verkeren;	
	U lof sal groyen, suete Marie,	
	Onder de zalege, sonder verseeren,	
	Van eewen tot eewen in ewigen tye!	
	Dies bidt vor ons, gebenedie.	925
MARIA	Danc hebt der visentacien reene,	
	Die my, lief brueders, van u gesciet.	
	Van groter bliscap dat ict beweene,	
	Die mijn herte toecomende siet;	
	Want ic weet wel, en twivels niet,	930
	Den tijt es nakende die dingel seye.	
	Na dat mijn kint my weten liet,	
	Eest nuttelic dat ic my bereye.	
	Dus waert dan goet dat men my leye	
	Op mijn bedde, in minnen devoet.	935
	Tes nuttelijc dat ic mij bereye	
	Den tijt, die mi mijn kint ontboet.	
JAN	Eerwerdige maget sonder genoet,	
	U begeerte die sal volcomen.	
	Hulpt alle de moeder des Heren groot	940
	Te bedde, brueders, het sal u vromen.	
	Haer duegden staen soe uutgenomen	
	Gewortelt uten paradise.	
	Uut Davids geslechte soe essi oec comen,	
	Bi Yesse gespruut in reynder wise.	945
	O suver seborie van hogen prise,	
	Marie, die droecht den hemelscen scat,	

MATTHEW	Protect us, lady, from despair	905
	When you are seated there next to your son;	
	Let the drops of your exquisite grace	
	Fall from heaven upon us here below.	
PHILIP	Rejoice now, lady, for your crown	
	Is richer than all other crowns:	910
	Such great joy nor any so beautiful	
	Was ever imagined in any heart.	
SIMON	Your fine and graceful nature is	
	So endowed with great gifts	
	And enhanced with such great wisdom,	915
	That it will illuminate all the earth.	
MATTHEW	You will repel the cruel fiend	
	To the good of those who honour you;	
	You will smooth the path of our life for us;	
	And so your praise will always be the greater.	920
ANDREW	Your joy will never diminish;	
	Your praise will grow, sweet Maria,	
	Amongst the blessed, without failing,	
	For ever and ever into eternity!	
	So pray for us, blessed lady.	925
MARIA	I thank you for this lovely greeting,	
	Which you, dear brothers, have bestowed on me.	
	It is great joy which makes me weep,	
	The joy my heart awaits;	
	For I know well, and doubt it not,	930
	The time the angel foretold draws near.	
	Since my child has let me know	
	It is needful that I prepare myself.	
	So it would be good to lay me now	
	On my bed, with heartfelt love.	935
	It is needful that I prepare myself	
	For the time which my child ordained.	
JOHN	Honourable virgin without equal	
	You desire will be fulfilled.	
	Brothers, let us help the mother of the Lord Almighty	940
	On to her bed; it will bring us joy.	
	Her virtues are so excellent,	
	Rooted in paradise.	
	She has come from David's line,	
	Descended from Jesse in noble fashion.	945
	Pure chalice, of great worth,	
	Maria who carried that heavenly treasure,	

	Wi bidden u dat u gracie rise	
	Op ons, reyn meegdelic suver vat.	
PETER	Lect daer alsoe, daer essi bat	950
	Op haer bedde dan ergens el.	
	O suver fonteyne, vol gracien nat,	
	Nemt ons voort in u bestel.	
	Versaecht u niet vor geen gequel,	
	Daar u de doot bi mach genaken;	955
	Want Vrouwe, ic weet te voren wel,	
	Ghi en seltse natuerlic niet gesmaken,	
	Ende dat mids dien, verstaet de saken,	
	Als u lief kint sijn passie leet,	
	Soe die propheten te voren spraken,	960
	Dat u sijn passie therte dorsneet.	
	Alsoet van u gescreven steet,	
	Soe leeddi daer soe groten pine	
	Van rouwe, die u was soe wreet,	
	Soe dat u herte verkeerde in tsine.	965
	Hoe souddi dan, godlike divine,	
	Noch eens gesterven, diet eens hebt leden?	
	Neen ghi, vorwaer, sijt dies te vreden.	
MARIA	In my moet bliken sijn groet begeren,	
	Sijn heilege gracie wil mi besprayen,	970
	Sijn wijsheit wil minen sin vercleren,	
	Sijn duecht wil al mijn erch verteren;	
	Ic en can my niewers af ververen,	
	Want in my voncken syn berrende layen.	
	Tot sijnder gelieften, soe mach hi sayen	975
	Selc saet als in my can becliven.	
	Laet hi sijn suetheit op mi wayen	
	Uut sinen goddeliken rayen,	
	Hi sal mi therte wel verfrayen,	
	Dat ic tot hem, om een verstiven,	980
	In allen saken volstentich sal bliven.	
JAN	Lof hebt, oetmoedege Vrouwe vercoren!	
	U groot begeren wort Gode bequame.	
PETER	Want ghi en vreest noch wee noch toren;	
	Lof hebt, oetmoedege Vrouwe vercoren!	985
PAUWELS	Ghi sijt de rose al sonder doren,	
	Ende moeder en maecht tot onser vrame.	
JAN	Lof hebt, oetmoedege Vrouwe vercoren!	
	U groot begeren wert Gode bequame,	
	Gebenedijt es dinen name.	990

	We pray you that your grace may fall	
	On us, perfect, virginal, innocent vessel.	
PETER	Lay her down, she'll be easier	950
	In her bed than anywhere else.	
	O chaste fountain, bedewed with grace,	
	Accept now our care of you.	
	Do not be frightened of any anguish,	
	Which death might bring to you;	955
	For I already know, my lady,	
	That you, naturally, will not suffer at all,	
	And that's because, you understand,	
	When your sweet child suffered his passion,	
	As the prophets had foretold,	960
	His passion pierced your heart.	
	So therefore it is written that you	
	Endured such pangs	
	Of grief which were so cruel	
	That your heart suffered as if it were his.	965
	Why would you then, divine lady,	
	Meet death again, having suffered it once?	
	Indeed you won't, so be consoled.	
MARIA	In me this great desire will shine	
	His holy grace will be laid upon me,	970
	His wisdom will enlighten my mind,	
	His virtue will undo my imperfection;	
	I need not be afraid at all,	
	For in me his burning flames are kindled.	
	As he desires, he may sow	975
	Such seed as can wax in me.	
	May he send his sweetness over me	
	From his heavenly rays.	
	He will make my heart rejoice	
	So that I will, without faltering,	980
	Remain constant to him in all ways.	
JOHN	Praise be, serene and special Lady!	
	Your great desire is pleasing to God.	
PETER	For you fear neither grief nor anger;	
	Praise be, serene and special Lady!	985
PAUL	For you are the rose without any thorn,	
	And mother and virgin for our sake.	
JOHN	Praise be, serene and special Lady!	
	Your great desire is pleasing to God,	
	And blessed is your name.	990

Selete. hier selen dapostelen in
bedingen liggen. Ende die wile
comt Lucifer ende roept sijn
dieneers, om te sinden na Marien
siele.

LUCIFER Ou! duvels, neckers, refuys van boeven,
Moetmen u aldinc voer besoeven?
Datmen u villen moet als een puut!
Waer sidi? Ou, seg!

ALLE   Hier meestere.

LUCIFER   Soe comt hier uut,
Valsce verraders, onnutte cockine,   995
Ghi ligt en mest, al waerdi swine,
Van ledicheden; crupt uten neste!
Wat bedrijfdi?

i VIANT   Wi doen ons beste,
Tormenten en pinen de sielen swaerlic,
Braden en stoken.

LUCIFER   Ghi doet den duvel baerlic 1000
Mi dunct ghi sijt de meeste deel stille.
Mochtic wel plagen na minen wille,
Ic soude meer sielen alleene beswaren
Dan alle de duvels die noyt gewaren.
Ghi en hebt geen werc meer inde le,   1005
Dat tachten es.

ij VIANT   Bi uwer weerdiche,
Lucifer, meester, wi sijn u getrouwe
In allen dienste.

LUCIFER   Dat sidi, vrouwe
Soet scijnt, ghi sijt van groten bedrive.
Maer wat segdi van desen wive,   1010
Tsmans moeder, die eens ons helle brac?
Daer moesti heenen.

BEIDE   Wy, meester?

LUCIFER   Ja, sonder gecrac
Si leit opt sceiden, trect rasch tot daer,
Tempteren, becoren, hebt genen vaer,
Doet al u beste in alder maten,   1015
Dat wi ons wreeken.

i VIANT   Dan sal niet baten,
Want onser geen tot enegen stonden
En costse noit gebringen tot sonden

Selete. Here the Apostles will
kneel in prayer. Meanwhile,
Lucifer arrives and calls upon his
servant to capture Maria's
soul.

LUCIFER   Hey! Devils, niggers, scum of villains,
                  Do I have to spell it out to you?
                  You should be skinned like toads!
                  Where are you? Come here!

ALL   Here, master.

LUCIFER   Come here at once,
                  False traitors, useless layabouts,   995
                  You're just lying about getting fatter like swine,
                  In idleness; get out of your nest!
                  What are you up to?

FIRST FIEND   We're doing our best,
                  Tormenting and plaguing souls, fiendishly
                  Roasting and stoking.

LUCIFER   You are behaving just like devils 1000
                  But half-heartedly, in my book.
                  If I were tormenting by my standard,
                  I alone would destroy more souls
                  Than all the devils that ever were.
                  You've got no spunk in you   1005
                  That's worth mentioning.

SECOND FIEND   Oh, your honour
                  Lucifer, master, we're ever so loyal
                  In every way.

LUCIFER   You're just like women
                  It seems; it's all talk.
                  What are you saying about this woman,   1010
                  That man's mother who once destroyed our hell?
                  Get yourselves there.

TWO FIENDS   Why, master?

LUCIFER   Just get on with it.
                  She's about to snuff it, get a move on,
                  Tempt her, seduce her, don't be scared,
                  Do your utmost without stint;   1015
                  That'll be our be revenge.

FIRST FIEND   It won't be any use,
                  None of us has ever managed
                  To get her as far as sinning

In geenre manieren, cleyn noch groot;
Maer si heeft ons menegen noot   1020
Beraden, als ghi wel wet; ic wane,
Dats pine verloren.

ij VIANT   Ic had liever te gane
In alde tormenten der heltscher pine,
Dan eens bi desen wive te sine,
Al hadden wijt alle te samen begrepen,   1025
Ja, die u dienen.

LUCIFER   Tes verloren gepepen,
Ghi moetter henen. Wat meyndi ghi,
Dat si soe mechtich mach sijn als hi?
Dats verre versceiden, want si es puere
Van erden, als mensce, en de natuere   1030
Es broesch ende oec de doot es wreet.

i VIANT   Tes waer, ic kent, maer ic en weet
Niemen ter werelt, met corten waerden,
Die ons meer scaet. My cremt de swaerden
Van vreesen, wanneer ic haren name   1035
Hoer noemen.

LUCIFER   Dats grote blame,
Keytijfs, voer u. Souddi ontsien
Een sympel wijf?

ij VIANT   Si hebbent goet gebien,
Diemen niet wederseggen en mach.
Mocht sijn, wi namens wel verdrach.   1040
Maer Lucifer, meester, eest u bevelen,
En twivelt niet, serteyn wi selen
De sake soe metten tanden gripen,
Machmense op enegen cant genypen,
Ghi selter af horen blide meere,   1045
Hoet ons vergeet.

LUCIFER   Dats dat ic beghere,
Daer sprecti als vriende, daer houdics mi an,
Ic saelt oec bekinnen.

i VIANT   Nu, gawi dan;
Dit werc es nu op ons versceenen.
Hier eest te doene. Brue! Brue!

MICHAEL   Waer wildi heenen,   1050
Ghi helsce draken? Vliet sonder blijf,
Terter niet naerdere.

In any way, not even a little one;
But she has caused us loads of trouble 1020
As you well know; I bet
It's a lost cause.

SECOND FIEND   I'd much rather go
Into all the pains and torments of hell,
Than go anywhere near this woman,
Even if we all went together, 1025
Every one of your servants.

LUCIFER   It's no good moaning;
You've got to go. Do you really think
That she's as strong as he is?
There's a hell of a difference, for she is pure,
Of the earth, like a human, and her nature 1030
Is fragile, and also death is cruel.

FIRST FIEND   I know, it's true, but I don't know
Anyone on earth, to be blunt,
Who hurts us more. My skin creeps
With fear when I hear her name 1035
Is mentioned.

LUCIFER   That's a great shame,
On you, you wretches. Are you scared
Of a simple woman?

SECOND FIEND   It's easy to give orders
When no one can argue with you.
If we could we'd like to give this a miss. 1040
But Lucifer, master, if it's your command
Don't doubt it, we're sure
To get our teeth into it,
If there's any way we can get hold of her,
You'll be pleased when you hear more of it, 1045
And of how we're doing.

LUCIFER   That's the ticket
Now you're talking like friends, I'll hold on to that,
I'll grant you that.

FIRST FIEND   OK, let's go.
We're saddled with the job now
Let's get on with it. Grr! Grr!

MICHAEL   Where do you think you're going 1050
You hellish dragons? Be off at once,
Don't come any nearer.

ij VIANT   Wy eisschen dit wijf
Van rechte, al esse in uwer hoe,
Als een puer mensce.

MICHAEL   Si en hoort u niet toe,
Satanas, want si es suver en reyne   1055
Van sonden, van smetten, als een fonteyne,
Alsoet van hare gescreven steet
In Canticis.

i VIANT   Ghi sijt ons te wreet,
Michael, laet ons gebruken ons rechte
Als over dmenschelike geslechte,   1060
Soet God geboet; dan mach niet bliven,
Wi eysschent u.

MICHAEL   En wil u niet verdriven
Van uwen rechte, verstaet wel my,
Want God seit selve in Genesy,
Datti viantscap sal setten claer   1065
Tusscen u ende dwijf.

ij VIANT   Ic kent, tes waer,
Maer oftse dit es, verstaet mi wel,
En weeten wi niet.

MICHAEL   Ten es geen el,
Want ghi hebtse altijt gehaet,
Soet blijct. Oec hebbense versmaet   1070
De Joden, die niet en geloven des,
Dat si moeder ende maget es,
Dwelc comt uut uwen valscen sae,
Dat ghi gesayt hebt, en mids den rae
Van u, heltsch viant, soe hebben de Joden   1075
Haer scaemte en confuse geboden
Onverdient; ende oec haer kint
Gedoot, gepassijt, alsoet scint.
Wat wildi meer, segt, valsch fenijn?
Es dit niet dwijf?

i VIANT   Saelt aldus sijn,   1080
Soe bliven wi met allen beroeft
Onser heerscapien ende verdoeft
Van enen wive, dwelc geet te naer
Den Gods rechte.

ij VIANT   Dat doet voer waer.
Tes hert om liden. Wist mens raet!   1085

MICHAEL   En wetti niet wel, datter noch staet
In Canticorum, dat si es

SECOND FIEND   We demand this woman
By rights, even if she's in your protection,
As she's a pure human.

MICHAEL   She's not yours
Satan, for she is pure and free   1055
From sins, from taint, as a fountain,
As is written about her
In the Canticles.

FIRST FIEND   You're too hard on us,
Michael, let us use our rights
Over the human race   1060
As God ordained; it has to happen,
We demand it.

MICHAEL   I won't come between you
And your rights, believe me,
Because he himself said in Genesis
That there will be great enmity   1065
Between you and the woman.

SECOND FIEND   I know, it's true,
But whether it's this one, believe me,
We don't really know.

MICHAEL   This is the one,
For you have always hated her,
That's clear. And the Jews too   1070
Have scorned her, because they don't believe
That she is mother and virgin;
And that's because of the false seed
Which you've sown; and because of your advice,
Hellish fiend, the Jews have   1075
Disgraced and shamed her
Undeservedly; and they've also killed
Her child, tormented him, as is clear.
Tell me what more do you want, poisonous fiend?
Is this not the woman?

FIRST FIEND   If that's how it is   1080
We'll all be robbed
Of our rule and crushed
By a woman, which usurps
The right of God.

SECOND FIEND   That's dead right.
It's hard to put up with. What can we do?   1085

MICHAEL   Don't you know that it is written
In the Canticles, that she is

               "Terribilis ut castrorum acies",
               Dats verveerlic, diet wel merke,
               Ghelijc den casteele of bollewerke.   1090
               Wien esse verveerlic el dan dy,
               Als haren viant? Tert achtere!

i VIANT   Ay my! Amy!
               Ligt af, Michael, ghi doet my seere,
               Ghi sijt ons te mechtich.

MICHAEL   Noch sprac God meere
               In Genesy, dat si soude onsoete   1095
               Dijn hooft bedrucken onder haer voete.
               Tes recht: al brac Eva bi dijnre list
               Tgebod Gods, tes al gecist
               Bider oetmoet der maecht Marien,
               De welke ons es, dit moetti lien,   1100
               Een moeder der salicheit, dits claere als glas
               Oec bescrijft Ysaias,
               Inden .X. cappittel, na claer bewisen:
               "Uut Yesse sal een roede op risen".
               Ende David in den Soutere seit voort   1105
               Inden persoen des vaders dit woort:
               "De here sal sinden de roede dijnre cracht
               Uut Syon, om te hebben de macht
               Ende heerscapie, verstaet dit wel,
               Inde middelt dijnre viande". Wie es dit el   1110
               Dan Marie, soet es in scine,
               Dijn gheesele ende dijn ewige pine?
               Si heefti alle dijn macht benomen.
               Wat doetstu hier?

ij VIANT   Wi moestender comen.
               Wi en dorsten Lucifer niet verhoren;   1115
               Hi es te wreet.

i VIANT   Ic seyt te voren.
               Maer watti seit, dat moet gehoort sijn.
               Hi sal nu overlic seere gestoort sijn.
               Wie sal voer hem nu dorren lien?

ij VIANT   Laet ons van achter in slupen besien,   1120
               Hi sal wel weeten hoet hier vaert.

MICHAEL   Ghi helsce honden, trect ongespaert
               Inden afgront dijnre forneyse;
               Want Jhesus Christus heeft bracht te peise
               Adaems mesdaet met sinen bloede,   1125
               Ende Maria mids haren oetmoede

               Terribilis ut castrorum acies.
               That means frightening, mind my words,
               Just like a castle or a bulwark.   1090
               For whom would she be terrifying except for you,
               As you are her enemy? Be off with you!

FIRST FIEND   Alas, alas!
               Leave off, Michael you're hurting me,
               You are too strong for us.

MICHAEL   God also said
               In Genesis that she would harshly   1095
               Crush your head under her feet.
               And that's justice: even though Eve through your trick broke
               God's commands, all that was put right
               Because of the nobility of the Virgin Maria,
               Who is for us, you must admit,   1100
               A mother of salvation, it's clear as glass.
               Isaiah also writes,
               In the tenth chapter, and clearly says
               'From Jesse a rod shall flower.'
               And also David says in the Psalms   1105
               In the person of the Father this word:
               'The Lord shall send the rod of your strength
               From Syon, in order that you have the power
               And the authority, notice this well,
               In the middle of your enemies.' Who else is this   1110
               But Maria, that is apparent,
               Your scourge and your eternal punishment?
               She has taken away all your power.
               What are you doing here?

SECOND FIEND   We had to come.
               We didn't dare disobey Lucifer;   1115
               He is far too cruel.

FIRST FIEND   I've said this before.
               What he says must be obeyed.
               He will now be terribly angry.
               Who will dare to go back to him?

SECOND FIEND   Even if we try to creep in at the back   1120
               He will know what's happened here.

MICHAEL   You devilish hounds, go back at once
               Into the abyss of your furnace;
               For Jesus Christ has reconciled
               Adam's crime with his blood,   1125
               And Maria in her humility

Es mechtich, wie haer sal roepen ane,
Alle u crachten te wederstane.
Op! rasch van hier! en ruymt de ste.

BEIDE   Amy! Amy! ghi brect ons de le.   1130
Des moet de leede duvel wouwen,
Die ons dit bierken dus heeft gebrouwen.
Al quamen alle de duvels met my,
En commer nemmermeer soe by,
Al gave my Lucifer oec dbevel.   1135

ij VIANT   Soe en salic oec, dat wetic wel.
Bue! hue! wech! wech!

Selete. Hier sal God spreken,
van boven oft onder, soe men
wilt, tot sinen hemelscen heere.

GOD   Marteleren, ingelen ende patrierken,
Maeghden, ghi heilegen, comt, hulpt mi werken
Een werc dat my voer al behaecht.   1140
Den kerstene gelove om een versterken,
Willic, invierich, mit hittegen vlerken,
Hier halen miere moeder, der suvere maecht.
Haer bi sijn mi soe wel behaecht,
Dat icse inden ewigen vrede   1145
Wil halen. Des wort u allen gewaecht,
Dats mijn begeerte. U niet en verdraecht,
Ghi en moet emmer trecken mede.
Ic wilse inder glorien stede
Stellen en doen haer spannen crone,   1150
Daer mense ewelic aenbede,
Doer die minne, die si mi dede,
Bi mi ende minen vader scone.
Dit willic dat haer gescie te loone.

i INGEL   Uwen heilegen wille, Here, moet becliven.   1155
Uwe gracie moet volstentich bliven
Op hem allen, die u minnen.
Lof moets gescien in u bedriven!
Van ewen tot ewen, in mannen, in wiven,
Moet men u gracie te vollen versinnen.   1160
Lof rise der hoger coninginnen,
Die u dus duegdelic heeft gedient,
Dat alle ingelen ende seraphinnen
Bliscap inde glorie gewinnen,

	Is powerful enough, to resist all your forces,	
	For the sake of all those who appeal to her.	
	Go! Be quick about it! Get out of here!	
BOTH FIENDS	Alas! Alas! You're breaking our limbs.	1130
	Let the devil himself suffer for it,	
	He who has brewed us this beer.	
	Even if all the devils came with me,	
	I will never come here again,	
	Even if Lucifer ordered me.	1135
SECOND FIEND	I won't either, I'm sure of that!	
	Alas! Alas! Let's go!	

Selete. God will speak here to his heavenly host, from
above or below, as you like.

GOD	Martyrs, angels and patriarchs,	
	Virgins, and you saints, come help me achieve a labour	
	That pleases me above all else.	1140
	To strengthen the Christian faith,	
	I want, intensely, with burning wings,	
	To bring here my mother, the pure virgin.	
	To be with her pleases me so much,	
	That I would like to bring her into eternal peace.	1145
	It's made clear to all of you,	
	That that is my desire. Do not resist it,	
	You will all have to be my helpers.	
	I want to sit her in the place of glory	
	And have her wear the crown,	1150
	So that she will forever be adored,	
	For the love that she showed me,	
	For me and also my noble father.	
	And this I want to be her reward.	
FIRST ANGEL	Your sacred will, lord, must be fulfilled.	1155
	May your grace remain constantly	
	With all those who love you.	
	May you be praised in all your works!	
	For ever and ever by women and men	
	May your mercy be fully understood.	1160
	Praise be to the noblest queen	
	Who has served you so virtuously,	
	That all angels and all seraphim	
	Will rejoice in the glory	

	Die ghi haer gunstelic toent als vrient.	1165
	Dies wort haer lof bi ons vercombient.	
ij INGEL	O hoge, vol gracien, sonder blame,	
	Geminde, eersame,	
	Daer God dese minne hier om doet risen.	
	Gebenedijt si dinen name,	1170
	Want selke vrame	
	En wilde hi noit aen niemen bewisen.	
	Aldus en machmen niet volprisen	
	U hoechde groot gebenedijt.	
	Du sels ons laven als voetsel der spisen	1175
	Ende verjolisen	
	Al themelsce heer verre ende wijt.	
	U lof moet groyen talder tijt.	
CONFESSOR	O hoge vercorne, salige bruut,	
	Comt bi ons in ons deduut.	1180
	Ghi werter ontfaen met selker eren,	
	Dat alle lovere, gers ende cruut,	
	Als tongen van clerken gaven geluut,	
	Si en souden den lof niet connen vermeren.	
	Die u es nakende sonder verseren.	1185
MARIA	O uutvercorne brueders, het naect	
	Seere minen ynde, ic hebt verstaen.	
	Gereetscap waer u goet gemaect,	
	Want sciere met my sal sijn gedaen.	
	Bereit de palme, daer seldi met gaen	1190
	Vor minen fiertere, God deet bevelen.	
	Mijns loofs hebbic gehoort vermaen	
	Hoge, van allen saligen keelen;	
	Oec horic de yngle singen en spelen	
	Soe suete, dat minen geest verlinct	1195
	Hier langer te sine, want sonder helen,	
	Hi wilt daermen dus suetelic sinct.	
	Och, lieve brueders, ic biddu, brinct	
	Alle gereetscap; in dat jolijt	
	Soe wilt mijn geest, het dunct hem tijt.	1200
PETER	Vrouwe, dats al te voren versien,	
	En moeyt u des noch cleyn noch groot,	
	Betrout ons dies; u sal gescien	
	Na ons vermuegen, soet u es noot,	
	Ent Gode gelieft, die ons geboot.	1205

	Which you so generously show her in loyalty.	1165
	That's why we proclaim her praise.	
SECOND ANGEL	O noble lady, full of grace, without blame,	
	You are beloved and honoured	
	For whose sake God shows this love.	
	Blessed be your name	1170
	For honour such as this	
	He has not ever bestowed on anyone.	
	Thus we cannot praise enough	
	Your supreme blessedness.	
	You will nourish us with the choicest food	1175
	And cause to rejoice	
	All the heavenly host far and wide.	
	May your praise grow for ever more.	
CONFESSOR	O noble, excellent, blessed bride	
	Come and join us in our joy.	1180
	You will be received with such honour	
	That if all leaves, grasses and herbs,	
	Could speak as if with tongues of scholars	
	They could not enrich your praise,	
	Which awaits you without any flaw.	1185
MARIA	O beloved brothers, my end	
	Now approaches fast, I well know.	
	It would be good if you could prepare,	
	For soon my time will be finished.	
	Prepare the palm with which you go	1190
	Before my bier, as God commanded.	
	I have heard my praise declared	
	In heaven, by all blessed voices;	
	And I hear the angels sing and play	
	So sweetly that my spirit grieves	1195
	To stay here longer, for quite openly	
	My spirit wants to be with those sweet songs.	
	O my dear brothers, I pray you make	
	All preparations; my spirit longs	
	To join that rapture: the time has come.	1200
PETER	Lady, all is prepared,	
	Don't be concerned for anything,	
	Depend on us for this; it will all happen	
	As you need as far as in us lies,	
	And as pleases God, who commanded us.	1205

GOD *tot sijnder moeder*   Comt, mijn weerde duve reyne,
                             Comt, ic werde u troest gemeyne
                             Ewich voort an sonder vermyen.
                             Comt, mijn uutvercorne greyne,
                             Comt, vol gracien bat en fonteyne,   1210
                             Daer ic af dwoech de sondege bleyne.
                             Comt hier metten gebenedien,
                             Die uwen lof selen belien
                             Voort aen met haren salegen monden.
                             Comt inder hoechster melodien,   1215
                             Comt te mijnder rechter syen,
                             Comt in alder yngelen verblien,
                             Ter groter bliscap sonder gronden.
                             Comt, ghi wort de hoechste vonden
                             Van alder ganser werelt wijt.   1220
                             Comt, uutvercorne, het dunct mi tijt.
MARIA   Lof, Here, ic hebbe u stemme gehoort.
                             Nu en willic hier niet langer leven.
                             Lof, kint, dat ghire mi toe vercoort,
                             Bi u dus hoge te sine verheven!   1225
                             Mijn brueders, nu wilt my orlof geven
                             Van hier te treckene, wy moeten sceyen;
                             Mijn sone ende alle sijn suet aencleven
                             Met groter bliscap na my beyen.
JAN   Vrouwe, soe wil hi u geleyen,   1230
                             Die Here vol alder crachten crachte,
                             Ende als ghi sijt ter weerdicheyen,
                             Soe doet ons, Vrouwe, in u gedachte.
MARIA   Orlof, vriende, die mijns hier wachte
                             Hebt genomen, lof rise u lien!   1235
                             Orlof, Jan, die mijns kints machte
                             In visioene hebt oversien!
                             Orlof, Symoen Peter, bi wien
                             Dit weerde geselscap wert bestiert!
                             Orlof, Andries, die mijns wout plien,   1240
                             Ende mi in minnen hebt gehantiert!
                             Orlof, Jacop, wel gemaniert
                             Soe hebdi u gedregen tot my!
                             Orlof, Pauwels, die ongeviert
                             Mi altoes stont getrouwelic by!   1245
                             Philippus, Matheeus, orlof! waer sy?
                             U duecht en es tot mi niet cleene.
                             Orlof, mijn vriende, verre en by!

GOD *to his mother:* Come my beloved, pure dove,
Come, I will be all your consolation
For ever more without stint.
Come my precious pearl,
Come, source and fountain full of grace, 1210
From whom I washed all sinful stain.
Come here with all the blessed,
Who will proclaim your praise
From now on with their blessed voices.
Come into the sweetest melody, 1215
Come to my right side,
Come where all angels rejoice,
To the greatest and everlasting bliss.
Come, you will prove to be the highest
Of all the whole of creation. 1220
Come beloved, the hour has come.

MARIA Praise, Lord, I have heard your voice.
Now I do not want to live here any longer.
Praise, child, that you have chosen me
To be raised up so high with you! 1225
My brothers, now give me permission
To go from here; we must part;
My son and all his sweet companions
Await me in great happiness.

JOHN Lady, he wants to accompany you, 1230
The Lord who is mightiest of all,
And when you're seated in your worthiness
Lady, keep us in your memory.

MARIA Farewell my friends, who took upon you
To protect me, praise be to you. 1235
Farewell, John, who saw in visions
All the powers of my child.
Farewell, Simon Peter, by whom
This worthy company was guided.
Farewell, Andrew, who cared for me, 1240
And served me with love.
Farewell, Jacob, irreproachably
You have behaved towards me!
Farewell, Paul, who constantly
Was always faithfully by my side! 1245
Philip, Matthew, farewell! Where are you?
For your virtue you are precious to me!
Farewell my friends, far and near by!

Soe groten bliscap haddic noit gheene.
Mijn geest wilt wech.

Hier sterft si.

JAN   Nu niemen en weene,   1250
          Want sagent de Joden, die ons benyen,
          Si mochten seggen, hoort wes ic meene,
          Wy daden dat wi hen castien,
          Dat es na der scriftueren belien,
          "Dat nyemen en sal ontsien de doot";   1255
          Dus mochtense seggen, sonder vermyen,
          Wi daden datmen hem verboot.
PETER   Tes waerheit bloet; maer laet ons beden,
          Ende loven den Here met bliden sinne
          Dat hi in selker weerdicheden   1260
          Bi hem wilt halen ons lieve vriendinne;
          Haer siele die vaert ten hemel inne.

              Hier selen dapostelen alle cnielen
              oft si haer gebet lasen ende de. . .

GOD   Sijt willecome, salige uutvercorne,
          Die welke in des viants toorne
          Verdiendet in gracien mids uwer duecht,   1265
          Dat ic van u wert de geboorne,
          Om [te] verlossene de verloorne.
          Sijt willecome te mijnre vruecht!
          Ghi hebt begrepen, reyn suver juecht,
          In uwen lichame suete ende reene   1270
          Die groote der werelt, dies ghi u muecht
          Verbliden, want al in u verhuecht,
          Dat ic ye sciep, tsi groot of cleene.
          Willecome, mijn uutvercorne alleene!
          . . . .
SINT JAN Mijn brueders, ter Gods weerdicheyen   1275
          Laet ons den lichaem doen bereyen
          Na sijn betaemte, alsoe men pliet
          Na onser wet.
PETER   Ghi, bruederen, siet,
          Dese drie maegden die selen gaen
          Den lichaem visiteren, wilt verstaen,   1280
          Alsoet costume es, ende cleeden

I never knew such great joy.
My spirit longs to leave.

Here she dies.

JOHN   No one must weep,   1250
For if the envious Jews saw this
They could say, listen to me,
That we are doing that for which we chastise them.
In this way we verify the scriptures:
That no one will fear death.   1255
Thus they could say, without doubt,
That we did what was forbidden to them.

PETER   That's certainly true; but let us pray,
And praise the Lord with joyful hearts
That he in such worthiness   1260
Will take to him our dear friend;
Her soul will journey into heaven.

Here all the Apostles will kneel down as if they were
saying their prayers and the...

GOD   Be welcome, blessed beloved,
Who to the fury of the devil,
Deserves in grace, because of your virtue   1265
That I was born from you,
To see free those who were lost.
Be welcome, to my glory!
You have contained, beautiful pure young woman,
In your sweet, unblemished body   1270
The greatest power in the world, therefore you may
Rejoice, for everything takes pleasure in you,
Everything I ever created be it great or small.
Be welcome my sole beloved!
. . . .

SAINT JOHN   My brothers, let's now prepare   1275
In honour of God, this body
As is proper, and as we are accustomed
According to our law.

PETER   You brothers, look:
These three virgins will now go
To attend to the body, you understand,   1280
As is the custom and they will dress

               Na haer behoefte ende bereeden,
               Altoes om haren lof vermeren;
               Seldi niet, kindere?

i MAECHT   Jawi, ghi heren,
               Wi selen geerne, eest u bequamelic,   1285
               Ons beste doen. Si was soe tamelic,
               Dat wijs u weten danc van dien,
               Dat wise geloeft sijn onder ons drien
               Te visenteerne. Wildijs betrouwen,
               Wi doent seer geerne.

PAUWELS   Jawi, jouffrouwen,   1290
               En bidden u om u hulpe van desen,
               Want claer, het sal vergouden wesen
               Vanden Here, daert al aen steet,
               Des sidi seker.

ij MAECHT   Wy sijn al bereet,
               U begeerte wort sciere gedaen,   1295
               Tot haren love wi gaent bestaen;
               Dies wilt vertrecken, ghi mans gemeene,
               Ende laet ons bider maecht alleene.

                        Selete. Die wile sullen sise bereyen.

iij MAECHT   Ghi brueders, waer si? ic coem u seggen:
               Comt, hulpt ons inden fierter leggen   1300
               Dese heilege maegt, vol gracien groot,
               Geen dwaen noch cuusscen en was haer noot,
               Dies moet haer ewigen lof gescien.
               Geen menselic ogen en mochten aensien
               Haer claerheit, die uut haer rayede, scinen.   1305
               Wi en sijn niet weert, des wi ons pinen,
               Dat wi haer meer genaken souwen;
               Comt ons te hulpen.

ANDRIES   Wi selen. Ghi vrouwen
               Ontdoet den fierter. Alsoe— daer—
               Legt suetelic neder.

PETER   Si en es niet swaer.   1310
               Dat was gedaen met cleinder pine.
               Lof hebs de Here!

	And prepare it as is necessary,	
	All that to give her greater honour;	
	Won't you children?	
FIRST VIRGIN	So we will, lords,	
	We shall gladly and if you desire it,	1285
	Do our best. She was so chaste	
	That we are very grateful you,	
	That we are allowed, we three,	
	To attend to her. If you will trust us,	
	We'll gladly do it.	
PAUL	Indeed, ladies,	1290
	We pray you for your help in this,	
	For certainly it will be rewarded	
	By the Lord, the foundation of all:	
	Be sure of that.	
SECOND VIRGIN	We are all ready.	
	Your desire will soon be fulfilled:	1295
	We'll do it out of love for her.	
	So take your leave, all you men,	
	And leave us alone with this lady.	

Selete. Meanwhile they will prepare her.

THIRD VIRGIN	Brothers, where are you? I've come to say:	
	Come and help us lay in the coffin	1300
	This holy virgin, full of grace.	
	No washing or cleaning was necessary,	
	May she be honoured forever.	
	No human eyes could behold	
	The bright clarity radiating from her.	1305
	We're not worthy, in doing this,	
	To be even closer to her.	
	Please come and help us.	
ANDREW	We will. You ladies	
	Open the coffin. So— there—	
	Put her down softly.	
PETER	She's not heavy.	1310
	It was easy to do that.	
	Praised be the Lord!	

JAN	Luuct toe de scrine.
	Alsoe. En laetse ons niet seer quellen.
	Brinct de bare.
BERTELMEUS	Hulptser op stellen.
	De bare es hier. Nu—daer—alsuetelic 1315
	Setse neder.
PAUWELS	Het valt al guetelic,
	Dat wi werken te harer vrame.
	Gebenedijt si dies haer name,
	Elken tot enen exemple bekint,
	Dat alle duecht uut hare begint. 1320
	Daer leitse eerbaer. Den hogen vrede
	Vloye haer toe! Waer willen wire mede?
	Jan, doet ons bediet van desen
	Waer sal den lichaem begraven wesen?
GOD	Mijn bruers, dat salic u gewagen: 1325
	Den suveren lichaem seldi dragen
	In dat dal, hoort wes ic meene,
	Van Josephat sonder versagen.
	Ghi selt daer vinden, reyn int behagen,
	Een nyeu graf, suet, suver en reene. 1330
	Maer blijft voort biden lichame gemeene,
	Tot leden sijn der dage drie
	Ende ic mijn gracie u verleene,
	Dat ghi verstaen selt, groot en cleene,
	Wat ic begeere dat voort gescie. 1335
	Soe edelen lichaem en was nye,
	Noch soe vol gracien van groten bedie,
	Ende nemmermeer voort geen sijn en mach
	Als dese, daer ic selve in lach.
	Hiermet latic u minen vrede. 1340
	Ic trecke in mijnder glorien stede.
JAN	Lof, Heere, dat u dit geweerde!
	Wes wi vermogen, wort tuwer eren.
PETER	Lof hebt, die ons dit selve vercleerde!
	Lof, Heere, dat u dit geweerde! 1345
PAUWELS	Lof u gescie in hemel ende erde!
	Glorie moet ewich in u vermeeren!
JAN	Lof, Heere, dat u dit geweerde!
	Wes wi vermogen wort tuwer eren,
	Want sonder verkeren 1350
	Soe es u vruecht ende sonder termijn,
	Reyn sonder verseren

JOHN	Now close the coffin.
	So. Let's not disturb her any more.
	Bring the bier.
BARTHOLOMEW	Come, help to lift it.
	The bier is here. Now—there—carefully 1315
	Put her down.
PAUL	It's all going well,
	We're all working for her good.
	Blessed be her name for this,
	Which is known as an example to all,
	That all virtue begins with her. 1320
	There she lies nobly. May great peace
	Flow towards her! Where shall we take her?
	John, now tell us about this,
	Where will the body be buried.
GOD	My brothers, I shall tell you that: 1325
	This chaste body you will carry
	In that valley, listen to my meaning,
	Of Jehosaphat without fear,
	And you shall find there a new grave,
	Beautifully made, sweet and pure and clean. 1330
	But remain now with the body, all of you,
	Till three days will have passed
	And I will give you my grace,
	That you will understand, young and old,
	What I desire should happen next. 1335
	There never was such a noble body
	Nor one full of such exceptional grace,
	And there will never be another
	Such as this, in which I was placed.
	And now I leave you with my peace. 1340
	I will depart to the place of my glory.
JOHN	Praise, Lord, that you did this!
	All that we do is for your honour.
PETER	Praise be, who explained this to us himself!
	Praise, Lord, that you did this! 1345
PAUL	Praise be to you in heaven and on earth!
	May your glory ever increase!
JOHN	Praise, Lord, that you did this!
	All that we do is for your honour,
	For unchanging 1350
	And without end is your glory,
	Pure without blemish

Met uwer leren.
Gedinct dan voort der knechten dijn,
Dat si uus loofs volstentich sijn.   1355

. . . .

PETER   Nemt op de bare, bi goeden avise.
Jan, gaet vore metten palmrise,
Dat de almechtege God ons sant.
Hout, siet, draget in u hant;
Dingel bracht, soet God begeerde,   1360
Uten paradise.

JAN   Bi uwer weerde,
Peter, vrient, het hoort u toe
Te dragene vor mi, ende seg u hoe:
Want doen Ons Here van henen sciet,
Ons allen hi u een herde liet   1365
Ende stelde ons, Peter, in uwer hoeden.
Aldus eest goet dan om gevroeden,
Dat ghi de hoechste sijt van ons allen.
Dus moets u nu de eere gevallen
Dit rijs te dragene na claer bedien   1370
Als ons overste.

PETER   Dan sal niet gescien
Bi rechte, alsic sal seggen, Jan.
Daer es noch veel meer redenen an,
Dat ghijt sculdich te dragen sijt
Ende ewelic ons overste blijt;   1375
Want God ons Here heeft u geseit
In visioene sijn heymelicheit,
Datti noyt te geenre stede
Negenen van ons allen en dede;
Ende oec soe sidi suver en reyne,   1380
Als maegt bekint, dwelc ic meyne,
Dat deser maegt oec wel betame,
Dat hi si suver van lichame,
Die dit edel rijs vorbaer
Vor haer sal dragen.

PAUWELS   Jan, hi seit waer.   1385
Wi begeren in rechter oetmoet,
Dat ghijt nu vor ons allen doet.
Peter heeft wel de redene geproeft:
Met meegden men meegden te eren behoeft.
Dus draecht dat rijs gebenedijt,   1390
Want u betaemt.

According to your doctrine.
Please now remember your servants
That they may steadfastly praise you. 1355

. . . .

PETER   Take up the bier, and take great care.
John, you go first with the palm branch,
Which Almighty God has sent us.
Look, carry it in your hand;
The angel brought it as God desired 1360
From paradise.

JOHN   With your permission,
Peter, my friend, it should be you
Who carries this, not me. I'll tell you why:
For when Our Lord left us here
He left you as our shepherd 1365
And put us, Peter, in your care.
Therefore it's good to remember
That you are superior to us all.
So to you should fall the honour
To carry this branch, that's clear, 1370
As our leader.

PETER   That should not happen
By right, as I will explain, John.
There are many more reasons
Why you should carry this
And continue for ever to be our leader: 1375
For God our Lord has shown you
In visions his revelation,
Which he has never otherwise done
For any of us up to now.
And moreover you are so pure and chaste 1380
Wholly innocent, by which I mean,
That it will please Our Lady
That he be pure in body
Who will carry aloft this noble branch
In her honour.

PAUL   John, he's right. 1385
And we desire respectfully
That now you do this for all of us.
Peter has convincingly established the reason:
One ought to honour virgins with virgins.
So hold aloft this holy branch, 1390
As befits you.

JAN   Ter goeder tijt,
                    Na dat ghire alle met sijt te vreden,
                    Ontfa ict in onderhoricheden.
                    Nu ga wi voort inden selven name,
                    Dat den Here moet sijn bequame.   1395
                    Peter en Pauwels, heft op de bare,
                    Looft alle Gode met stemmen clare.

                                Hier heffense de bare op ende
                                singen: Exit de Egypto. Alleluia.
                                Ende dinglen inden trone selen
                                oec singen ende orglen. Dan
                                comen de Joden als sijt horen,
                                en maken contenancie.

i JODE   Wat rampe es ditte? tuten mi doren?
                    Of droemet mi? wat tes verloren,
                    Al hordictic tot morgen, tes seker sanc;   1400
                    En hoordi niet singen, gebuere?
ij JODE   Ic hore groet geclanc.
                    En weet niet wat mi selven gesciet es,
                    Noch wat dinge dat hieraf dbediet es.
                    Ic ben recht in mi selven vereent;
                    Wat willet wesen, gebuer?
i JODE   En weet wat meent,   1405
                    Som duncket mi orgelen en somtijts snaren,
                    Ende somtijts sanc.

ij JODE   Het sal hem verbaren
                    In ander manieren eer lanc termijn,
                    Dat seldi vinden.
i JODE   Wat maecht oec sijn?
                    Om waer seggen, tes een vremt geveert.   1410
                    Eest boven oft ondere?
ij JODE   Tes meest derweert.
                    Mi lanct te wetene, wat sal gescien
                    Bi deser vruecht.
i JODE   Hoo! ic hebt gesien.
                    Nu weetict meest, dits goet bestel,
                    Het sijn de kerstene, dat merkic wel,   1415
                    Die ginder dus comen tenen versame
                    Al singende, ende bringen den dooden lichame

JOHN
                    Now then
Since you are all content with that
Obediently I'll take up this branch.
Now let us proceed in the same spirit
So that it will please the Lord.   1395
Peter and Paul, lift up the bier,
And all praise God with ringing voices.

    Here they lift up the bier and sing Exit de Egypto. Alleluia.
        And then the angels from the throne will also sing and
                                make music.
  Then the Jews come as they hear this and make a disturbance.

FIRST JEW
    What catastrophe is this? Do my ears deceive me?
Or am I dreaming? Hey! All is lost,
Even if I listen till tomorrow, this singing won't go away: 1400
Don't you hear singing, neighbour?
SECOND JEW
                      I hear an awful lot of noise.
I don't know what's happened to me,
Nor what all this signifies.
I'm really upset about it:
What does all this mean, neighbour?
FIRST JEW
                   I don't know what it means, 1405
Sometimes I think they're playing the organ, and
    sometimes strings,
And sometimes it's singing.
SECOND JEW
                    It'll become clear
In one way or another before long,
As you'll find.
FIRST JEW
            What can it be?
To tell the truth it's a strange event.   1410
Does it come from above or below?
SECOND JEW
                  Mostly from that direction.
I'd really like to know what's going to happen
After all this rejoicing.
FIRST JEW
             Hey, I've got it.
I do know what this is, it's a good thing,
These are the Christians, I'm quite sure,   1415
Who are coming together over there
Singing all the while; they're bringing the dead body

	Vanden wive, die Jhesum droech,	
	Den groten prophete.	
ij JODE	Wi hebbens genoech.	
	Rasscelic lopen wijt doen verstaen	1420
	Den Potestaet; tsal anders vergaen	
	Metten lichame, hebben wijs geval,	
	Dan si wanen.	
i JODE	Dat peynsic dat sal.	
	Wistense onser liede meenen,	
	Al singense nu, si mochten wel weenen	1425
	Eer lanc; wi mochten van haren sange	
	Wel droefheit maken.	
ij JODE	Wi beiden te lange,	
	Eer tvolc versaemt wort int gemeyne,	
	Trijst somwijls lanc.	
i JODE	Te wapenen! te wapenen! groet en cleine!	
	Haestelic, die ons vriende sijt,	1430
	Te wapenen! te wapenen! het es tijt;	
	Oft neen, wi hebbent aenden hals.	
	Te wapenen!	
POTESTAET	Wat maecti gescals!	
	Hoe roepti soe? hoe leelic gebeerdy!	
ij JODE	Waer om, here?	
POTESTAET	Al tfolc verveerdi	1435
	Met uwen gelate. Hoe hebdi u soe?	
	Tloept al te hope!	
i JODE	Lacen, tes van noe,	
	Want en beletti niet de daet,	
	Wi seggen u wel, her Potestaet,	
	Ons allen sal naken veel verdriets.	1440
	Dat wijf dat du dy vermiets	
	Te verberrene, waerse doot,	
	Die draechtmen nu met vrouden groot	
	Te grave, ende meynense met groter weerden	
	Na haer costume gaen doen ter erden.	1445
	Dus, pijndijs niet haestelic te wederstane,	
	Tsal volcomen.	
POTESTAET	Elc sciet wat ane!	
	Deen een jacke, dander een pansier,	
	De derde een huve! Dits goet bestier,	
	Tes juust bespiet, laetse ons omringen,	1450
	Maect battaelgie!	
DOUWERE	Laetse ons bespringen	

	Of the woman who bore Jesus,	
	The great prophet.	
SECOND JEW	That's all we need to know.	
	Let's go quickly and inform	1420

SECOND JEW   That's all we need to know.
Let's go quickly and inform   1420
Our High Priest; if we have our way,
What happens to the body will be different
From what they think.

FIRST JEW   I'm sure that's so.
If they knew the intention of our people
They will be weeping before long, even if they're singing. 1425
Now, we are going to change their song
Into grief.

SECOND JEW   That's taking too long
And before we've got all the people together,
That'll take time too.

FIRST JEW   To arms! To arms! Young and old!
Quickly, all who are our friends,   1430
To arms! To arms! It's time;
If not, we'll suffer for it.
To arms!

HIGH PRIEST   What a racket you're making!
What are you shouting about? Why are you carrying on so?

SECOND JEW Are you asking why, Lord?

HIGH PRIEST   You're scaring everyone   1435
With your goings on. What's it all for?
Look at the crowd coming!

FIRST JEW   It's got to happen,
Because if you don't prevent this,
We're telling you, Lord High Priest,
We're all going to have much grief.   1440
That woman, about whom you were so bold as to say
Should be burned, after she died,
She's now carried, with great honour,
To her grave, and they intend to bury her
With great ceremony, according to their custom.   1445
If you don't quickly make an effort to prevent this
That's exactly what will happen.

HIGH PRIEST   Put on your armour:
One person a jacket, another a harness,
The third a helmet! That's the thing to do.
This was just in time. If they surround us,   1450
Prepare for battle!

THE ELDER   If they rush us

Op daverechte met onsen maetsuwen.
Willense hen weeren, wi selense duwen;
Soe wee hen, datse noyt waren geboren,
Ons wet te cranckene.

ij JODE   Wie geeter voren,   1455
Siet toe, en make hem niet te breet,
Want, serteyn, si sijn seer wreet;
Ic duchte, als wise willen verlasten,
Si sullen ons na ons scaduwe tasten;
Si hebbent som tanderen tiden gedaen,   1460
Dat ic wel weet.

POTESTAET   Ic sal voren gaen
Ende vaense als prince met cloeken moe.
Maer volgt mi corts, en siet wel toe,
Al sijnse wreet, hets al gedwas.
Weerense hen, smyt inden tas,   1465
Dats mijn begeerte. Doet mijn bevelen.
Weest onversaecht.

i JODE   Wel here, wi selen,
Want sterc genoech soe es ons scare.
Datter XXX werven meer ware,
Wi selen hen seylen aen haer boort.   1470
Staet stille bi een, ic hebse gehoort
Si comen, maer nyemen en wil hem ververen
Si blivender alle.

POTESTAET   Laet my gebeeren,
Ic sal vernemen van haren bedrive
Ende wat si meynen. — Segt mi, ketive,   1475
Hoe hebdi u dus? wat moegdi jagen
Met uwen sange? wat bringdi gedragen,
Daer ghi maect dit geveerte mede?
Ghi brinct in roeren al de stede
Ende doet ons allen grote blame.   1480
Wat draechdi daer?

JAN   Den dooden lichame,
Die den eerwerdegen God almechtich
In haer selven besloot warechtich,
Als scepper des hemels ende der erde;
Dien willen wi na haer hoge weerde   1485
Begraven. Wi sijnder toe gestelt
Van Gode almechtich.

We'll hit them from the side with our clubs.
If they try to defend themselves we'll press hard on them;
They'll be sorry that they were ever born,
And broke our laws.

SECOND JEW   Whoever advances,   1455
Be careful; don't lay yourself open,
For surely they're very fierce;
I fear if we want to bring them to bay
They'll try to steal our shadows;
That's what they've done at other times,   1460
I do know that.

HIGH PRIEST   I will go first
And capture them fearlessly, as a prince should,
But follow on my heels, and watch out.
They may look fierce, but it's all empty bluster.
If they fight back, hit them hard,   1465
That's what I want. Do as I say.
Don't be afraid.

FIRST JEW   Sure, Lord, we'll do that,
Because our army is strong enough
Even if they were thirty times as many,
We'll press hard on them.   1470
Stand still all of you; I can hear them;
They're coming, but no one should be frightened,
They'll all perish.

HIGH PRIEST   Give me a moment
I will find out what they're doing
And what they mean by it. — Tell me, scoundrels,   1475
What's your game? What are you after
With your singing? What is it you're carrying
For which you are making this commotion?
You're upsetting the whole town
And you're causing us great trouble.   1480
What exactly are you carrying?

JOHN   The body,
Which at one time harboured
The most noble God Almighty,
The creator of heaven and of earth;
Her we would bury, in accordance with   1485
Her great merit. We have been charged with this
By God Almighty.

POTESTAET   Ic weds, her, ghi en selt
Oft ghi en sijt sterker te wederstane
Dan wy alle. Ic slader hant ane
Als prince, dat ic u calengiere.   1490
Den lichaem wert gedaen te viere,
Sijns ondancs, dies noit pine bestoet
Haer te verheffene.

DOUWERE   Worptse onder voet
Ter blamen van hen, die aldus gecken
Met onser wet.

POTESTAET   Comt, hulptse af trecken,   1495
Worpt inde more de partroeldie,
En slaet al doot dan de ramoeldie.
Ter droever tijt deet hen begonnen.
Smyt inden tas!

ij JODE   Ay lacen! wy en connen.
Ic en weet niet waer si sijn gevaren,   1500
En sier nyemene; mijn ogen staren,
Al waert bi nachte. Recht als den catere,
En weet waer duken.

POTESTAET   Ach water! watere!
Mijn hande verberren mi aende scrine
Van desen like.

DOUWERE   Soe doen de mine,   1505
En sijn veel droger dan een bast;
Si sijnder aen verdorret soe vast,
En canse getrecken uter hitte
Vander fiertere.

i JODE   Wat duvel es ditte!
Benic nu dul? [*dits my onsoete*].   1510
Ic en sie nyemen, ic ligge [*en wroete*]
Al waric een puyt. Dits wonder groot,
Mijn lede sijn swaerder dan een loot.
Achermen! my es in lanc soe swaerdere,
En mach niet op.

i GEBUER   En com er niet naerdere,   1515
Ic sal mij. . .

[Hier ontbreekt in het handschrift een gehele katern,
dus ongeveer 350 verzen.]

HIGH PRIEST	I bet, sir, that you won't	
	Unless you are stronger than all of us	
	And can resist us. I as high priest	
	Will claim this body according to the law.	1490
	This body will be burned,	
	Notwithstanding him, who ever made an effort	
	To elevate her.	
THE ELDER	Overpower them	
	And blame those, who thus mock	
	Our law.	
HIGH PRIEST	Come, help to pull the body down,	1495
	Throw this rubbish into the mud	
	And then kill the rabble with her.	
	It was a stupid thing to do anyway.	
	Chuck it away.	
SECOND JEW	Alas! We can't do it.	
	I don't know where they've gone to;	1500
	I can't see anyone; I'm straining my eyes	
	As if at night. Dazzled like a cat,	
	I don't know where to hide.	
HIGH PRIEST	I need water! Water!	
	The coffin of this corpse is burning	
	My hands.	
THE ELDER	And so are mine.	1505
	They're much drier than bark;	
	And they're so firmly stuck to it,	
	That I can't pull them from the heat	
	Of the coffin.	
FIRST JEW	What the devil is this!	
	Am I going mad? [This really hurts.]	1510
	I can't see anyone, I'm lying here [wriggling about]	
	As if I were a frog. This is scary,	
	My limbs feel heavier than a lead weight.	
	Alas! They are getting heavier and heavier.	
	I can't get up.	
FIRST NEIGHBOUR	I won't go any nearer to it,	1515
	I shall . . .	

[Here a whole quire is missing from the manuscript,
about 350 lines.]

En hebt geen twivel aen mijn woort,
Maer doet dit wonder voort vermaen
En wilt in gansen gelove volstaen.

THOMAES *cnielende*   Lof, ombesmette
        Reyn violette,   1520
        Maria Vrouwe,
        Maegt ende moeder,
        Daer ons behoeder
        In rusten wouwe.
        Uut shemels douwe,   1525
        Reyn kersouwe,
        Sidi gegroyt
        Tot onsen behouwe,
        Altoes getrouwe
        Met ons gemoyt.   1530
        Ic biddu, fonteyne, die overvloyt
        Van gracien, reyne maegt Marie,
        Vergeeft mi, want my seere vernoyt,
        Dat ic bi u niet en was te tye.
        God kint, dat ics mi seere vermye   1535
        Vor alle mijn brueders, groet en smal.
        Doch willic bi hen gaen, wats gescie,
        En doen soe dingel my beval.
        Ic hopicse tsamen vinden sal.

                                                 Selete.

PETER   O Here, alder menscen confoort,   1540
        Wat vruechden mach inden hemel risen?
        Ic hebt seer lange wile gehoort.
        Lof alder creatueren confoort,
        Tes al in vrouden, suyt ende noort,
        Al themelsce heer wilt verjolisen.   1545
        O Here, alder menscen confoort,
        Wat vruechden mach inden hemel risen?
        Wat maecht bedien?

JAN   Tes een bewisen
        Van groten saken en boven natuere,
        Hoordijs niet, brueders?

PAUWELS   Jaic, wel ter cuere.   1550
        Jan, ic hebber verwonderen in,
        Wat wesen mach.

	And you mustn't doubt my word,	
	Go and proclaim this miracle	
	And remain steadfast in honest belief.	
THOMAS *kneeling*	Praise immaculate	
	Pure violet,	1520
	Lady Maria,	
	Virgin and mother,	
	In whom our protector	
	Chose to dwell.	
	From heaven's dew,	1525
	Pure marguerite,	
	You have grown	
	To our benefit,	
	Always faithful	
	Concerned for us.	1530
	I pray you, fountain, which overflows	
	With grace, pure virgin Maria,	
	Forgive me, for I am sorely grieved,	
	That I did not reach you in time.	
	God knows that I am very ashamed	1535
	Before all my brothers, young and old.	
	Yet whatever the outcome I want to join them,	
	And to what the angel commanded.	
	I hope I shall find them gathered together.	

Selete.

PETER	O Lord, comfort of all people,	1540
	What is this rejoicing in heaven?	
	I have heard this of old.	
	Praise, comfort of all creatures,	
	All is in joy, south and north,	
	All the heavenly host is rejoicing.	1545
	O Lord, comfort of all people,	
	What is this rejoicing in heaven?	
	What can this mean?	
JOHN	It is evidence	
	Of great matters beyond nature,	
	Can't you hear it, brothers?	
PAUL	Yes, I can, very well.	1550
	John, I greatly wonder,	
	What this may be.	

ANDRIES   God geefs gewin
                  Alle sonderen ter sielen vramen,
                  Oft Gode behaecht.
JAN   Dies seggen wi amen
                  Met goeder herten, soet redene si.   1555
                  Geminde brueders, elc hoort na mi:
                  Mi tuycht den sin claerlic van desen
                  Dat Maria sal sijn verresen,
                  Met siele met live, als nu ter tijt,
                  Ende vaert int hemelsce jolijt   1560
                  Bi haren geminden sone vercoren.
                  Dit es de vruecht die wi hier horen,
                  Daer en hebbic genen twivel in.
PAUWELS   Tmach soe wel wesen.
JAN   Ten es niet min.
THOMAES   Mijn brueders, Gods vrede si tewiger tijt   1565
                  Bi ons! Want ghi nu druckich sijt,
                  Soe comic tot uwen troeste, eylaes!
                  Al merric lange.
JAN   Ey, Thomaes! Thomaes!
                  Lieve uutvercorne, geminde broeder,
                  U mach wel rouwen, dat ghi ons moeder,   1570
                  Marie, die reyne suver maecht,
                  Van deser werelt niet sceyden en saecht;
                  Want noyt gesien en was vor desen
                  Deerliker, sueter doot.
THOMAES   Ic en mochter niet wesen,
                  Lieve brueders, ic was in Yndia   1575
                  Na Gods bevel; ic bidde gena
                  U allen te samen als van dien.
                  Niet min ic sal u claer bedien,
                  Wat ic gesien hebbe ende verstaen
                  Onder wegen.
PETER   Doets ons vermaen,   1580
                  Lieve Thomaes. Om cort recoort,
                  Wi hebben soe groten vruecht gehoort
                  Van sange ende melodiosen acoorde,
                  Dat noyt mensce tsgelijcs en hoorde.
                  Dus staen wi hier in twivel groot,   1585
                  Wat wesen mach.
THOMAES   Tes sonder genoet,
                  Want, sonder twivel, om cort verclaren,
                  Maria die es te hemel gevaren

ANDREW   May God give benefit
To all sinners for their souls' profit
If it pleases him.
JOHN   To that we say Amen
With all our hearts, as is right.   1555
Dear brothers, now listen to me.
I am wholly certain in my mind
That Maria will ascend
With soul and body, at this moment,
And progress toward the heavenly joy   1560
Beloved by her beloved son.
This is the joy that we now hear,
I do not doubt it all.
PAUL   That must be it.
JOHN   It can't be anything else.
THOMAS   My brothers, May God's peace be with us   1565
For ever! Because you are now sad
I come to console you,
Even if I am come late, alas!
JOHN   Ah, Thomas! Thomas!
Dearly beloved, cherished brother,
You will be sad, that you did not see   1570
Our mother Maria, that pure chaste virgin,
Leave this world behind;
For never before has been seen
A more moving, sweeter death.
THOMAS   I could not be here,
Dear brothers, I was in India,   1575
As God commanded; I beg forgiveness
For that from all of you together.
Nevertheless I shall explain clearly
What I have seen and understood
As I came along.
PETER   Do tell us,   1580
Dear Thomas. In short,
We have heard such great joy
With singing and melodious harmony
Which no human being has ever heard.
So we stand here full of doubt,   1585
What this may mean.
THOMAS   It's without parallel
Because, to sum up,
Maria has journeyed to heaven

	Met siele, met live. Hout dit gewaerlic.	
	Ic hebt gesien, gehoort soe claerlijc.	1590
	Oec eest mi mondelinge geseit;	
	Ende, om te meerder sekerheit,	
	Es my haer gordelken gegeven	
	Van den ingle. Dus wilt begeven	
	Alle twivel ende dolinge hier ave,	1595
	Ende laet ons tsamen gaen ten grave,	
	Eer dat wi voerder mormereren.	
JAN	Lof God almechtich, Here der heren!	
	Hoe wonderlic es u werc om gronden!	
	Thomaes, ic hulpt u selve orconden,	1600
	Dat dit haer gordel was, sonder waen,	
	Datse te dragen plach.	
PETER	Laet ons dan gaen	
	Ten grave, sonder langer beye.	
ANDRIES	Tes cleerlic soe. Want de Here seye	
	Hi wilde haer doen selc weerdichede	1605
	Gelijc als hi hem selven dede;	
	Ende oec betaemt haer alder eere;	
	Dus nyemen en twivele.	
PETER	Met corten keere,	
	Laet ons beginnen dit graf tontdeckene;	
	Soe weten wi claer vanden verweckene.	1610
	Gods gracie en mach geen werc ontswichten.	
	De erde es af, hulpt mi af lichten	
	Van deser scrine suetelic den sceele.	
	Siet, esser wat ynne?	
PAUWELS	Neent, luttel noch vele	
	Van haren lichame; lof hebs de Here,	1615
	Diese verwecte!	
JAN	Hier sijn haer cleere,	
	Suver en scone noch bleven int graf.	
	Nu laet ons Gode dancken hieraf,	
	Datti ons dese miracle groot	
	Heeft willen bewisen.	
PETER	Ende hemels broet	1620
	Es hier oec in, mijn broeders, besiet,	
	Op dat ons en soude twivelen niet.	
	Dies moet hi ewigen lof gewinnen!	
ANDRIES	Ghi brueders, comt, siet alle hier binnen,	
	Dat nyemen en twivele in sinen waen	1625
	Des wercs, dat God hier heeft gedaen	

	In soul and body. Take this for true.	
	I have seen it and heard it quite clearly,	1590
	And I have been told it as well;	
	And, to make it more real,	
	I have been given her little girdle	
	By the angel. Therefore let go	
	Of all doubt and uncertainty upon this,	1595
	And let us go together to the grave	
	Without creating further doubt.	

JOHN   Praise God Almighty, Lord of Lords!
Your works are miraculous to grasp!
Thomas, I will help you to testify,   1600
That this was her girdle without doubt.
Which she used to wear.

PETER   Let us go then
To the grave, without more tarrying.

ANDREW   It must be so. For the Lord says
He wants to raise her to the same extent   1605
As he did for himself;
And indeed all honour befits her:
No one doubts that.

PETER   Quickly then,
Let us begin to open this grave.
Then we will be certain about this resurrection.   1610
With God's grace no work is too burdensome.
We've cleared the soil, help me to lift
Gently the lid of this shrine.
Look, is there anything there?

PAUL   There is no trace
Of her body; praise be the Lord   1615
Who resurrected her!

JOHN   Here are her clothes,
Which remain clean and pure in the grave.
Now let us thank God for this,
That he has wanted to show us
This great miracle.

PETER   And there is also   1620
Heavenly bread, my brothers, look,
So that we would not doubt.
Therefore God must be forever praised!

ANDREW   You brothers, come, look inside this,
So that no one will have any doubt in his mind   1625
Of the work that God has wrought here

Bi siere mogentheit, ende wat eren
Hi sijnder moeder bewijst.

BERTELMEEUS   Heere alder heren!
Hoe riect dit graf! Alsulken virtuut
En gaf ter werelt nie specie no cruut,   1630
Noch sulken guer als hier uut slaet.

MATHIJS   O moeder, nu sijt ons advocaet
Voer uwen sone, die u in desen
Soe hogen gracie hier heeft bewesen;
Dies moet u ewigen lof toe vloyen.   1635
Laet u te biddene niet vernoyen
Vor alle sondaren, tsi cleyn of groet,
Die u aanroepen in harer noet.

JAN   Lof, lieflike bruut des vaders gemint!
Lof, moeder, die hebt gebaert dit kint,   1640
Maegt blivende, des Heilichs Geests vriendinne!
Lof, suete fonteyne, daeruut dat rint,
Soe ons de heilege Scriftuere ontbint,
Dese iij rivieren groet van gewinne!
Lof hebt, die hemel ende erde hadt inne,   1645
Alsoet den Here gelieven wouwe!
Lof, tabernacle, daer God sijn minne
In goet met gracien, tonsen bekinne.
Wi loven u alle, jonge ende ouwe,
Lof, lieflike, suete, suver kersouwe!   1650

ANDRIES   Lof, suete, eerwerdege balsemiere,
Reyn van bestiere,
Werdich al loofs in ewiger tijt;
Wel riekende specie, reyn goedertiere,
Diet al verchiere   1655
Bi uwen sone gebenedijt!
Lof, druve, die vol van gracien sijt!

PETER   Lof, cederen rijs, dat bloyende blijt
Int hoge jolijt,
Boven alle bomen gestade.   1660
Lof uus, leitsterre der werelt wijt:
Sonder respijt
Leert ons treden de hemelsce trade.
Lof, die inder natueren grade
Die Gods genade   1665
Verdiendet tonser alder vramen!
Want mids uwer oetmoedegher dade
Gesciet de scade

	In his great power, and the honour	
	Which he shows his mother.	
BARTHOLOMEW	Lord of Lords!	
	How fragrant is this grave! No spice nor herb	
	In all the world has such perfume,	1630
	Nor such fragrance as comes from here.	
MATTHEW	O mother, now be our advocate	
	Before your son, who has in this	
	Shown you such wondrous grace;	
	Eternal praise may come to you.	1635
	Please do not cease to pray	
	For all sinners, great and small,	
	Who call upon you in their need.	
JOHN	Praise, lovely bride, beloved of the father!	
	Praise mother who has borne this child,	1640
	Eternal Virgin, dear to the Holy Spirit!	
	Praise, sweet fountain, from which flows	
	That which Holy Scripture reveals,	
	These three rivers of great worth!	
	Praise be, who was in heaven and earth,	1645
	As it pleased the Lord!	
	Praise tabernacle into which God	
	Poured his love with grace, as we believe.	
	We all love you young and old.	
	Praise, lovely, fair, pure marguerite.	1650
ANDREW	Praise sweet tree of balsam,	
	Pure in nature,	
	Worthy of all praise for ever;	
	Fragrant spice, pure in kind	
	Which enhances everything	1655
	Through your blessed Son!	
	Praise, grape, which is full of grace!	
PETER	Praise cedar branch, always in blossom	
	In great joy,	
	Steadily above all other trees.	1660
	Praise to you, lodestar of all the world:	
	Without ceasing	
	Teach us to tread the heavenly road.	
	Praise, who in nature's plan	
	Deserved	1665
	God's grace to our benefit!	
	For because of your humility	
	The damage is done	

	Den viant, dat wi te boven quamen	
	Van onser quetseliker blamen!	1670
JAN	Nu laet ons tsamen, alsoet betaemt,	
	Den Here dancken siere melder gracie,	
	De welke ons allen dus heeft versaemt,	
	Elc onversien, in corter spacie.	
	Wi moeten dit dal der tribulacie	1675
	Noch wandelen na des Heren gebien.	
	Dus niemen en heb geen mormeracie:	
	Den wille Gods die moet gescien;	
	Sijn gracie sal ons wel versien.	
PETER	Orlof, lieve brueders, wi moeten sceyen,	1680
	Niet langere en mogen wi tsamen bliven.	
PAUWELS	Wi moeten gaen Gods wege bereyen.	
	Orlof, lieve brueders, wi moeten sceyen.	
JAN	Elc bidde den Here met weerdicheyen,	
	Dat ons sijn gracie wille verstiven.	1685
PETER	Orlof, lief brueders, wi moeten sceyen,	
	Niet langer en mogen wi tsamen bliven.	
ANDRIES	God doe becliven	
	Sijn hoge gracie in onsen werke,	
	Datter sijn heilege gelove bi sterke	1690
	Tot alder menscen salicheden.	
	Adieu! dits wech, blijft alle in vreden!	
	Amen.	

DE NA PROLOGHE

Eerbaer notable, die hebt verstaen	
Dbewijs van onser materien soet,	
Al hebben wijt slichtelijc gedaen,	1695
Wi bidden u allen, elc neemt vor goet.	
Dits dleste spel, sijt dies wel vroet,	
Van .vij. blijscapen principalen,	
Die Marien vol der oetmoet	
Gescieden ter werelt, om cort verhalen.	1700
Dierst was: hoe God liet neder dalen	
Gabriel, uut reynen gedachte,	
Om ons te lossene uter qualen,	
Die haer de salige bootscap brachte.	
Dander was: hoe hy in kerstnachte	1705
Van haer, als mensce wordt geboren	
Tot vramen den mensceliken geslachte,	
Als moeder ende maegt, in sviants toren.	

	To the enemy, and it rescued us	
	From our wounding sinfulness.	1670
JOHN	Now let us together, as is proper,	
	Thank the Lord for his benign grace	
	Which has brought us all together,	
	Unexpected for each of us, and quickly.	
	We will still have to roam through	1675
	This vale of tribulation as the Lord commands.	
	So let no one protest against this:	
	God's will must prevail,	
	His grace shall watch over us.	
PETER	Farewell, dear brothers, we must part,	1680
	No longer can we stay together.	
PAUL	We must go and prepare God's way	
	Farewell, dear brothers, we must part.	
JOHN	Everyone should pray respectfully to the Lord	
	That his grace will strengthen us.	1685
PETER	Farewell, dear brothers, we must part,	
	No longer can we stay together.	
ANDREW	May God increase	
	His holy grace in our work	
	So that his sacred faith will be strengthened	1690
	For the salvation of all mankind.	
	Adieu! Peace be with you!	
	Amen.	

THE EPILOGUE

Worthy audience, who have understood	
This play of our cherished subject,	
Even if we did it rather simply,	1695
We pray you all, see our good intent.	
This is the last play, be aware of this,	
Of the seven principal joys	
Which Maria, always humble,	
Received in this world, and we'll sum them up.	1700
The first was how God sent down	
Gabriel, bringing her the blessed message	
With the wonderful aim,	
To free us from our sins.	
The second was how he, from her	1705
Mother and virgin, was born as man	
On Christmas night to the benefit	
Of human kind, to the Devil's fury.	

Ten derden male, na toebehoeren,
Hoe die .iij. coninge uut verren lande 1710
Versaemden ende alle een sterre vercoren
Ende brochten de heilege offerande.
Haer vierde bliscap was selkerhande
Uutnemende ende alder vruecht exempel,
Dat haer geen liden noch druc en ande, 1715
Doen sine vant sittende inden tempel.
Sijn hoge verrisen en was niet sempel,
Dat es de vijfste, dat elc versta.
De seste, op tcorte sonder omwempel,
Dat was de sinxendach daer na. 1720
Nu mach elc weten, sladijs wel ga,
Dat dit de .vij^de. dan moet wesen.
Wi bidden dat elc in dancke ontfa
Wes ons gesciet es nu in desen;
Want weert gelachtert si of gepresen, 1725
Dbeginsel ende dynsel in alder wijs
Es tuwer liefden uut minnen geresen,
Ter eeren der stat, hebt dies avijs.
Van allen duechden geeft Gode den prijs.
Sijn gracie doet dwerc in allen steden. 1730
Die wil ons int salege paradijs
Versamen hierna met vrolicheden!
Hiermede een slot, elc ga in vreden!

The third one, as it should be,
How the three kings from far away   1710
Came together and followed a star,
And brought the holy gifts.
Her fourth joy was so great,
And an example of all joys,
That gave her neither suffering nor sorrow   1715
When she found him sitting in the temple.
His great resurrection was not simple,
That is the fifth, everyone should know.
The sixth in short, and without further ado,
That was Whitsuntide, hereafter.   1720
Now each should know, and mark my words,
That this should then be the seventh.
We pray that each gratefully receives
What has been shown us here;
For whether it's blamed or praised,   1725
From beginning to end in all respects
It's done out of love for you,
And to the honour of the city, you can be sure.
Praise God for all good things.
His grace works in every place.   1730
He shall gather us hereafter
In joy in blessed paradise.
We've reached the end: go in peace!

Notes

First Joy Notes

8   **prince** Philip the Good, Duke of Burgundy (1396–1467).

8   **lady** Isabella of Portugal (1397–1471).

9   **lord** Charles the Bold (1433–77).

10   **lady** Either Catherine of France or Isabella of Bourbon. If this refers to Catherine, the first performance ever must have been 1441; if to Isabella, it was 1448 which is more likely.

24   **bower . . . Troy** Legendary attribution that the city owed its origins to those escaping from Troy.

30   **Zavel** The Church of Our Lady was built on the Zavel, an area in the centre of Brussels, by the Guild of Crossbowmen in the fifteenth century.

109   **gnaws** The iconography of Envy frequently incorporates a figure gnawing itself.

257sd **Selete** A pause in the action, often a change of narrative or mood indicated or introduced by singing and playing or other appropriate noises.

413   **eternal life** The Devil could not bestow eternal life, but this is a parody of the promise made to Adam.

487   **free will** The exercise of free will was a central Catholic doctrine much opposed by Protestants.

597   **cauldrons of hell** This suggests that there may have been a representation of hell onstage, possibly the traditional hell mouth below the stage.

638   **Seth** The journey of Seth is found in the *Gospel of Nicodemus* and is dramatized in the Cornish *Ordinalia* where the seed he plants turns into the tree at Calvary.

916   *drilling . . . heaven* Drilling a hole in heaven by prayer is a notable allegorical motif. The stage direction implies that Heaven was on an upper level and the drilling was done from below.

951   The last three Dutch words have been overwritten.

961   MERCY *speaks to* GOD This begins the Debate of the Four Daughters of God, which eventually inspired the Incarnation: see 1109. For the dramatic context, see P. Meredith and L. Muir, "The Trial in Heaven in the *eerste bliscap* and other European plays," *Dutch Crossing* 22 (1984): 84–92.

1299   the enemy The Devil was kept in ignorance of Christ's divinity, but the dramatizations of the Temptation of Christ in biblical cycles show him seeking to find out the truth.

1345sd   kiss The kiss of reconciliation is a feature of the debate between the Daughters in non-dramatic writings as well as in several plays including *The Castle of Perseverance* and the *N Town* Passion. It originates in Psalm 84:11 (Vulg.).

1378   flowering shoot i.e., Christ.

1385   Balaam His prophecy appears at Numbers 14:17.

1456   En The capitalised E is possibly rhetorical.

1615   eighth day of September Traditional date, first noted in the second century, for the feast of the Nativity of Mary.

1745   Solomon The Song of Songs describes the spotless beauty of the beloved at 4:7.

1830   wand In the apocryphal legend about Mary's marriage, Joseph's wand is the only one to flower among those of the other suitors, in spite of his humility.

2064   another *Bliscap* This passage, which links the play to other episodes, is a feature of the cycle. Because the performances lasted over a seven-year period it must have been necessary to make such links. But equally the material performed was drawn from a corpus of beliefs and memories which would be common to most people in the audiences.

Seventh Joy Notes

19	**I won't repeat** Though the earlier narrative is not mentioned in detail it is apparent that memory of the previous episodes was likely to be stimulated, especially as the performance occurred in the same place.
68	Though there is no obvious break in the sense of the Dutch, it appears that metrically a line is wanting.
95	**remember the words** This is another way of summoning recollection. The words recalled are in John 19:26–7.
165sd	**places** This suggests that the acting area was arranged so that Mary could go to a number of different places, as well as having her own room as at 305sd.
184	**King of the Jews** A reference to the inscription placed by Pilate on Christ's cross which was rejected by the Chief Priests, and which Pilate refused to change: John 19:19–22.
386	**daisy** traditional symbol for Mary as chaste.
421	**palm branch** The palm was associated with victory and was also an emblem appropriate to the procession of virgin martyrs.
479	**Habakuk** According to the Apocrypha account he was carried to Daniel in the lion's den by an angel with food he had cooked: Daniel 14:32.
516	**weeds** Recalls the Parable of the Tares in which the enemy, who is specifically identified by Christ as the Devil, sows weeds among the seed planted by the good man: Matthew 13:24–43.
909	**crown** Though the crown is mentioned here, the Coronation of the Virgin is not enacted in the *Bliscapen* as it is in the *York Plays*.
986	**rose without any thorn** proverbial for innocence and purity: Milton, "and without thorn the rose," *Paradise Lost* 4.256: derived from Genesis 3:18, and cf. *First Joy*, 299.
1057	**Canticles** Song of Songs 4:7.
1059	**our rights** The Devil's rights of possession over humanity (see *First Joy*, 583–4) were thought to have been generated because it sinned through free will, and ultimately they were forfeited because of the Devil's participation in the death of Christ.
1064	**Genesis** For the enmity between Satan and the seed of Eve, see Genesis 3:15.
1088	*Terribilis ut castrorum acies* "Terrible as an army in battle," Song of Songs 6:9.
1095	**Genesis** 3:15.
1102	**Isaiah** 11:1.

1105   **David** Psalm 109:2 (Vulg.).

1271   **werelt** Beuken states that the manuscript between 1263–75 is difficult to read because of the reagent.

1274   three lines of stage directions written in red have been obliterated.

1328   **Jehosophat** This Valley is held to be the place of the Last Judgement: Joel 3:12.

1355   A stage direction has probably been deleted here as the rhyme scheme is not interrupted.

1398   **Exit de Egypto** Psalm 114:2 (Vulg.).

1504   **My hands** This legendary incident appears in the *Legenda Aurea* and was the subject of the lost *York* Funeral of the Virgin performed by the Linenweavers.

1601   **girdle** In the *York* Assumption of the Virgin, Mary gives her girdle to Thomas, who uses it as proof to the other disciples that he has seen her.